# Critical inventions

General Editor: John Schad
*University of Lancaster*

PUBLISHED

Heidegger's Bicycle
Interfering with Victorian Texts
*Roger Ebbatson*

The English Question; or, Academic Freedoms
*Thomas Docherty*

The Prodigal Sign
*Kevin Mills*

Rapture
Literature, Addiction, Secrecy
*David Punter*

GIVEN: 1° Art 2° Crime
Modernity, Murder and Mass Culture
*Jean-Michel Rabaté*

Someone Called Derrida
An Oxford Mystery
*John Schad*

FORTHCOMING

The Medium is the Maker
Browning, Freud, Derrida
*J. Hillis Miller*

In Search of Vinteuil
Music Writing and the Literary Act of Creation
*James Holden*

The Habits of Distraction
*Michael Wood*

**John Schad** is Professor of Modern Literature at Lancaster University. He is the author of *The Reader in Dickensian Mirrors*, *Victorians in Theory*, *Arthur Hugh Clough*, and *Queer Fish: Christian Unreason from Darwin to Joyce* – this last published by Sussex Academic Press. He is also the editor of *Dickens Refigured*, *Thomas Hardy's A Laodicean*, *Writing the Bodies of Christ* and co-editor of *life.after.theory*.

**Other selected works by David Punter**

*The Literature of Terror: A History of Gothic Fictions from 1765 to the Present Day*
*Romanticism and Ideology: Studies in English Writing 1765–1830* (with David Aers and Jonathan Cook)
*Blake, Hegel and Dialectic*
*The Hidden Script: Writing and the Unconscious*
*Introduction to Contemporary Cultural Studies* (ed.)
*William Blake: Selected Poetry and Prose* (ed.)
*The Romantic Unconscious: A Study in Narcissism and Patriarchy*
*William Blake: The New Casebook* (ed.)
*Gothic Pathologies: The Text, the Body and the Law*
*Spectral Readings: Towards a Gothic Geography* (ed., with Glennis Byron)
*A Companion to the Gothic* (ed.)
*Writing the Passions*
*Postcolonial Imaginings: Fictions of a New World Order.*
*The Gothic* (with Glennis Byron)
*The Influence of Postmodernism on Contemporary Writing: An Interdisciplinary Study*
*Metaphor*
*Modernity*

# Rapture

## Literature, Addiction, Secrecy

DAVID PUNTER

SUSSEX
ACADEMIC
PRESS

*BRIGHTON • PORTLAND*

2 4 6 8 10 9 7 5 3

*First published 2009 in Great Britain by*
SUSSEX ACADEMIC PRESS
PO Box 139
Eastbourne BN24 9BP

*and in the United States of America by*
SUSSEX ACADEMIC PRESS
920 NE 58th Ave Suite 300
Portland, Oregon 97213-3786



*British Library Cataloguing in Publication Data*
A CIP catalogue record for this book is available from the British Library.
*Library of Congress Cataloging-in-Publication Data*
Punter, David.
Rapture : literature, secrecy, addiction / David Punter.
p. cm. — (Critical inventions)
Includes bibliographical references and index.
ISBN 978-1-84519-102-3 (h/c : alk. paper) —
ISBN 978-1-84519-103-0 (p/b : alk. paper)
1. Ecstasy in literature. 2. Addicts in literature. 3. Literature—History and criticism. I. Title.
PN56.E27P86 2009
820.9′353—dc22

2008047291

FSC
Mixed Sources
Product group from well-managed forests and other controlled sources
www.fsc.org Cert no. SGS-COC-2482
© 1996 Forest Stewardship Council

Typeset and designed by SAP, Brighton & Eastbourne.
Printed by TJ International, Padstow, Cornwall.
This book is printed on acid-free paper.

# Contents

# Series Editor's Preface

'The question remains,' says David Punter, 'how can we address, or be addressed by, rapture?' To put this another way: how can we read the text that is rapture if reading itself is, as Punter will show, a form of rapture, a form of addiction, even a form of dissolution, so-called because we who read (we the dissolutes, as it were) do, in the end, dissolve into the text that we read. In fact, we dissolve so thoroughly that it becomes impossible to know, says Punter, whether we are reading or 'being read'; and indeed, if it is also the case that even as we read our minds are forever running elsewhere, forever distracted by the whirlpool of echoes that is literature then, in the end (if there is an end) we must all become those 'most astute readers, the readers who are lost in the rapture of having no idea what it is that they are reading.'

And that is precisely the rapture to which Punter calls us; for he is so enraptured by rapture, so carried away with being carried away, that to read this book is often to have no idea what it is we are reading. I am not sure if you would call it philosophy, poetry, psychoanalysis, self-analysis, confession, or even (believe it or not) a bestiary? 'Rapture cannot be achieved,' he says, 'without a sinking or rising into the trajectory of the animal.'

This book is, I think, all the above and yet it is, at the same time and all the while, a species of reading, or attention - attention to the vast and various literature of rapture. It is, though, an improvisatorial reading, a reading-in-process, a form of reading that is to conventional academic reading what 'thinking aloud' is to, well, . . . thinking. In this book, we might say, Punter is 'reading aloud' and what we hear, or over-hear, is the noise of everything, or what George Eliot would have called 'the roar on the other side of silence.' In Punter's case, it is the roar of all the loose ends and distracted thoughts which live just the other side of the silence that is the orderly travesty of reading we might call orthodox literary criticism.

So, what we have here is the heterodoxy of disorder, or (to echo Punter) the heresy of hearsay – a form of reading in which words grow wild and meanings go astray among the echoes, and echoes of echoes, that resonate through the labyrinth of language even (or above all) when . . . absolutely no-one is speaking. We must listen, says Punter, for 'the sound we would hear if all other sounds were shut out'; this, he says, is the 'sound of rapture, a mere buzzing, a tinnitus of the soul,' or indeed the tinnitus that is the soul, or at least the soul of rapture. And the genius of Punter's book, this astonishing act of reading aloud, is that it eavesdrops upon itself so deftly that we do, very gradually, become aware of this tinnitus, or what he calls 'the pattering of life in language's wainscot.'

Punter's father was, we learn, a naval radio-operator, a man who listened in on the Second World War, and that may be just one reason why the pattering we hear is not just of life but also of death or, at least, life-in-death, life lived within the labyrinth of the tomb. Punter, you will find, is invariably reading 'that which is inscribed on the inside of the grave-door.' To read the book that follows is, then, to hear the noise made by Punter's beautiful reading of this door. It is a pattering or puntering that enraptures.

# Preface

I am not sure what sort of book this is. I hope that it follows a series of threads through its title words; some readers may prefer to see it as a series of linked essays. I have no problem with that; it seems to me possible that the period of the critical monograph is, partly for theoretical and partly for technological reasons, nearing its end, its inevitable occlusion by some other form, the delineation of which is, necessarily, not yet clear.

If it is a series of linked essays, then it might be possible to think that each essay follows a slightly different critical trajectory, and I have been tempted to try to identify those; but that that would be to succumb to a taxonomic impulse which would be directed by a rage for order. This book, though, is an attempt to deal in some way with questions of disorder, with the limits of what we might take the law to be.

But this book, like some of my previous ones, is concerned with questioning the writ of the law; which, I suggest, places it firmly within the mainstream of literature, if not of literary criticism. As far as literary criticism and literary theory is concerned, I have not much to say in this Preface, because it may be that we currently lie in a fallow period: the great wave of deconstruction has broken on the shore. A period of recovery may be in order; or a period when we can use the absence of clear markers to strike out for something different. I am struck by the fact that we live in a time when, in some sense, anybody can write: the concomitant question would be, who can read?

I also need to say that there is a way in which this book can be read as a companion to my previous book, *Writing the Passions*; even though it approaches a different topic, there are similarities in terms of arrangements and emphases. And finally (as we begin): 'rapture' is an impossible topic, the soul of impossibility; but I shall be saying more about that as time and the text go on.

# Acknowledgements

My first acknowledgement must be to the general editor of this series, John Schad, who approached me with the disarming line that I could write and publish a book which would not be published anywhere else. How could one refuse such a challenge as well as such a signal honour?

My second is to my wife, the art therapist and child psychotherapist Caroline Case, clinician, artist and writer, without whose help, thought and love this book would not have been written.

Some parts of the book have seen the light of day before in previous incarnations, mostly in the form of conference papers and guest lectures, including ones at the University of Stirling; St Mary's College Strawberry Hill; the University of the Algarve (Portugal); Leeds Metropolitan University; the University of Central Lancashire; the University of Santiago de Compostela (Spain); the University of Bristol; the University of Wales Swansea; the Centre for Studies in Romantic Literature, Jadavpur University, Kolkata (India); and the University of Exeter. In terms of publication, earlier versions of some parts have appeared in *The Malahat Review*, *Foreign Body*, *Gramma* and *Cambridge Quarterly*.

# The Critical Inventions Series

Do I dare / Disturb the universe?
(T. S. Eliot, 'The Love Song of J. Alfred Prufrock', 1917)

In 1961 C. S. Lewis published *An Experiment in Criticism*; over forty years later, at the beginning of a new century, there is pressing need for a renewed sense of experiment, or invention in criticism. The energies unleashed by the theoretical movements of the 1970s and 1980s have been largely exhausted – many now say we are experiencing life after theory; some, indeed, say we are experiencing life after criticism. Criticism, we might say, is in crisis. But that is where it should be; the word 'criticism' comes, as we know, from the word 'crisis'.

Talk of crisis does not, though, fit easily within the well-managed contemporary academy; with its confident talk of 'scholarly excellence', there is a presumption that we all know, and are agreed upon, what scholarship and criticism is. However, to echo Paul de Man, 'we don't even know what reading is'; and what is, potentially, exciting about our present crisis is that now we really know that we don't know what reading is. It is, then, in a spirit of learned ignorance that we propose 'critical inventions', a series which will feature books that, in one way or another, push the generic conventions of literary criticism to breaking point. In so doing the very figure of the critic will shift and change. We shall, no doubt, glimpse something of what Oscar Wilde famously called 'the critic as artist', or what Terry Eagleton called 'the critic as clown'; we may even glimpse still more unfamiliar figures – the critic as, for example, autobiographer, novelist, mourner, poet, parodist, detective, dreamer, diarist, flaneûr, surrealist, priest, montagist, gambler, traveller, beggar, anarchist . . . or even amateur. In short, this series seeks the truly critical critic – or, to be paradoxical, the critic as critic; the critic who is a critic of criticism as conventionally understood, or misunderstood. He or she is the critic who will dare to disturb the universe, or at least the university – in particular, the institutionalisation of criticism that is professional, university English.

Establishment English is, though, a strange institution that is capable of disestablishing itself, if only because it houses the still stranger institution of literature – which, as Jacques Derrida once wrote, 'in principle allows us to say everything/ anything [tout dire]'. We, therefore, do not or cannot yet know of what criticism may yet be capable – capable of being, capable of doing. 'Critical inventions' will be a series that seeks to find out.

> Read the text right and emancipate the world.
> (Robert Browning, 'Bishop Bloughram's Apology', 1855)

JOHN SCHAD, Series Editor

1

# Enraptured

In this book, I shall be suggesting that 'rapture' is a critical term in two senses of the word 'critical'; it is a term capable of being used critically, and it is critical to the experience of the writing and reading of literature. Let me begin with some excerpts from the *Oxford English Dictionary* definition of 'rapture':

- The act of seizing and carrying off as prey or plunder
- The act of carrying, or fact of being carried, onwards; force of movement
- The act of conveying a person from one place to another, especially to heaven
- Transport of mind, mental exaltation or absorption, ecstasy
- The expression of ecstatic feeling in words

In terms of the reading act, there is a specific trajectory being described here, from rapine through to 'being carried (away)'. In terms familiar to contemporary psychiatry, a 'state of rapture' is a definition applied to episodes in conditions of extreme psychosis.[1] These will form poles between which I shall try to move. There will inevitably be a movement also towards the apparent impossibility of recounting 'rapturous states', and of fixing them in words or in time within cultural expectations. There is a question, which might have to do with 'ghostly presences', as to what we do with those who are 'enrapt', and what we do inside ourselves with reading moments of rapture.

This trajectory could clearly take us through 'states of heightened awareness', which at the same time seize us, carry us off, and not at all necessarily towards heaven; there would also be a question of 'transport to hell', a journey on which one might well see, for example, William Burroughs or the less well-known but equally hallucinogenic writer John Rechy reporting as best they can. There would also be a series of questions arising from what T. S. Eliot refers to in his poem 'Marina' (1930) as the 'ecstasy of the animals', and how states of rapture might invade and distort our assumptions of the 'human', so that they have to be 'held in secret', becoming resistant to interpretation even at the same time as communication, perhaps beyond the human, might seem to be the utmost imperative.[2]

## After Poetry?

A suitable preface, in terms of the relation between rapture, ghostly presences and the afterlife, might be found in Jacques Derrida's brief work, 'Che cos'è la poesia?', part of which runs as follows:

> *Sans sujet: il y a peut-être du poème, et qui* se laisse, *mais je n'en écris jamais. Un poème je ne le signe jamais. L'autre signe. Le je n'est qu'à la venue de ce désir: apprendre par coeur. Tendu pour se résumer à son propre support, donc sans support extérieur, sans substance, sans sujet, absolu de l'écriture en soi, le 'par coeur' se laisse élire au-delà du corps, du sexe, de la bouche et des yeux, il efface les bords, il échappe aux mains, tu l'entends à peine, mais il nous apprend le coeur.*[3]

This essay, 'Che cos'è la poesia?', has a contorted history, explanation of which is offered by Elisabeth Weber in her Note to the translation available in *Points . . . : Interviews, 1974–1994* (1995). It was first published in the Italian journal *Poesia* in 1988, and republished in a French journal the following year, where it was preceded by a note explaining that *Poesia* 'begins each of its issues with the attempt at or the simulacrum of a response, in a few lines, to the question "Che cos'è la poesia?"'.

Yet already, it is possible to begin to speculate on this. What is the 'simulacrum of a response'? Is it a simulacrum in the sense that it is not a response at all, not the 'real thing', whatever that might be, some 'virtual response' that is, perhaps, addressing a quite different question – or none at all? Is it a simulacrum in that it is not in fact Derrida's response, but somebody else's – some ghostly presence who, perhaps, for purposes of his or her own, is 'simulating Derrida' (the essay itself provides some hints as to how this might inevitably be so)? And what is this about 'a few lines'? The English translation in *Points . . .* runs to over 200 lines, although they are lines, admittedly, not of poetry.

But all of this, perhaps, is not really 'to the point'. What is more remarkable is that 'Che cos'è la poesia?' inserts itself into a dialogue with the dead. Again, Weber explains; the question itself is addressed to a 'living person',

> while the [other] question 'Che cos'era la poesia?' is addressed to the dead, this time to the 'Odradek' by Kafka. At the moment he or she is writing, the living respondent does not know the answer given by the dead one: it appears at the end of the issue and is the choice of the editors.[4]

And so here might be an 'end of the issue' in an address to the dead, except that again one might put questions to this 'mediated dialogue'. If the 'living' respondent (whatever that might be) is unaware of the answer (already) provided (but later, in the issue, in the event) by the 'dead' one, does it follow that the 'dead' respondent is unaware of the (preceding, but later) response of his or her *confrère*?

There is here, perhaps, something of an auditory hallucination going on, a deaf dialogue around the rapturous but ghostly time and space of poetry. That the 'authoritative' text cannot be single-mindedly (or monolinguistically) reproduced is underlined by the fact that, in *Points . . .* , 'Che cos'è la poesia?' is the only piece reproduced in both French and English. This appears to be explained by Weber as something, surprisingly, to do with hedgehogs. But of that I have nothing to say here.

It would be possible to sense something quite playful going on in the positing of this question, in the garnering of perhaps ill-matched answers from the living and the dead; something that might, at all events (and no doubt in every issue) afford the editors (and readers) some amusement at a kind of dramatic irony of the cemetery, an epitaphic reversal. Within this structure, it would obviously be difficult to know what company one was keeping, what specific ghost was going to (is going to? will be about to?) provide an 'afterword' to your own unwitting, perhaps witless, prologue.

It might be better not to get, as it were, carried away, but instead to try to go back to the beginning. The English translation of the Derrida quotation runs as follows:

> Without a subject: poem, perhaps there is some, and perhaps it *leaves itself*, but I never write any. A poem, I never sign(s) it. The other sign(s). The *I* is only at the coming of this desire: to learn by heart. Stretched, tendered forth to the point of subsuming its own support, thus without external support, without substance, without subject, absolute of writing in (it)self, the 'by heart' lets itself be elected beyond the body, sex, mouth, and eyes; it erases the borders, slips through the hands, you can barely hear it, but it teaches us the heart.[5]

The sense of the playful, perhaps, is already ambushed by this declaration, this painful yearning in a cemetery, over an abyss where the ghost of poetry writhes, forever without body, unable to incarnate. You can barely hear its cries as it moves perennially towards a body which it will never achieve.

What can I do about this, what is there that could possibly be done to alleviate the suffering? I cannot write Derrida's lost poems for him. Besides, I think, actually, that he does it (when the occasion arises, when the spirit moves and he is carried away, enraptured) perfectly well himself. What about these closing words to his essay 'Typewriter Ribbon: Limited Ink (2)' (2001):

> I am so sad that Paul de Man is not here himself to answer me and to object. But I can hear him already – and sooner or later his text will answer for him.
>
> That is what we all call a machine.
>
> But a spectral machine
>
> By telling me I am right, it will tell him he is right.
>
> And sooner or later, our common innocence will not fail to appear to everyone's eyes, as the best intentioned of all our machinations.[6]

Will it not? Will a combined innocence come out in the end, in the wash, at the end of the issue, in a ghostly response from and to the dead? Perhaps; but anyway this is surely a fine elegy, a textual mourning for . . . a dialogue which is, in some sense, irredeemably past; in another time, ongoing without finitude, a machine set to run which has no end, no moment of closedown.[7] This is the terror of the textual/spectral artifact: speech without end, a never-ending cycle of simulacra of response, text-messaging to a virtual respondent – who may be dead, may be deaf, or perhaps there is no longer any difference between the two.

## Empty, Absent Organs

At all events, Derrida says, and this much we can exhume without controversy from this apparition of a dialogue – poetry *is* the heart – heart without boundaries, heart which is not an organ but perhaps the simulacrum, the hypostasis of an organ. But, as I have said, this keeping up of appearances is difficult, and my mind runs elsewhere, through other defiles, towards a poet who has something to say about the enraptured heart, although what he says is perhaps elliptical (as is befitting in the context of an organ that has to bear such a freight of ascribed, inscribed meanings):

> Finely, brush the
> sound from your
> eyes: it rests
> in the hollow
>
> as looking in
> the shops at both
> reflections, in

the glass
how
to move and the
sun slanting over
the streets: shielded
from the market

in the public
domain, as
taking the pace
of movement

in the hollow
furnished with that
tacit gleam, the
cavernous heart.[8]

'That/tacit gleam, the/cavernous heart'; I have written something about this poem before, I am sure I have; I would not want to repeat myself, to contribute to some burgeoning scenario of echoes. But I do find that I suggested that this poem (by J. H. Prynne, called 'On the Anvil' [1969]) suggests that we are

> unwilling subjects caught in a signal flux of language – a language, to be sure, which is not foreign to the discourse of the 'gleam' and the 'heart' but in which such romantic images figure merely as the 'tacit', the silent, the empty, the 'cavernous', places where language cannot probe even though we suspect that all the time its surfaces, and thus our own self-positionings, are being formed by pressures beyond our ken?[9]

And it seems, from that strayed question mark, as though I was formulating a question, although not one that I can now grasp again with real clarity. Did I really say that? In response to whom, or what? What called it forth? Let us have another try at the 'cavernous heart': this would be the heart waiting to be filled, the cavern from which all sign of habitation has gone – it would be asking the question of whether the poem is always a relic, an afterlife, an evacuated site, perhaps an archaeologised phenomenon, a system of runes from which we attempt to recreate lost civilisations, or even the phantasm of a lost 'civility', a civility within which questions might be suitably responded to instead of hanging on, in a state of uncertainty, of undecidability.

It is obviously possible. As Derrida says elsewhere, with a fine disregard for his professed difficulties with the personal pronoun, 'I always have the feeling that, despite centuries of reading, these texts remain untouched, withdrawn into a reserve, still to come'.[10] He is talking here of certain specific texts; but perhaps also describing a general condition, the spectacle of the poetic spectre, the uncertainty of what these texts – any texts – might 'become' – if 'to become' is their fate – unless, of course, they are to remain 'tacit', a 'tacit gleam', and our prospect of a rapturous apocalypse of reading is indeed a phantasm, an impossibility – like Derrida's writing of poetry, the gleam left by an already vanishing apparition. In response to a question, asked in the course of an interview, as to what form his 'great work' would take (a question that in terms of Derrida's achievements might seem otiose, but which would also signify a certain waiting, an incompleteness, a way in which extant texts are nevertheless always haunted by the promise of that which is to come, of a further ramification of life) – 'Would it take the form of a poem, of fiction?' – he replies (or replied, I am getting confused here, perhaps a little tense – one might sense a certain lifting of fatigue at the prospect of this apparently approaching apocalypse, the rapture):

> It would be at least a crossing of multiple genres. I am looking for a form that would not be a genre and that would permit me to accumulate and to mobilise a very large number of styles, genres, languages, levels . . . That's why it is not getting written.[11]

Not getting written here, at any rate; maybe it is being written somewhere else within the order of ghosts. Heart like a cavern, yearning to be filled. But to be filled with what, in the absence of an origin? Why, of course: to be filled 'virtually', to be filled with reverberation, with echo, with apparition.

I shall make a new start (promises, promises).

Prynne, as has already become, presumably, apparent, is a contemporary poet, usually perceived as one of the most 'difficult' in the English language. Derrida also, of course, has something to say about such attributions of 'difficulty', although in this particular case he is talking about Paul Celan (or perhaps, of course, about himself and his difficulties with the crypt, the cryptic):

> That is what I try to underscore about Celan, who is supposed to be a difficult and cryptic poet, for example, in the way he arranges dates, allusions to experiences he has had, and so forth, with all the problems of decipherment that this supposes . . . What I suggested is that he didn't do it out of calcu-

> lation, in order to put generations of academics to work looking for the keys to a text. It is the experience of writing and language that is involved in this crypt, this cryptics.[12]

But that, I suppose, is still what you get in a 'cryptics' – you get echoes, you cannot make them go away, and as you listen to them (if you are not involved in a dialogue of the deaf) they only intensify, even to the potentially psychotic point where dates (and tenses) are obscured, where the origin of the sound is lost; or is loss. Prynne (I am trying for the moment to stay with Prynne, although Derrida's voice keeps calling me away, or at any rate it appears that it does) is distinguished in many ways, and one of them is that although he is by profession a literary academic, he rarely writes literary criticism or gives guest lectures on literature. One of the very few he has given is called 'Stars, Tigers and the Shape of Words' (1993), and it is at least in part about voice. But it is also about the final vicissitude of voice and the afterlife: echo. In the context of Alexander Pope's oft-quoted reflection on sound effects in *An Essay on Man* (1733–4) ('The *Sound* must seem an *Eccho* to the Sense'), in the eighth of 161 notes on a lecture-text only 35 pages long (but I have not counted the number of lines), he comments as follows:

> There is some ambiguity here about how Pope understood the acoustics of the echo. Properly, his formulation seems to suggest that managed sound may provide a kind of instant echo, or a confirming effect of related or resembling sound coming close after its sounded original and reinforcing it by varied repetition; or alternatively it may suggest that the idea in the mind of the writer comes into a potentially sounded form as the words are inscribed on to the page, and to this silent image of sound the phonetic performance (realised tacitly in the mind of the reader) provides a matching echo.[13]

## Echo, the Stilled Heart

Some ambiguity: indeed there is, and it would be difficult to think of a context in which some ambiguity did not accompany the idea of echo, as it would be difficult to think of a context in which some ambiguity did not accompany the echo of an idea. But it is the notion of a 'silent image of sound' that stays the attention, stops the heart, engages with rapture; this notion of an interior singing, an unstilled voice, a tinnitus of the soul. 'You can barely hear it, but it teaches us the heart', Derrida says; the idea, the image, the poignant almost-hearing of a continuing poetic, of something *going on*, responding to its own voice perhaps, never sure of whether there is another participant in the poetic drama, but nevertheless not about to end its own participation, because to do so would mean . . . that 'something is happening here/But you don't know what it is/Do you, Mister Jones?'[14]

But alas, early-mid-period Bob Dylan is no place to be in the course of an exploration like this. Back to 'would mean': would mean what? Not death, presumably: that would be too glib. Besides, poetry itself already partakes of death, it looks towards death, it elegiacally frames the death of, for instance, Paul de Man and says that 'sooner or later his text will answer for him'. I find myself wondering (I am losing track amid all these echoes, I am worried about being stranded in this cavern when the last wisps of daylight cease to filter down, I am frightened what voices I might hear – am I intruding, for example, on the site of an oracle with all its connotations of a rapturous afterlife?) – I find myself wondering what that 'answer for' really means. We can be 'answered for', in the sense that something or someone elsewhere might answer on our behalf (depending on what the questions might be, what kinds of response are recommended or elicited); we can also find ourselves answerable for our sins, our derelictions, our words, our poems. It might be that some unimaginable court of law will hold us answerable for positing unanswerable questions, we might ourselves be cut short, *tout court*, unready to confront an end to these apparitions, unwilling to look beyond them into the cavern.

'A poem, I never sign(s) it'. Well, indeed: the poem, as Derrida says, is in one sense something that 'leaves', or is carried away, it goes off to make new friends; but it might be that one would still like to feel that one's own poems still have a small place in their cavernous heart for their progenitor, even if they may well prefer the ubiquitous fantasy of the changeling, which is that they were brought into this world by faery means and that their parents have never been worthy of them.[15]

But let me return to Prynne; is this my fourth beginning? In 'Stars, Tigers and the Shape of Words' he makes some alarming comments on a peculiar and distorted after-lively echo to be discovered in the researches of, of all people, the great linguistician Ferdinand de Saussure. While Saussure was giving the lectures that were to become known as the *Cours de Linguistique Générale* (1916), devoted to demonstrating the arbitrariness of the sign, he (according to Prynne)

> was also engaged in a rather different direction of linguistic research and enquiry, which concerned the possible linguistic evidence for a systematic use of verbal anagrams in the composition of classical literary texts. Saussure

> himself published nothing of this work, which he seems to have pursued with a complex mixture of determined fascination and sceptical disbelief; but his documentation fills over a hundred notebooks . . .[16]

A hundred notebooks (how many lines?), devoted to an exploration which, had it come to a conclusion (provided or elicited a response), would have overturned, or at the very least challenged, responded to before, as it were, the fact, the vast structuralist enterprise which coloured the intellectual developments of the second half of the twentieth century; yes, I see now that 'Che cos'è la poesia?' is indeed, by comparison, only a few lines. But perhaps we can let go of that. Likewise, we can probably let go of Prynne's tantalising phrase 'verbal anagrams', with its implicit assumption that there are other types of anagram, a worrying thought; but not as worrying, perhaps, as the thought that seems to have assailed Saussure, which is that he might have been entirely on the wrong track, that the apparent pursuit of an 'opening' in the vast field of discourse might instead have been pointing determinedly in the wrong direction, that meanwhile all had been happening 'on another scene', that the rules were always different. There is an urban myth (but 'urban' is entirely the wrong word) about the anthropologist who, having observed and written up a complicated ceremonial in Papua New Guinea, sent his academic article to a local colleague who complimented him while gently remarking that he had in fact obviously been observing not the ceremonial itself but the refreshments provided for the spectators.

I am not sure, on reflection, what the word is that should replace 'urban'; I am still less sure of the force of the phrase 'local colleague'. Perhaps one might be led into choosing to concentrate instead on what all these evasions, these eloquent slidings-away, these verbosities are about:

> When one writes, one is always trying to outsmart the worst. Perhaps so as to prevent it from taking everything away, but the last word, you know, always belongs to non-mastery, for both the reader and oneself.[17]

What would this 'worst' be? Would it be the fantasy of there being no audience, no possibility of hearing, no possibility of being heard – from, perhaps, inside the coffin, or inside the home, inside the place where one lives (*demeure*, as Derrida might have it)?[18] Only today (as I write) I read in the newspaper about the discovery of the body of a man, a body that had been lying in the 'undiscovered country' for fifteen months, a body whose cries – from beyond the grave – had not been heard. This was in an urban flat. The worst, one might say, does not 'take everything away'; rather, it prevents it from being 'taken away', it leaves everything exactly where it is, immoveable, unmoved; dead to the world, freed of echoes, severed from its own ghost or demon, perhaps enjoying its own unrecountable rapture.

What we have here might be referred to as the 'last word', and at the very least that might prevent me from beginning yet again (which might be tiring). The last word. What are the 'last words' in the first edition of Prynne's so far collected work, the volume called simply, of course, *Poems* (2005)?

> Fissile drag under gang profile, all
> brows raised at surround inhibition of the tonic
> yellow signal; the arrays lie packed in a dark light
> defect of strictness set to a little head or button:
> patterns matching the surveillance shape in bright
> shadow under wing chalking the egg yolk cartoon.[19]

I do not really know what much of this means. I have said it before, and the feeling seems to be intensifying, echoing back to me: I am tired. As a reader, it is easy to tire of complexities, evasions, complicities of which I am never part. I sign (up to) nothing. I am tired, when in a state of rapture, of my computer repeatedly telling me that my spelling is unconventional and my grammar unacceptable. But to think of signing (up to; or even of being, or feeling, 'up to' signing): what other kind of signature can there be, except one that signifies total evacuation, a promise of oblivion? Yet – and yet. There is presumably a tape recorder here (it is still there, still running, at the end of this book, on the last pages of a work called *Soul Mountain*), lurking (evasively) within these lines, perhaps listening to them, or tracing them; some kind of machine with heads and buttons, creeping on and round in the night, in the darkness, Krapp's very last, perhaps, sticking to its last afore night come; or some such composite of echoes in the afterlife.[20] Perhaps there is music in them too, an obscured, darkened music, signified in the 'tonic', echoed and re-echoed in the replacement of the egg carton by a 'cartoon', sound stretched out beyond meaning, operating only under the rules of poetry, the regime of echo, sound captured in the empty room, the coffin, of soundlessness. Sound; echo; sense. Sen(surround) – sent where? Nobody knows (as Derrida says, so flippantly, so colloquially, 'you know').

## Tape, Spool, Toxic Remembrance

I wonder: why does 'tonic' slide off into the 'toxic'? Is it the 'yellow', is it the thought of waste here, or am I getting too enmired in the thought of

Samuel Beckett's character Krapp, in the endless spooling of the image, of the word that detaches itself from thought, that goes on to a different kind of life as it is repeated, as it seeks the repetition, the echo, which is poetry? The 'yellow signal', I suppose, is a kind of sign of life, a tiny, almost moribund avatar, a yolk which will (almost) never come to be born, which will instead be consumed, the fruit of seven minutes (the average human requirement for reproduction) or three and a half minutes (perfect boiling, but only, of course, if the egg has not been in the fridge, if technological support has been withheld). I feel the need to defend myself a little here, lest it be thought that I getting off the point, or indeed going off the boil: Prynne's poetry is a masterwork of incorporation, within which all things technological and virtual are consumed, it constitutes a discourse to which nothing is alien, precisely a 'crossing of multiple genres' which at the same time recognizes that at the right point of forging, the correct application of heat, the very notion of 'crossing' becomes invisible, even its apparition is melted, rapture is achieved. My computer told me sternly when I wrote this that I meant 'heart', not 'heat', but it is wrong; I am not (yet) entirely a creature of echo.

'Shape' and 'shadow' ('bright shadow', admittedly; shades of John Donne's rapturous 'bracelet of bright haire about the bone'[21]) – but that is odd, it is the title of an essay I wrote years ago on the uncanny in poetry, and especially (if my memory serves me well, and I have not been misled by the echoes of words) on Thomas Hardy and Walter de la Mare, and which had something to do with a course Nicholas Royle and I were teaching together at the time.[22] Shape and shadow.

> So I write in order to keep. But keeping is not a dull and dead archiving. It is at bottom a question of infinite memories, of limitless memories which would not necessarily be a philosophical or literary work, simply a great repetition.[23]

Thus Derrida: writing as loss; writing as retention – the great Freudian escapade[24] – but 'writing in order', what would that mean? In what order, or, perhaps, to whose order? An order of ghosts? Let us (try to) be clear: the spectre referred to here, one that hovers over all writing, and particularly over poetry, as well as over all academic exploration, is known under another name as Asperger Syndrome, the need to collect examples and tie them together – it is there in model trains, it is there in the fate of stamps ('arrays . . . packed in a dark light'), it is there in Walter Benjamin's attempts to collect together the scar tissue of a damaged life, it is there in rhyme and rhythm.[25] It is there in the work of, for example, the great Edwardian anthropologists, who thought that the end of collection would be the beginning of research and understanding, and who died like Henry Wellcome, with his million 'things', as he endearingly called them, uncatalogued and doomed to their current re-dispersal around the world's museums, in many cases back whence they came.[26] It is there as a travesty, or perhaps as a cartoon; as the image of a disparaging displacement.

'Disparage'; now, what does that remind me of? Ah – Derrida on *parage*, again in the context of the apparent echoing of an interview:

> It is perhaps this conceptual criterion that one must interrogate at the moment one attempts to decide between literature, philosophy, and poetry. Now, if we come back to philosophy, literature, or poetry, you mentioned *parages*. *Les parages* means a vicinity; it is a metaphor that comes to us from nautical or maritime language; it names a vicinity at a distance that is difficult to measure: that which is neither near nor far.[27]

Oh dear. Why are those two lists that name (and echo) literature, philosophy and poetry changed from one instance (echo) to the next? And why is poetry here held up as separate from literature? Is poetry near to literature, or is it far from it? What kinds of distance do these observations invite us to plumb, and how shall we feel safe as we fall into the gaps between, enter into these 'crossings of genres', these voyages of exploration without maps?

Then again, perhaps it is my faulty attempt to echo 'parage' and 'disparage' that is to blame, for certainly 'disparage', in English, although it comes from the Old French, has very little to do with 'vicinity' in any obvious way; its reference rather is 'to match or cause to marry unequally'. But then again: the Latin root *vicinus* translates into French as *voisin* ('cousin') – perhaps there is more to this dangerous consanguinity than meets the eye – or, indeed, the ear. Poetry, then, as problematic matching of blood relations; working more by an incestuous system of echoes than by 'sound' good sense (which way round should those last three words be? Sound/poetry? Good/literature? Sense/philosophy?).

I think I may be verging here onto what I would like to call the 'etymospectral' (which might, or might not, show that I have at last begun; or alternatively, that this thinking is already in its afterlife). Derrida does too, in *Points . . .* , for example, where he speculates on the etymology of 'cramp', and cites as an example of the 'really beautiful' this passage from an etymological dictionary:

> *Crampe*, 11th cent., in addition, adj. 13th cent., notably in the locution *goutte crampe*, still in dictionaries; *crampon*, 13th cent. Frankish **kramp* "curved"

> (cf. High German *kramph*, id.). The two nouns, which surely come from a same root, very probably already existed in Frankish. The Middle Dutch *cramp*, Ger. *Krampf*, Eng. *cramp* allow one to restore the Frankish word **krampa* id.; likewise the Anglo-Saxon *krampo* "crochet" {bracket, hook} and the Eng. *cramp* render the existence of a Frankish **krampo*, masc., probable. Der.: cramponner, 15th cent.[28]

My computer did not like that one bit; it thought I had been carried away. However: what would it be like, one might passingly wonder, to be 'still in dictionaries' – to lie still – or still to lie – or to be still, or stilled, while the floodtide of meanings passes over; to 'still' (or distill) the wonder or rapture to a succession of numbers, the substance of an apparently endless but paradoxically constrained catalogue, a collector's list? What, again, would it be like to conceive of 'a same root' – not, we notice, 'the same root' or a 'similar (or consanguineous) root' but 'a same root' – would this be the kind of root of which we might be thinking while we are experiencing 'vicinity', *voisinage*? It is noticeable that the unnamed questioner in this interview (which is called 'Between Brackets I' [1975]) passes at this point, and with seeming haste, onto an entirely different question (which is, as it happens, a question about 'the question').[29]

But let us leave further questions out of the question; except that one might reasonably ask what, if anything, is out of the question. Disparagement, disparity between cousins, perhaps; or echoes that do not quite seem to return the sound with which they started. Or, to put both of these together, seascapes, nautical expeditions, which can neither acknowledge or understand returning to their starting-point nor give a satisfactory account of where they have been.

## Brow of the Sea

Here is another voice of the lost, an echo from the heart of poetry:

> In those words through which I move, leaving a cry
> Formed in exact degree and set dead at
> The mingling flood, I am put forward on to
> Live water, clad in oil, burnt by salt
> To life. Here, braced, announced on to the slow
> Heaving seaboards, almost I am now too
> Lulled. And my watch is blear. The early grey
> Air is blowing.

It is that first pallor there, broken, running
Back on the sheared water. Now the chill wind
Comes off the shore sharp to find its old mark
Between the shoulderblades. My eyes read in
The fixed and flying signs wound in the light
Which all shall soon lie wound in as it slowly
Approaches rising to break wide up over the
Brow of the sea.[30]

This voice is that of W. S. Graham, Scottish/Cornish poet, artist and sailor. A sailor, it would appear here, on the 'mingling flood' of language, through or upon which he leaves a 'cry', as of a seabird, perhaps, or more specifically as in the ghostly 'crying' of a gull, itself an echoic description supposed to remind us of the crying of a baby abandoned to the gales, of a soul unhoused, unprotected in the afterlife. Yet here too, alongside the loss, the waste of waters, the inexorable and inexplicable flood, there is also 'exact degree', the collector's mania, the placing of one word beside another in symmetry, in a relation which seeks all the time to contradict the dangerous uncertainties of 'vicinity', of that hovering, unclear sense of closeness that could also be distance, a mere telescopic error, a mistake of distance or of sight.

Oil and salt, a malign protection and a stinging return to life, seabirds enmired and (perhaps) freed. Poetry here, as often for Graham, swings between these two poles: between that which serves as an outer coating (oilskin) and that which irritates from within but thereby prevents one from succumbing to the blearing, the blurring of vision. Clarity is nowhere; but this makes the search for clarity all the more profound, the more precious. 'Braced' and 'announced': two stilled moments, and between the two, between the readiness and the sound, everything has already occurred, there is nowhere else left to go, the whole of the mapless sea has infiltrated itself into the bone.

Oh well. At any rate, it is clear, if anything is, that the water is sheared, marked by the boat and by the wind; it is also marked as the page, the 'leaf', is marked by the word; but in the end, all is uncertainly signified in the 'wound' – or the 'wound'. How can we tell, in this ghostly afterlife of the poem, how the word should be pronounced? What would pronunciation even mean in this watery world where the markings on the surface of the sea fall away, fall apart as we look at them, and where the echoes that return might be mere figments of the underwrought imagination?

What seas what shores what grey rocks and what islands
What water lapping the bow

> And scent of pine and the woodthrush singing through the fog
> What images return
> O my daughter.[31]

And so back to Eliot, but I confess I have no idea; what images *do* return? And why cannot you phrase it as a question rather than as an oracular pronouncement? But then, this is after all Eliot, or at least a collection of his fragments, a confabulation of sea-voyages from Odysseus on, under the name, the sign of 'Marina'. Perhaps it betrays the fact that Eliot, unlike Graham, never was a sailor; whatever voyage there was, whatever vicinity was to be sailed through, he never sailed/signed it; but we must not fall here into a realist heresy, that would never do. How close, after all, in the world of echo 'heresy' is to 'hearsay'.

Right: here we go, casting off again. These signs which are 'fixed' (perhaps this is what caused poor Saussure his hundred notebooks of anxiety) are also signs which are 'flying' – reminiscences, echoes perhaps, of the 'fixed and flying constellations', but also reminders that the word is committed not to the page but to the sea, like the final sign to Joseph Conrad's secret sharer, cast upon the waters, subject to constant and immediate erasure.[32] What then, under these circumstances, where everything is carried away, can be 'kept'?

As Derrida puts it,

> To write (of) oneself is to cease to be, in order to confide in a guest/host [*hôte*] – the other, a reader – who will henceforth have as charge and as life nothing but your inexistence.[33]

And yet, one is free to wonder. At least, one is free to wonder, 'Is one free to wonder?'. Another thing one might wonder, if there were time, would be whether this 'inexistence' is the other face, the other voice, the distorted echo of monumentalisation; the concept of posterity (the hope of immortality) is perhaps not so easily fazed (no, dear computer, not 'faxed'. We are dealing in the possibility here of a less immediate kind of communication, of something held in reserve, of something that never quite gets round to constituting an apparition; of the rapture of poetry). And anyway, is it possible to write '(of) oneself', in any of the multitude of meanings one might ascribe to that phrase?

Since it now rather seems as though we might be in danger of being becalmed, going round in circles, I will interject within my own discourse. My father was killed by a dictionary. It is true (in some sense of the word 'true'; but how shall I convince you of that?). Let me try. My father suffered from angina (the word bears looking up; I shall come to that in a moment. Who knows: perhaps we shall all come to it). He also liked crosswords (mild Asperger, or the dominance of meaningless echo; I also suffer that liking myself, because it makes words 'fade into their own parade', echo of Dylan again[34]). One day, suffering chest pains, he stayed home from work; he was found later, dead, leaning out from his bed with a crossword beside him and a dictionary in his hands. Appropriately to heart disease, I think it was Chambers'; but that, of course, is only hearsay.

Oh dear. What more to (hear)say? Did I mention that he, like Graham, was a sailor – twenty years at sea, in destroyers? But not a combatant; he was a radio operator, all those years in a tiny cabin; listening. I wonder what he heard? Perhaps he heard heartbeats, sailors' heartthrobs, the rapture of the sea: listen to what the dictionary has to say about angina:

> A dangerous disease, the paroxysms of which are characterised by sudden and severe pain in the lower part of the chest, towards the left side, with a feeling of suffocation and alarm of impending death; they are brought on by over-exertion when the heart is diseased; called also *breast-pang*; *heart-stroke*, and *spasm of the chest*.[35]

Well, goodness me. There are almost too many echoes here to be registered; counted; collected. For example (and let us put it in the form of a series of questions): is consulting a dictionary to be counted as over-exertion? Are feelings 'of suffocation and alarm of impending death' to be registered alongside thoughts of premature burial; coffins; or perhaps burials at sea, with all the panoply attendant on such occasions? Is angina, the feeling attendant on an over-stretched heart, to be associated with poetry – poetry which (and here I am echoing myself) *is* the heart, as Derrida tells us (do we believe him?)? What are we to make of this 'lower part of the chest', with its all too obvious connections with the lower part of the sea-chest that Jim Hawkins discovers in *Treasure Island* (1882), and which sets the whole mechanism of the archetypal adventure story in motion – or which puts it, as we may alternatively say, all at sea, demonstrates how all story issues from the crypt?

But I apologise; perhaps I have become too personal, have breached a rule of decorum. I have (perhaps) gone too far in the region of 'fixed and flying signs' (although when I get there, I find myself accompanied by Derrida and Graham; yet I find this to be of only limited reassurance. We all share the problem of limited ink). However, this does at least give me a cue to recall myself again to Derrida:

> . . . without the *possibility* of this fiction, without the spectral virtuality of this simulacrum and as a result of this lie or this fragmentation of the true, no truthful testimony would be possible. Consequently, the possibility of literary fiction haunts so-called truthful, responsible, serious, real testimony as its proper possibility. This haunting is perhaps the passion itself, the passionate place of literary writing . . . [36]

So: there is (again perhaps) no possibility of 'truthful testimony', there is only the ghostly presence, the virtuality of such a thing. In place of 'fixed and flying signs', we have only flying fish, momentarily glimpsed, already the stuff of hearsay, or indeed of legend, a different kind of reading – rapturous truths of the heart which are not amenable to further ratification. And then, of course, one is confronted with the difficulty of thinking beyond this panoply, this array, of phantasms (nothing is ever wound up, sometimes I wonder whether that is what texts do, they wind me up, and then again I suppose the payoff is that they also set me going, though not, I think, to heaven):

> What remains to be thought and presently resists thinking thus passively exposed, in its very passivity, is not only the *phantasm*, the phantasm that operates, *fait oeuvre*, makes the work (at the crossing of the unconscious, the phenomenological *phainesthai*, the noema as an intentional but not real component of consciousness, and of spectrality [*phantasma*] of phantoms). How is one to think the durable hardness, the until now invincible, though always threatened, effectivity of an onto-theologico-political phantasm – sovereignty, for example?[37]

## Fictions of Sovereignty

I am not sure I want to follow Derrida onto this terrain of sovereignty (I am not at all sure that I want to follow this paragraph at all). Perhaps I am afraid. Perhaps (to try to catalogue, to collect, the fear) I am not certain that this hypostasised, quasi-essentialist category of sovereignty has anything by way of real existence. I fear it is a snare, another aspect of enmirement, and a delusion, the result of an over-nice conscience and an anxiety (no doubt induced by echo) about the heresy of the reality status of the text.

But I am more interested in the phantasm, the ghostly presence, because I believe it to be more powerful than sovereignty, which is constantly under siege. The phantasm can say to the sovereign – and does, often, perhaps most recently in, for example, Iraq – 'I know your name, and I know where you live'. Under this pressure, sovereignty has no recourse; it reveals its dumbness and its impoverishment, for it has set itself outside the circle of echo, it has set itself apart and therefore its power is the ultimate sign of its inevitable vulnerability, it has nowhere at all to go but down. If the phantasm rises from the grave, if it comes to demonstrate that the power of the apparition is never banished by firepower (no matter what our anthropological and psychoanalytic sophistications might whisper to us about the power of fire[38]), then the sovereign is always already dead, its power only succoured by that monumentalisation with which poetry too is (ambiguously) involved, in a dance of the afterlife where the real power-lines (engraved, no doubt, in water) become entwined around each other; like, no doubt, some ancient myth of the bard and the chieftain, the perpetual sale of echo to the highest voice (sorry, I seem to have meant 'the highest bidder').

And so: I am not interested in sovereignty (though that is no doubt an evasion, a treason, a heresy), which is temporary, echo-less, and doomed; it is the antithesis of rapture, its psychotic, megalomaniac pole. What interests me in Derrida, and in the whirlpool of echoes and resonances which his words stir, is the ghost, which I take also to be the unattributable spasm of the heart, the moment of angina which will clarify and kill, while it reminds and echoes. There is no durable hardness – this is a triumphalist myth, constantly proved faulty; instead there are moments of echo, rhyme, repetition, never simple to interpret, never certain of voice or origin; there is, we might say – and Derrida does say, elsewhere, as we have seen, but only under the deepest of occlusions – poetry.

Or, to put it another way:

We take up with the black branch
in the street, it is our support and
control, what we do with life in
the phase now running on. From here
each time the glitter does settle out,
around some lamp, some fried-up
commercial scene we live in
support of and for. Who is this
that may just do the expected
thing; not the magic silence
of the inward eye you may be quite
positive. TV beams romantically into
the biosphere, plant food is our

daily misery. Mine: light & easy,
the victim-path is not so absurd.[39]

Well well. Where to start (begin again). This (wet) black branch: is it Ezra Pound's, and do we here come again upon the motif of sale, of capitalism, of capitalism's serving-men of prejudice?[40] And this 'running on', this lamp, are these the substance of Graham's wish to catch the flood-tide (of language, of the sea, of that which bears us away to the province of the night-ghosts)? Neither, of course, of these, *strictu sensu*; this is (again) Prynne. But that does not help. Is 'fried-up' a misprint for 'fired-up', or are we back again with the carton of eggs?

At all events, we are here on the terrain of a certain externality, a discourse that is outside its objects, its objections, which seeks to delineate a territory where 'plant food is our/daily misery', and this might serve as a change of wind, a change of tide, that might enable me to come back again to Derrida, who, on these wilder shores, and perhaps paradoxically, may signify as a 'point' of anchorage, a point on a map, a point indeed of resistance so that we may be able to orientate ourselves. Yet the critical thing, the absolute orientation, is that we are never where we think we are, we have always been carried away elsewhere (of course; this is not the 'expected thing' or the 'magic silence'), instead we (but here I have substituted, slyly, the plural, indeterminate 'we', by a no doubt unforgiveable sleight of hand, for that occluded singular personal pronoun with which Derrida in fact (?) begins this sentence)

> live this relation with a disinterestedness that is more and more distracted, an accelerated forgetfulness that is more and more profound, and with the certainty that the essential thing, as it is called, is going on elsewhere. Elsewhere: not simply in general, outside of me, which goes without saying, but also for me, in 'me', or if not totally elsewhere, then at least in a place whose paths are infinitely multiplied and confused by the 'texts'.[41]

I am not frankly sure that I agree with Derrida's ascription of these phenomena of virtuality (as I see them) to a relation with 'disinterestedness'; in fact, I am sure I disagree, insofar as I can be sure, because I think that what is here being underestimated is the romantic beaming of Prynne's TV screens and/or the downside of the genre cross-dressing that might constitute the simulacrum, the apparition, of the 'great work'. Nevertheless: the 'elsewhere':

> Do be serious they say, all the time
> in the world mounts a deficit
> of choice moments fluffed and spilled.
> Is misery worse than not knowing its cause,
> the wrong fuel in a spirit lamp?[42]

Or, finally:

> The scene of 'I am dead' – with all of its investments – maintains for a long time a very general value. Universal structures are interpreted throughout it. But somewhere – and hence the signature effect – they 'shift gears' not just into my readable proper name (that is easy to decipher), but into a particular, if not absolutely singular phantasmatic organisation. Even if I had many things of an idiomatic sort to say about the 'I am dead' that manipulate me, or which I try to outsmart, something of them remains absolutely hidden, unreadable . . . [43]

Enraptured.

# 2

# Romanticism and the Open Secret

When we speak of being 'rapt' in, or before, a work of art, and we assume that this entails a suspension of the critical faculties, it is perhaps inevitable, at least in the European context, to think of the moment of romanticism, which will help us to think through some of the questions to be addressed. What do we mean when we say that we are 'carried away' by a book? What have various writers meant when they assert that they are 'rapt' in their creativity? How do we deal with the 'secrets' of writers – because, for everything revealed, there is surely always something 'held in secret', something unsaid, something unknown, something which continues to fascinate?[1] What, indeed, is the nature of our addiction as we read – in other words, what is the meaning of our 'dependence' on the text? When we speak, often negligently, of 'escapism', is it possible that we touch lightly upon a truth, at least in inverted form: how can we escape (as readers) from the toils of the writer; how can we escape (as writers) from the imagined trammels of the destined reader – or are we all complicit in these acts of mutual bondage, inseparable addiction?

The *Oxford English Dictionary*, as we have seen, has a substantial entry on 'rapture', and the major uses can be arranged under the five headings already mentioned: the act of seizing and carrying off as prey or plunder; the act of carrying, or fact of being carried, onwards, or force of movement; the act of conveying a person from one place to another, especially to heaven; transport of mind, mental exaltation or absorption, ecstasy; the expression of ecstatic feeling in words.

And so we are taken, necessarily, to the relation between rapture and the secret. There is, of course, a wealth of critical literature on the secret; probably the best-known is the book by Frank Kermode, *The Genesis of Secrecy* (1979). Much of it is informed by psychoanalysis, although, perhaps surprisingly, Freud himself had little directly to say on the topic. The crucial developments arise with Nicolas Abraham and Maria Torok's work on the notion of the crypt and, in a very different way, with some of Jean Laplanche's comments in his *Essays on Otherness* (1998). Abraham and Torok's version of the secret is probably by now familiar, centred as it is around the notion of a psychic realm below the unconscious to which access cannot be gained, which is 'guarded', like, say Abraham and Torok, and Derrida, a cemetery, a place to which we have no access but which continuingly signifies its presence by its 'imprint' on the world of the living, the apparently hermetic gestures of the 'cemetery guard'.[2]

Laplanche's version is, I think, more interesting.[3] His central argument begins with a rejection of Jacques Lacan's famous dictum that the unconscious is structured like a language; according to Laplanche, the very notion of structure is foreign to the unconscious and is simply an effect of the recuperation. Instead, Laplanche speaks of 'messages', messages which are sent crucially down through the generations. But these messages are of a complex type (and, to my mind at least, William Blake's enduringly mysterious 'The Mental Traveller' [c. 1803] is relevant here[4]): it is not simply that a message can be passed consciously from parent to child, because where those messages are important, where they touch, for example, on sexuality, then the unconscious of the parent is also involved, which inevitably means that the message arrives, if it does at all, in a skewed format, 'awry' as Slavoj Žižek would say.[5]

## Beckoned by Ignorance

It seems to me critical to say of 'The Mental Traveller' that, in an important sense, Blake does not know what he is talking about, and here there are links with Andrew Bennett's ground-breaking work on literary ignorance.[6] Something, certainly, is sensed in 'The Mental Traveller'; perhaps as readers we become rapt as we observe the procession of the generations evolving, grasping for a structure within which to contain the mysteries of human development but always failing to do so as the 'Woman Old' repeats her acts of binding, repression, 'nailing down', as Blake puts it. For me the poem is encapsulated in the phrase 'the wild game of her roving Eye': as we stare, entranced, at the phrase 'wild game' we are inevitably led in two different, and quite possibly mutually exclusive, directions: first towards the notion of dangerous seduction, second, via the slightly later phrase 'Like the wild Stag she flees away', towards a *topos* of hunting. But what actually 'flees away' as we gaze at this piece of writing is meaning itself, if we consider meaning to be a matter of the stabilisation of forms; instead we are confronted with a kind of play of the unconscious, a secret which, however hard we try, cannot be let out. The last line of the poem, of course, is 'And all is done as I have told', which is a beautifully circular message which arrives, has its destination, precisely at the point where we began.[7]

Or we may choose to 'hunt down' the secret in Blake's 1807 notebook where we find the quintessentially alarming entry for January 20th, which simply reads 'between Two & Seven in the Evening – Despair'.[8] What are we to make of this? By what strange right, indeed, are we impelled or required to make *anything* of it, since it is a notebook entry and not, apparently, in a genre dedicated to public apprehension or consumption? What are we to do with the combination of chronological precision and emotional depth with which we are presented? Can we move beyond being simply 'rapt' by it? I am reminded of Iris Murdoch's *Metaphysics as a Guide to Morals* (1992). Amid the many (some would say endless) chapters which go on and on about the ineffable concept of 'the good', there is one short chapter called 'Void', which appears to be an attempt to account for the terrible lacuna, the gap in the world, which troubles and destabilises the search for the good as soon as its name is uttered, which signifies the impossibility of the transmission of the message, the moment, we might say, of negation.[9]

I now want to venture into another brief excursion on etymology: in Blake I am, obviously, particularly interested in the term 'rapt' and its homonym, 'wrapt' with a 'w'; but also in the words 'secret' and 'sacred'. The two spellings of 'rapt' have, etymologically, nothing in common. 'Rapt' with an 'r' is one of the many derivatives from the Latin root which has also given us 'rape, 'rapine', 'raptor' and of course 'rapture'. 'Wrap' with a 'w' comes, on the contrary, from a different root: that root is obscure, so the *OED* charmingly confesses, but is certainly of Germanic origin. But if this is an apparently unassailable distinction, it is also one which has proved unable to stand the test of time. To take two examples, Madame d'Arblay in her *Camilla* of 1796 speaks of a person being 'absorbed in . . . wrapt expectation', with a 'w';[10] in a translation of *Gil Blas* in 1809 we hear – rather interestingly – of a character reading 'with so grave and wrapt a silence', again with a 'w'.[11] We could say of this latter that it is simply a misspelling (if, after Freud, we any longer believe in simple misspellings); but is it? How would it make any less sense if we were to affirm that we can indeed be 'wrapped [with a 'w']' in silence? Would, in fact, the meaning be any different? From both points of view, we would be 'wrapped', or seized, or stolen, away from the world, we would be living in a sequestered, secret place, where there is nothing but the self and the book.

And so to 'secret' and 'sacred'. Again, the words have separate roots. 'Secret' and all its many cognate and semi-cognate forms traces back in the end, through many diversions, to the Latin root *secernere*, meaning 'to separate, or divide off'. 'Sacred' is also evidently Latinate, from the different root *sacer*, meaning (obviously) 'sacred'. But here again, the meanings begin to waver. What is the sacred if it is not that which is 'separated', 'divided off', placed in a 'different' location from the quotidian? What is the secret if it is not held in a different, consecrated space? And what, indeed, does, 'consecrate' mean? Well, it means to 'dedicate', to 'devote as sacred', to 'deify', and it does, supposedly, come from the same root as 'sacred'; but somewhere along the way, in (at least) French, Spanish, Portuguese and Italian, as well as English, the 'a' has eloped and been replaced by an 'e'. We find this passage, written in 1828: 'We have consecrated this prejudice in our institutions and our hearts':[12] 'consecrated' in the same sense, presumably, as the apparently separate word 'secreted'. The consecrated place is, then, one which is set apart, one which is, in a critical sense, unknown, perhaps unknowable except to the initiate, to the person or people who are in on the secret.

## Secrets of the Chamber

I will return to Blake via a very brief quotation from Derrida: 'I call secret not only that which is intimate but that which is like a style: inimitable'.[13] Thus the most overt of the literary distinctions which we try to make, distinctions of style, become also held in or as a secret, there is something sacred and inimitable about a style: any other view would merely sanction plagiarism, would assert the full and unassailable control of language over the human subject, would lead in the end to the inhuman, which also, of course, is precisely the threat and promise of contemporary technology, as our students know so well.

In Plate 79 of *Jerusalem* (1804–20), we find part of Jerusalem's great lament for a lost paradise.

> The river Severn stay'd his course at my command:
> Thames poured his waters into my basons and baths:
> Medway mingled with Kishon: Thames reciev'd the heavenly Jordan.
> Albion gave me to the whole earth to walk up & down, to pour
> Joy upon every mountain, to teach songs to the shepherd & plowman.
> I taught the ships of the sea to sing the songs of Zion.
> Italy saw me in sublime astonishment: France was wholly mine
> As my garden & as my secret bath: Spain was my heavenly couch,
> I slept in his golden hills; the Lamb of God met me there,
> There we walked as in our secret chamber among our little ones,
> They looked upon our loves with joy, they beheld our secret joys
> With holy raptures of adoration, rap'd sublime in the Visions of God.[14]

As we look at those last lines, we may presume that one of their meanings is that in the paradisal past Jerusalem and Albion 'walked as in our secret chamber', in other words, given other moments in Blakean discourse, 'walked naked'. We then have an immediate tension placed on the term 'secret'; what is now hidden is what was previously displayed, the human form (the 'human form divine') was not to be 'held in secret', rather it was seen as the source of joy. The 'little ones', of course, are in one sense all the peoples of Europe; but in another they are surely children, and as we go on we find that 'they looked upon our loves with joy'; in other words, I presume, the sexual act was itself not hidden, not 'secreted', but rather served as a model for enjoyment, for ecstasy. Instead of the secret, coded messages transmitted according to the Laplanchean model, there was a time when there was a direct line from parent to child which was characterised by an uninhibited eroticism. 'Secret' then, here in both of its uses, seems to mean 'now secreted': the secret is what happens when the most common of human activities disappears behind the veil, vanishes into a hidden room, a room which we may indeed like to think of as 'sacred' but which is characterised more importantly by its being a 'guarded space', a place which is separated off from the commonalties of life: in some, but perhaps negative, sense 'consecrated', the bedroom, to put it crudely, as cemetery.

The effect of this absence of inhibition, we are told, is 'rapture', the transport of the 'little ones' to another place. But Blake almost literally spells out for us here the cultural accommodation between the two etymologies of 'rapt'/'wrapt': as the little ones are entranced, seized by the primal scene – and not always, as of course Freud pointed out, merely frightened out of their wits by its apparent proximity to violence[15] – so they are also 'wrapped' (with a notional 'w') in the 'Visions of God' – in the sense, presumably, of being sequestered in innocence and thus unable to fall into the Freudian trap. 'Rapt' without a 'w' is to be seized away; 'wrapt' with a 'w' is to be hidden away. But here the two are elements in the same dialectic: even as we are transported, we are simultaneously protected; but of course, it is precisely this dialectic which, so Jerusalem tells us, has now fallen away, to be replaced by all the panoply of the 'pompous High Priest', the effects of a repressive consecration which prevents any experience of 'Comingling'.[16]

These complex linkages between rapture and secrecy also occur in *Vala, or, The Four Zoas* (1795–1804). This is a conversation between Los and Enitharmon:

> Enitharmon answer'd: 'Secure now from the smitings of thy Power, demon of fury,

> If the God enraptur'd me infolds
> In clouds of sweet obscurity my beauteous form dissolving,
> Howl thou over the body of death; 'tis thine. But if among the virgins
> Of summer I have seen thee sleep & turn thy cheek delighted
> Upon the rose or lilly pale, or on a bank where sleep
> The beamy daughters of the light, starting, they rise, they flee
> From thy fierce love, for tho' I am dissolv'd in the bright God,
> My spirit still pursues thy false love over rocks & valleys'.
>
> Los answer'd: 'Therefore fade I thus dissolv'd in raptur'd trance.
> Thou canst repose on clouds of secrecy, while o'er my limbs
> Cold dews & hoary frost creep tho' I lie on banks of summer
> Among the beauties of the World'.[17]

Well, one response to these lines would be to suspect that all marital rows are much the same, and amount to the essential line from a Travelling Wilburys song, 'Where were you last night?'[18] However, aside from a recommendation of marital therapy, my concern here is again with the trajectory of rapture. 'If the God enraptur'd me infolds', says Enitharmon; but what is she saying? Does the word 'enraptur'd' apply to God? Surely not; it would be difficult to think the possibility of God himself being enraptured: where on earth (or in heaven) would he be enraptured, seized away, *to*? But this leaves us with the equally unthinkable – because ugly – phrase 'enraptur'd *me* [my italics]'. One is forced to think – at least I am forced to think – that something very odd is happening in that line, and one obvious symbol of this is its metrical peculiarity. It is as though something is trying to get expressed which cannot be contained within conventional syntax: there is God, there is 'me' (Enitharmon), and there is rapture: but what there is not is any clear way of expressing the relation between the three terms.

## Of Seizure and Festivity

For Los, of course, things look otherwise: he is emphatically *not* (or so he protests) having a good time with the 'virgins/Of summer', or the 'beamy daughters of the light', yet that word 'rapture' creeps in again. He certainly sees himself as being 'seized' by something, but his sense of his agency in the matter is very different from Enitharmon's. As too is his sense of Enitharmon's position and stance: while she sees herself as dedicated, consecrated, to God, what Los sees is that she is wrapped in 'clouds of secrecy', these being, of course, the clouds which Enitharmon herself registers as 'clouds of sweet obscurity'. Enitharmon's bliss is Los's perception of her removal of herself from contact, her placing of herself in a secret, sacred space which forces him out into the 'cold dews & hoary frost'.

The ambiguities of consecration occur later again in *The Four Zoas*, this time in the context of Urizen:

> Thus in the temple of the Sun his books of iron & brass
> And silver & gold he consecrated, reading incessantly
> To myriad of perturbed spirits.[19]

There is nothing, of course, that Urizen likes more than to get wrapped up in a good book. In this case, he 'consecrates' the books: he 'dedicates' them in the temple of the sun. By doing so, he continues to perform what is his essential function in Blake of hiding things away; but at the same time this act of secretion is simultaneously an act of display, 'reading incessantly/To myriad of perturbed spirits'. It reminds one of the worst kind of literary festival, a kind of Hay-on-Wye of the soul.

A further quotation from Derrida reads:

> *Death* is always the name of a secret, since it signs the irreplaceable singularity. It puts forth the public name, the common name of a secret, the common name of the proper name without name. It is therefore always a schibboleth, for the manifest sense of a secret is from the beginning a private name, so that language about death is nothing but the long history of a secret society, neither public nor private, semi-private, semi-public, on the border between the two.[20]

I wonder why the phrase 'clouds of sweet obscurity' comes back to mind. Anyway, the way I make sense of this is that the very act of 'naming' involves a complex operation between the private and the public, or perhaps the sacred and the profane. The name is, in a sense, like style, inimitable: it patrols the boundary between what is known and what is not known; in its very public availability, in the way in which we are ourselves inevitably named by our name, it simultaneously involves the private, the secret, the fantasy of a name known only to ourselves – which would, perhaps, not be a name at all but some other, unnameable thing.

It would be possible to take this back to another of the poems from Blake's Pickering manuscript, 'William Bond' (c. 1803).[21] I would want to do so because the poem seems to me contain a kind of what Derrida would describe as a 'signature effect',[22] the repetition-with-difference from

'William Blake' into 'William Bond'. What the poem appears to produce is a kind of sacred, hieratic act; but whether it is possible for the meaning of this act – which seems also to be, in some sense, an act of sacrifice – ever to become fully public seems doubtful. It is held, as it were, in secret: 'I wonder whether the Girls are mad,/And I wonder whether they mean to kill,/And I wonder if William Bond will die,/For assuredly he is very ill'. Thus the poem begins, but we as readers may indeed find ourselves continuing to wonder, for the poem answers none of these questions; what is does do is to enact a secret and to conclude, I think, with a rapture:

I thought Love liv'd in the hot sun shine,
But O, he lives in the moony light!
I thought to find Love in the heat of day,
But sweet Love is the Comforter of Night.

Seek Love in the Pity of others' Woe,
In the gentle relief of another's care,
In the darkness of night & the winter's snow,
In the naked & outcast, Seek Love there!

To return, thus prompted, to the question of the relation between rapture and communication, we may find helpful a brief comment by Martin Heidegger in his 'Letter on "Humanism"' (1947): 'the liberation of language from grammar into a more original essential framework is reserved for thought and poetic creation'.[23] In Heidegger again, then, we find an emphasis on the role of poetry as something which 'carries us away', which transports us to a place where linguistic and generic conventions have little or no place: in stark opposition to a notion of poetry as, for example, the 'highly wrought', these kinds of idea about poetry put the reader in a type of suspension, a place where the usual coordinates by which we measure experience no longer apply, within which we are 'rapt', in either or both senses of the term.

And the great type of the poet, for Heidegger, was of course Friedrich Hölderlin, whom we may also fairly describe as a poet of rapture. Here, for example, are some lines from his poem 'Sunset':

Where are you? Dazzled, drunken my soul grows faint
 And dark with so much gladness; for even now
  I listened while, too rich in golden
   Sounds, the enrapturing youth, the sun-god

Intoned his evening hymn on a heavenly lyre.[24]

'Enrapturing', being carried away, being rendered faint and dark: the task of the poet here is not to enlighten but to attempt to convey an experience within which words fail, where a secret is intimated but one which is too powerful to convey; meaning is not so much transmitted or rendered public as hidden, placed in a secret space, within which the role of the reader is as, in Conrad's endlessly ambiguous term, the 'secret sharer' – the sharer in secret, the sharer of secrets. Blake knew this, of course, in part in his strange relation to a supposedly 'hermetic' tradition, a relation which has since driven critics into equally strange and baroque interpretative contortions,[25] and in part in terms of his all-important concept of 'self- annihilation', a process to which Hölderlin's contemporary Novalis also refers when, for example, he says:

> The true philosophical act is suicide; this is the real beginning of all philosophy, in that direction all the needs of the philosophical apprentice tend, and only this act corresponds to all the conditions and characteristics of transcendental action.[26]

It is interesting to pause and note that reports of psychotic rapture also continually emphasise its own opposite, the moment of disaffiliation, the long come-down which succeeds the rapturous ineffable, which is also the realisation of the incommunicability of that which rapture brings: like the long, perhaps endless, addictive moment, the psychotic episode is also conducive to despair, perhaps that despair of which we have just heard Blake speaking (if indeed we are 'hearing' the text, a point to which I shall return later). But Michael Hamburger, who translates Novalis thus, also makes the point that 'suicide' is probably the wrong translation (although, in an interesting moment of non-translation, or failed translation, he repeats it himself) for the German word *Selbsttötung*, literally the 'dying of the self', the snuffing out of the candle, we might say following the dictates of high romanticism, in the light of a greater flame.[27] The secret, then, insofar as it is a secret which can be communicated, is the secret of absence, of absenting: behind the words on the page, the apparent recording of experience, lies the awareness of a lacuna, and whether this is 'translated' as rapture or despair, or as an inevitable compound of both, might fairly appear to be a precarious decision.

## At Home with Dr Autenrieth

As, perhaps, is the relation between rapture and silence, the silencing of the poet before, perhaps, the power of poetry – or language. To turn again to Hölderlin, we find this passage in his long poem 'Bread and Wine':

> Where is the swift? And full of joy omnipresent, where does it
> Flash upon dazzled eyes, thundering fall from clear skies?
> Father Aether! one cried, and tongue after tongue took it up then,
> Thousands, no man could bear life so intense on his own;
> Shared, such wealth gives delight and later, when bartered with strangers,
> Turns to rapture; the word gathers new strength when asleep . . . [28]

Above all it is the last line here which fascinates me: 'the word gathers new strength when asleep' ('*es wächst schlafend des Wortes Gewalt*'). Whatever is going on here in terms of rapture, it is, as we might expect, not under control: we might in Freudian terms say that it arises from the unconscious, but it is also true that one might regard that act of cultural translation, or recuperation, as suspect; maybe there are equally valid renditions of experience available within romantic discourse itself. What is at stake here, more significantly, is a process of secrecy, perhaps of secretion: below the surface something is growing, something perhaps reminiscent of the hidden multiplicity of Gilles Deleuze and Félix Guattari's rhizomes:[29] it forms itself according to a different order from the quotidian and it manifests itself in a different sort of connection; it is, as it were, 'rapt' (with a 'w') in sleep, and in this state the boundaries of the individual waver and are transformed.

Now this, we might say, is precisely typical of the kind of high romanticism of which Hölderlin's poetry is emblematic; much of that poetry is what we might call a 'poetry of transport', a reaching out towards the ineffable. But it would be implausible to separate this from the wider question of Hölderlin's fate, and here, of course, we need to tread carefully on the brink – patrol the boundaries, we might say – of life and work, of the textual and the experiential. For example, we hear that when Hölderlin was removed to what is usually referred to as a 'mental home' in 1806, 'there was drug treatment of a sort, belladonna and digitalis, but also the notorious Autenrieth mask, applied to stop patients from screaming, besides the straitjacket and long forcible immersions in cold water inside a cage'.[30] A drug regime ('of sorts'): a set of attempts to redirect and refuel addiction, prophylactics against a 'different' dependency.

We can listen also to this salutary judgement on Hölderlin's later poetry, from David Constantine:

> Some of the Tübingen poems are beautiful and touching, and some have

> moments of the purest immanence such as the preceding poetry had always striven to achieve; but the inexorable trend is downwards and away.[31]

'Striven to achieve'; 'downwards and away'. What seems to be at stake here is a phenomenon which we might term the 'rebuff of rapture': the moment when, for example, a certain kind of striving is abandoned and the result is a movement of contradiction. On the one hand, there is the putative effortless achievement of that which no amount of striving can ever produce; on the other there is the long slow slide away from rapture, the abandonment, as Blake might put it, of Eden for Beulah,[32] the inevitable regrowth of the skin of contentment when aspiration has proved, Icarus-like, too dangerous and scorching to be borne.

Rapture then, we might say, can also be considered to be, among other things, the birth-pangs of its own opposite. We might also use the relevant psychological terminology here; we might say that rapture is an unthought protection against despair, a structure of guarding, a Gothic fortress within which we may be 'sequestered' away from the pull of the quotidian, and indeed the pull of time. Within rapture, as within the regimes of addiction, time falls under a 'different' god, we walk, like the protagonist of Algernon Blackwood's short story 'The Pikestaffe Case' (1924),[33] in ellipses rather than straight lines, we adopt, or fall prey to, a different geometry. The notion, then, of removal to another plane is inevitably constructed on the postponement of a feared descent into the mundane, the vertiginous fall from the high tower known in the Tarot reading. And so we begin to glimpse the ways in which the dialectic of rapture would be identical to the dialectic of addiction; it is, for example, the custom of alcoholics to refer in private – in secret, indeed, albeit of course an open secret, as all secrets are – to non-alcoholics as 'earth people', people who are bound by everyday ties, who are therefore unable to experience the moment of floating free, who are unable to 'subject' themselves to the 'being carried away', to a mode of transport which is always on the brink of being out of control, of threatening a suspension of subjectivity.[34]

There is then at stake here a certain state of exemption, of being freed from earthly bonds. On this topic, if somewhat obliquely, Heidegger again has something to say:

> Being [capitalised in Heideggerian rhetoric] is also called the holy, the ultimate source of the conserving power that guards beings in the integrity of their Being. It is neither God nor the gods; it is 'beyond' both gods and men, granting to both the integrity of their Being in the sense that it opens up the domain in which both gods and men may come-to-presence as what they

> are. It is the overflowing source which gives rise to all beings. As such, Being is also ground.[35]

Not unusually for Heidegger, this passage is not without its difficulties: but in the context of what I am trying to talk about, it is in particular the word 'overflowing' (which, of course, Blake also uses in one of the better-known Proverbs of Hell[36]) which should attract the attention. Rapture is, among the many things I have mentioned, also the moment of overflowing: the moment of *Selbsttötung*, of the dying of the self. Is the result of this condition a kind of madness? In the case of Hölderlin, as in the case of Blake, the possibility hovers, although one might fairly enquire of the safety of a diagnosis which ensues from a combination of digitalis and cold water; or indeed precisely what it was that Hölderlin might have screamed had it not been for the pressure of the ghastly Autenrieth face mask. What is certain is that rapture represents, in some sense, an encounter with the incommunicable, and as such, to hark back for a moment to a previous quotation from Derrida, an encounter with death – within which, one might add, the question of 'style' becomes irrelevant, as though one could choose the colour of one's skin as a gesture of style.[37] But also here Heidegger is seeking to effect a highly significant discursive loop: precisely that which 'floats free' is also the guarantee of the 'ground', the way through which we recognise the 'groundedness' of all being: thus rapture, considered from one (or another) point of view is not simply a moment, or mode, of escape, but is instead a moment of recognition of inexorability, within which what is realised, above all, is how one is 'tied' to a condition of humanness which can never be free except insofar as freedom is the mere recognition of being bound to a higher power. Which is, of course, the definition of freedom put forward by many religions ('whose service is perfect freedom', to take but the Christian example[38]); and yet this definition remains one which astounds by virtue of its very circularity, asserting the absence of the transcendent even at those moments when the possibility of transcendence appears most closely on the horizon, appearing to perform an ambiguous act of beckoning which threatens the very space into which we may find ourselves, Icarus-like, projected.

## Chime

But to revert to an earlier point: if there is no question of style within rapture, if rapture menaces style's particularity, its separateness, its own refusal of the one, unified body, perhaps even its singularity,[39] if style and rapture figure as opposing means of dealing with the imminence of death, through, we might say – developing on Derridean terms – signature and the erasure or deletion of signature, what there certainly is in relation to rapture, at least as some of the romantic writers conceived it, is a question of harmony. One of Hölderlin's most frequently used tropes, which is of relevance in this regard, is of 'ringing'. He speaks (or tries to speak, on a terrain on which all speech appears to be prematurely ended) of the way in which the 'ringing' of the heavens (whatever, and wherever, they may be) is in some sense answered, during the moment of rapture, by the 'ringing' of the earth.[40] I should say here that I am not alluding directly to a multiplicity of ring-tones, of the strange harmonies which sometimes break out in train carriages, especially, it seems, when going into, or coming out of, a tunnel, although maybe that too is relevant. What I mean to refer to is rather a sense of resonance, literally therefore of resounding, of 're-sounding', such that the individual voice becomes – as it also does in, for example, Blackwood's strange novel *The Human Chord* (1910) – subsumed into a wider harmony of voices (or indeed of voice, since all individuality is here lost, under erasure). On this point it is useful to remember that we talk conventionally of the psychotic moment as one in which the subject (if there is a subject) may 'hear voices', voices which command this or that from some hypothesised superhuman perspective; but one of the technical terms which has been deployed clinically in the course of the long series of attempts to understand this process is perhaps more apposite: 'thought broadcasting'[41], which more aptly captures the way in which under conditions of psychosis (which is nowadays considered more frequently to be a kind of 'interruption' within more usual modes of communication rather than as the condition or 'ground', in Heidegger's sense, of personality) the normally narrow boundaries of communication dissolve in what one might term – again searching for a contemporary equivalent, and one which might go beyond Avital Ronell's sustained investigation of the relation between the psychic and the telephonic[42] – a quasi-eternal broadband of the soul.

And I do not mean that as merely a mawkish attempt at contemporary reference: I think it carries a greater signification, because one of the things broadband does is to relativise the issue of what might alternatively be called, in that term of even more mysterious provenance, 'eavesdropping' – or, as P. B. Shelley and other romantics had it, 'overhearing'.[43] What is it to 'overhear'? In one obvious sense, it is to hear that which one is not intended to hear (and this is, of course, an underlying if paradoxical condition of all fiction). Certainly this is true, even if that apparently obvious sense of presumed intention might also be under a certain erasure; but overhearing is also to 'hear too much', to hear, perhaps, sounds and harmonies which threaten to overwhelm, to hear that which one is not 'authorised' to hear (and that which, therefore, threatens one's 'authority', one's being as an 'author', or indeed as the 'author of one's own fate', in that striking if clichéd phrase which hints, if one can still hear it aright, at the literary as the ground of experience). It is therefore indeed to hear (and here the distinction between 'hearing' and 'listening' might begin to demonstrate itself) that which Heidegger might refer to as the 'ground of all being' (or 'Being'), the sound we would hear if and when all other sounds were shut out, the sound, we might therefore say, of the rapture (and here I should say that I am not unaware of the recent quasi-religious coinage of the image of 'the rapture' as the seizing away of a kind of post-Calvinist elect, since it is obviously part of the ground of the neo-Christian fundamentalism which now plays so large a part in global politics, and which is probably, through its resistance not so much to scientific discovery and advance as to broad-based human and organic sympathy, the major threat to the planet's future). Rapture, however, as the ground of all being: one might instead refer to the sound of one hand clapping.

We need, however, to return to the question of this apparent 'indifference' of language, to the point at which language ceases to be a mode of differentiation and instead assimilates itself to the low buzz, the slow hum of static on the communicative wires. We may again quote Heidegger, in what appears to be rather desperate mode, a mode which in Heidegger is fundamentally estranged yet bizarrely familiar:

> We speak and speak about language. What we speak of, language, is always ahead of us. Our speaking merely follows language. Thus we are continually lagging behind what we try to 'capture'. Thus when we speak about language, we remain entangled in a speaking which is persistently inadequate.[44]

The key terms here would be 'rapture' and 'capture': the 'being seized away' and the 'being seized back'; liberation and incarceration, considered as the twin moments of our encounters with language. Of course, we might say, and especially if we were to try to 'capture' the moment of a post-structuralist consensus (although perhaps it is one which, of necessity, is now in a process of 'passing'), language seizes us all the time: in syntactical terms in particular, to venture even a few words off the strait and narrow of conventional grammar places us at risk: of misunderstanding, certainly, but much more than that – of severe risk to our lives and liberty. The modern variations of the Autenrieth face mask beckon. 'Colourless green ideas', to quote Noam Chomsky, may indeed 'sleep furiously'[45]: but at the same time they are held together on the thin thread of syntax, they may butt against but they do not break the chain of signification.

But at the same time, to consider matters in a more diachronic than synchronic light, language is continually in the process of being reborn and remade: in Blakean terms, Los's activity on the anvil can never cease, and yesterday's language is never our own. My children listen to what they call R&B; but Otis Redding or James Brown it is not, and neither do they recognise what I am talking about when I mildly suggest that there might have been wildly different acronymic avatars of the current music (that is, naturally, not exactly how I express it).

## Overflow/Overdose

But to return (again; and again). Perhaps – and there is always this danger when trying to think about Hölderlin and Heidegger – I seem to be verging on the unduly mystical. In fact, reviewing the past pages, there is no doubt about it: the mystical has an unmistakable presence here. And it would seem probable that such a danger hovers whenever rapture appears (which, ironically, means that the mystical may not be so secret or 'consecrated' a realm as it may appear). Perhaps this tendency may be somewhat alleviated if we turn to a passage from Novalis' 'novel' – or perhaps prose poem – *Heinrich von Ofterdingen* (1800), which may put matters in a more carnal perspective. Novalis is speaking here of the baptism of the poet in the fountain of language – that very fountain, perhaps, which in Blake's 'proverb' continually overflows:

> He dipped his hand into the basin and wet his lips. It was as though a spirit breathed through him and he felt deeply strengthened and refreshed. An irresistible longing to bathe seized him, he undressed and stepped down into the basin. It seemed as if a sunset cloud was enveloping him; a heavenly sensation flowed through his soul; with voluptuous delight countless thoughts strove to mingle within him. New images never seen before arose and interfused and became visible beings around him, and every wave of the lovely element clung to him like a tender bosom. The waves appeared to be charming girls dissolved, which embodied themselves as they touched the youth.[46]

Any psychoanalyst, experienced or inexperienced, confronted with this passage (in default of its defunct human avatar) ought presumably to thank whatever gods seem appropriate for presenting such an extraordinarily overt set of sexually revealing symptoms. The youth, to begin with, undresses (and Novalis' writing is throughout his brief career a writing of youth, or of prolonged and postponed adolescence; it would indeed be strange were it not); he experiences feelings which, he claims, he has never experienced before, as if in some condition of half-understood awakening after, one presumes, a period of anticipatory latency; he, it would appear, 'mingles', although with whom or indeed what remains unclear, unless this is a 'self-intertwining', an awakening of the auto-voluptuousness of the previously unfelt, or at least unrealised, body; a bosom mysteriously, yet perhaps not entirely to the reader's surprise, appears and, lo and behold, resolves itself, developing now from the recourse to the mother to a more adventurous exercise in the polymorphous, into a flow of 'charming girls'. That this is a moment of adolescent sexual fantasy hardly needs underlining; repression is barely (so to speak) an issue. Here again we have the overflowing fountain, the seizure of (or by) rapture; but, according to one very obvious psychological explanation, what it is overflowing *with* is an all too palpable desire, an over-excitation of stimulus which might, almost literally (and to quote the Travelling Wilburys again), take one's breath away.[47]

But through this *topos* we can again return to rapture, and to the notion that when one is seized, transported, one's breath is indeed taken away. But that, of course, would also be the condition of death; or, perhaps, as Edgar Allan Poe knew so well, of those states of suspended animation (which literally, of course, imply the suspension of breath or spirit) which are to all intents and purposes indistinguishable from death.[48] 'To all intents and purposes'; or perhaps, more accurately, they are distinguished by one thing, and that is the most important thing of all, namely the possibility that one might live to return and tell the tale.

And so we might perhaps come upon a hypothesis, which is relevant to rapture: which is that the telling of the tale, the recounting of the story, as so many writers, romantic and other, tell us, requires a prior moment of suspended animation, a moment in which our breath has been taken away. The story of story, therefore – if one may put it like that – would then always be as it so often is in western classical myth, the story which remains to be told (the remains of a story, always merely the remains, for the story itself has been forever lost, within the rapture, from which nothing can be remembered) after a return from the dead, carrying with us, if we are lucky enough and the underworld has not claimed us as its own, some more or less recognisable residue of an otherwise incommunicable experience which is, seen from another angle, not experience at all but precisely that which comes to challenge and relativise the very concept of experience:[49] 'life', as we might say, 'Jim, but not life as we know it'. And *Star Trek* is perhaps not as irrelevant as it might seem; an apparently endless series of encounters with other, more or less indecipherable worlds which continue to hold their own, non-narrativisable secrets may be one of the best of critical accounts of the secretive process of creativity.

Perhaps, however, it is not appropriate to conclude a chapter either with Novalis's sexual fantasies or with *Star Trek*. Instead I will return for a moment to the notion of rapture. For to be seized away, as we have seen, is also to be wrapped up: or perhaps, as the Christian religion appears to assert in its complex, convoluted and probably only half-understood discourse about the body of Christ, it is in the opposition between the two that the numinous can be felt, the body wrapped and the body seized away. We might recall that after Blake's brief mention of despair in his notebook, he goes on to make some interesting, but entirely mundane, points about printing. Despair, it would appear, is not necessarily the end, any more than rapture can be 'the end'. The end, if there is an end, can only be constantly postponed, and rapture is perhaps one of those modes of postponement, seizure and capture as a way of representing a longed-for stoppage in time.

## Judgement Day

Yet there cannot be an end to a discussion of rapture without also at least bringing onto the stage a notion of paranoia, because the sense of a 'different' life can hardly be separated from a radical doubt as to the bearability of the present one; and here perhaps our best witness is Judge Schreber – or better, the composite personality of Schreber and Freud which we need to unravel as we read the surprisingly short text of Freud's 'Psycho-analytical Notes on an Autobiographical Account of a Case of Paranoia' (1911). In it, Freud attempts to unravel Schreber's 'theologico-psychological system'. Part of this consists in the belief that:

> Souls that have passed through the process of purification enter into the enjoyment of a *state of bliss*. In the meantime they have lost some of their individual consciousness, and have become fused together with other souls into higher unities. Important souls . . . may have to retain their sense of identity for hundreds of years to come, before they too can become resolved into higher soul-complexes, such as 'Jehovah rays' in the case of ancient Jewry, or 'Zoroaster rays' in the case of ancient Persia.[50]

It is clearly not very far from Schreber's 'state of bliss' to a state of rapture; neither is it difficult to see this potential as 'wrapt' within the possibility of the loss of individual identity – ironically more difficult if one has made the most of that individuality during one's 'ordinary', time-bounded lifetime. But Freud goes further than this, and in a remarkable pronouncement he alludes to the possibility that Schreber's 'concept of the state of bliss is derived from a condensation of the two principal meanings of the German word "*selig*" – namely, "dead" and "sensually happy"'.[51] Here we have an immediate (or unmediated) glimpse directly into the 'mechanics of rapture': the refusal of a separation between sensual fulfilment and death, the ready assumption that what may be required for the rapture is the annihilation of the self. Is this a metaphorical or a literal annihilation? This is perhaps precisely where the intervention of rapture dwells, in a refusal to acknowledge the persistence of such a distinction. In the realm of rapture, there is no obvious distinction between the literal and the metaphorical, and this, of course, is also the most basic description of the psychotic episode or state, the submersion in 'concrete thinking' which acts to prevent the drawing out of the fine thread on which the attribution of the metaphor might be based.[52]

One of the principal elements in Schreber's delusional system is, as it is also with some romantic poets, his relation to the sun (at which he believed he could, under certain circumstances, look directly). Freud wishes to

> draw attention to the subject of the *sun*, which, through its 'rays', came to have so much importance in the expression of [Schreber's] delusions. Schreber has quite a peculiar relation to the sun. It speaks to him in human language, and thus reveals itself to him as a living being, or as the organ of a yet higher being lying behind it.[53]

'Has quite a peculiar relation to the sun'; what, one has to ask, would an 'ordinary' relation to the sun be like? How 'familiar', in any sense of that word, might it be? But more importantly, perhaps, we have here the sense that even the sun may only be an avatar of something beyond; and thus we have a sense of the continuous movement in rapture, whereby any apparent object (of our desire, of our communication) may be only standing for (revealing and concealing at the same time) some 'other' thing, some different source of revelation, the reality, the presence of which we are always on the verge of grasping, yet never without the menace that it may elude us, it may demonstrate to us that we are, in the end, unworthy. And so, we may ask, is it really the case that the realm of rapture is entirely opposed to the demands of the moral law:[54] or may it be a figure for a taking to the highest extreme of that law, involving discovering and inhabiting a realm where, despite the apparent irrelevance of one's 'just deserts', some phantomatic remnant of such a process – a process of 'judgement' perhaps, especially in the 'case' of Judge Schreber, precisely an exemplar of the derangement of 'due process' – remains to haunt us just as the moment of bliss invites to seek the succour of transcendence?

# 3

# The Scene of Addiction

I have already suggested that rapture and the secret are bound together with questions (some would say 'issues') of addiction, and it would seem important, in any consideration of addiction, and especially any consideration of the relationship between addiction and rapture, to turn to William Burroughs. Burroughs's texts provide us with one of the most self-conscious of guides through an addicted world which is violently dislocated from linear time, while at the same time, and crucially, undermining the reliability of any such guide. We cannot, Burroughs tells us, trust the account of the addict; but this also implies, in a further phantomatic reticulation, that we need to question to what extent we can trust ourselves in the moment of addiction to reading. While we are secretly communing with the text, for example, we may also be liable to 'forget', or to ignore, the outer parameters which comprise the moral universe; we are freed – in the moment of addiction (which is an endless moment), in the moment of reading (which may also be an endless moment) – but, paradoxically, we find an equally endless problem when we have to account for the difficulty in reporting the content of this freedom. Here may be, for example, an essential link to the definition of 'rapture' as a psychotic phenomenon; I mean here to refer to 'rapture' as a critical ingredient in the complexities both of reading and of addiction. In the work of Burroughs, as in the condition of the psychotic episode, there is a more or less violent dislocation between the force of the messages 'broadcast' to us from the outside and the alignment of these messages with the counterforce of the world of apparent experience.

A further argument would be that we are here in some sense in a Gothicised world; this would rest to an extent on an absence, or better a draining, of trust, which includes (or is based on) a 'forgetting', or forgoing, of trust in ourselves.[1] While we are, therefore, secretly communing with the secrets within the text, we are also liable to 'forget', or to ignore, the outer parameters which comprise the moral universe and its various genres; we are freed but, paradoxically, we find the utmost difficulty in reporting the content of this freedom, as do so many Gothic protagonists, straining as they so frequently do against the presumed disbelief of their auditors.[2] Here we find one aspect of this essential link, which can also be found across

Gothic fiction, to the notion of psychotic rapture, which may be, among other things, an emblem for the force reading has in dislocating us from a world, in placing us in a position (through interpellation or vocation) in a realm not of our choosing; which will uncannily replicate our suppressed sense that that is where, if we were only to admit it, we are anyway, in a realm which is fully comprised of 'habit'.

## Crave

I would like, then, to address some questions that might arise from a reading of Burroughs, and these are, at least initially, of a very general kind. What, we might ask – as Burroughs implicitly but constantly does – is the condition of literature? What is the condition of reading? To take this a stage further, and to focus on the 'medical' quality of Burroughs's writing, what, therefore, is the nature of the term 'condition'? What, indeed, as we move through Burroughs's texts, might 'our' condition be – as readers, as citizens, as – in at least some sense of the word – addicts?[3] Or, to put it in another way which is all too typical of Burroughs, what is my doctor's condition, and how does it relate to mine, how does it affect or 'condition' mine? Are we speaking here of the possibility of a cure, or of the perpetuation, albeit perhaps through altered means, of a dependence – or, to put it in more overtly Gothic terms, do we finish the text feeling as though we have been 'freed', or rather as though what we need is precisely another dose, another fix? What, finally, might the condition(ality) be of any (potentially fatal) meeting with 'the doctor' – what is 'conditional' about this, and 'conditional' upon what?[4]

Yet of course even this is not in any sense final. For as Burroughs' texts spin it out (as they weave through themselves, as they effect their own curiously intertwined textuality), how might we become (or already be) 'conditioned' to the uncertainties of these questions, which would amount to a conditioning to paranoia, an absence of ground on which to pass judgement? Burroughs's fictions – like, again, so many Gothic fictions – are obviously paranoiac, or at least overtly concerned with the imagery of persecution, and in both cases we can fairly ask in what 'condition' might we at any time be in a 'market' situation, in a hidden economy of drugs or visions, and what might it be like (for the purposes of commerce, or re-sale) to be (technologically) re-conditioned?[5]

Perhaps we have, then, for the moment to continue the questions; and this would seem apposite for, after all, Burroughs's fiction is a fiction of questions, an interrogative fiction. For all of its apparent assertiveness, its arrogance, its deliberate and excessive supply of offence, we are already knowingly undermined by the bringing on stage of a radical uncertainty about the nature, or remains, of subjectivity. How then, we might also ask, might we be served here by a concept or practice of secrecy – after all, everything in Burroughs appears to be overt, even blatant, angrily charged with the narcissistic necessity for display; what world, we might therefore ask, is there which does not know of, or at least suspect, our 'condition'? Let us look at an example:

> White sat quietly beaming 'humanity's condition' – Wise Radio Doctor started putting welfare officers in his portable – The Effects Boys to see if they can do any locks over the Chinese – Told me to sit down – .[6]

Where here (if anywhere), we might ask of Burroughs, is the rapture; how are we 'taken away', how are we seized by (or of) the text – or, to put it in a different register, how are we 'subjected' to (Gothic) nightmare; and if we are indeed 'taken away', is it only, for example, on a hospital trolley or stretcher – on which we might eventually die?

Rapture, as I am beginning to suggest, is a critical term in Burroughs (as it is in the Gothic). A question which is often posed is whether the rapture, in Burroughs' terms, might be a postponement or recapitulation of death, and specifically of the endlessly contested scenario of the death of his wife at, it would appear, his own hands – or rather at the barrel of his own gun.[7] And a further question, indeed, might be of how this might re-enact the violent rapture of the Gothic – the sense of being removed from, or relieved of, all responsibility as we watch the unstoppable drama unfold – or explode – beside our hospital bed. This would return us to the question of what the condition might then be of the reader as patient – in Burroughs, with his overt, yet still secret, medicalisation of the text; in Gothic, with its frequent reliance on the terrors of fractured bone, invaded flesh, the hint of postponed healing.

How are we 'enrapt', Burroughs goes on to ask, by drugs? Or to put it another way, what might it mean *not* to be thus? After all, the drugs, as we are now well aware, are in the water, they are, we might say, in a condition of dissolution (which in turn pre-mirrors the always imminent dissolution of the body, the morbid return to fluidity[8]). To speak both pharmacologically and theologically, the apparently pure water of life is already contaminated, we are 'conditioned' to our intake – just as, indeed, were the early readers of Gothic, accustomed to a 'different' world, a world where conventional parameters were in abeyance, where our assumptions about history, about cause and effect, about a certain immunisation in the face of contamination, have succumbed to a more 'o'er-mastering' logic. To what, again, are we 'conditioned'? What might it mean (to look at the issue of conditioning a little awry) to be 'ill-conditioned'? Could addiction be referred to as, for example and to rejuvenate again an alcoholic rhetoric, 'air conditioning'?

## Free Toxins

Burroughs refers us, as he often implies, to a molecular level, to a level, a stratum, where we find ourselves apprehending the virus, living what has now come to be thought of as a viroid life,[9] a creeping, crawling kind of life, which, on later reflection, would be an avatar of the kind of 'pharma fiction' represented, for example, in recent films like *Blood Diamond* (2006) or in John LeCarré's *The Constant Gardener* (2005). For, in ways that Burroughs perhaps foresaw (if he could indeed foresee, or see, anything, given the self-imposed blindness, or at least narrowing of vision, which is the outcome of junk), addiction has now become politically critical. The crucial issues that Burroughs dwells on – how political and corporate mastery are predicated upon, and conduce towards, a guarantee of an addicted future which is the ultimate goal of consumerism; how dependency can reach a point where it is 'independence' that should be regarded as perversion, since it pretends to deny desire; how subjectivity can be drained and then reconstituted in a form wholly assimilable to capitalist needs – seem to have greater resonance now than ever before. The structure should be read like this: if the embracing system appears to be, or to be on the point of becoming, total, does that mean that we are no longer capable of perceiving it straight, that Herbert Marcuse's anxieties about one-dimensionality have reappeared in a different form, that we have lost our bearings, or indeed our minds;[10] or does it mean that we are at last in fact receiving the true message, the message which comes down the wires but simultaneously tangles the wires, which is a message of despair, a message that tells us, in the least uncertain terms possible, that, as so frequently in the depths of the Gothic labyrinth (a labyrinth which will further entangle us later) or of the mazes of the opiate, there is no chance of escape?

'Word begets image and image *is* virus', Burroughs says in a telling phrase in *Nova Express* (1992),[11] thereby calling attention, among other things, to the curious logic of the replica, whereby information itself becomes a deflection, novelty an unnecessary complication in the predestined life of the organism. It is probably impossible to think (which is why Burroughs's texts to such a large extent abandon, or prohibit, anything which we conventionally recognise as thought) what a radical suggestion this is, for we consider ourselves, as a species, to be bound to a project which we refer to as 'civilisation', or as modernity, to be predicated on the new; this has been the basis of modernity, at least in the West, down the ages.[12] But perhaps the irruption of the new should be seen differently, looked at through a different lens; perhaps it is merely a way of avoiding destiny, which really resides endlessly in 'more of the same', in a feared succumbing to the repetition without alleviation, the chronic anxiety of the desert or of the ocean.

As a 'test case', so to speak, we might consider the 'alnorphine test', to which Burroughs alludes, again in *Nova Express*. It does not exist (as we might indeed expect), except in the realm of dysfunction and the realm of narrative (such as Gothic, and especially nineteenth-century medicalised Gothic) which might be brought to bear on such dysfunction. Apomorphine, on the other hand, which is a staple of Burroughs' *pharmakon*, is used now mostly for erectile dysfunction and Parkinson's disease[13]; a far cry, one might say, from the apparent delights of the hallucinatory, from the moment of the mind's fortress yielding up its horrific yet, in the end, edifying secrets. I used the term 'medicalisation' loosely above: certainly there is medicine in Burroughs, as, disturbingly, there is also surgery, but it is with the 'pharmacological', in the broadest sense, that his writings – like, arguably, Derrida's – are chiefly concerned.

Here is Burroughs, still in *Nova Express*, describing the psychological and political force of the 'cut-up' technique:

> This is machine strategy and the machine can be redirected – Record for ten minutes on a tape recorder – Now run the tape back without playing and cut in other words at random – Where you have cut in and re-recorded words are wiped off the tape and new words in their place – You have turned time back ten minutes and wiped electromagnetic word patterns off the tape and substituted other patterns – You can do the same with mind tape . . . [14]

The question would be, Can you? Can you rewrite the past, substituting 'other words' for those conventionally used? This could seem to be to do with the Orwellian, with the rewriting of history; as it could also seem to be about the Gothic, about the complex processes of reinscribing a different view of history, about considering the 'remains' under a different light, from a different point of view, or with the colourings of a different chiaroscuro. Gothic, it has often been said, is distorted history;[15] in Burroughs, history itself figures merely as a distortion, a recuperation, a way of asserting a progression of or from subjectivity which the quasi-eternal facts of addiction and rapture serve to challenge or deny. It would also, of course – looking towards the present and the future rather than the past – seem to be about virtual reality, about a radical textual instability which would itself announce the instability of the subject, which would also be the moment of the perception of persecution which would re-colour the surrounding universe.

It could therefore also be an attempt – perhaps always doomed – to interrupt the pattern of repetition (the pattern of the addict), an attempt to find a way out of the 'dungeon of the self', wherein we are always being confined by Burroughs's 'Nova Guards'. But the question also arises: of what are the Nova Guards themselves frightened, how is fear revisited onto the custodians of a suspect, state-sanctioned sanity? Might they, Burroughs speculates, nonetheless be scared, be in a condition of basic fear – fear, perhaps, of the 'scorpion gods',[16] of insectile life, of the reptilian, for this is where the fears in Burroughs appear to reside – perhaps indeed of everything to which Deleuze and Guattari refer as the rhizomatic, the creeping, crawling, omnipresent life which radically undermines the 'arborescent', progress- and development-oriented myths by which we are taught to live our lives? For the truth of the addict – and if this is a repetition, then it is a deliberate one – is that there is no escape; it is not as though one can detach the 'substance' from the subject, for the substance has already become that from which the fabric of the subject is woven. Junk comes to announce the rule of the cyborg; the cyborg comes to announce the enduring success of junk.[17]

A further quotation from Burroughs:

> Time: The night before adventurers who hope to form another blazing photo – Injury Headquarters Concentration with reports from Hiroshima – Some of the new hallucinogens and Nagasaki – Slight overdose of dimethyltryptamine – Your cities are ovens where South American narcotic plants brought total disposal – Brain screams of millions who have controller lives in that place screamed back from white hot blue sky – Can always pull the nova equipped now with tower blasts from Hiroshima and Nagasaki – In such pain he has only one turnstile – [18]

This is not merely – or perhaps not at all – a description, rather it is a textual enactment, an incarnation, of the phenomenon Burroughs knows as Nova Express. But, it might be argued, it is pointless to write (about) Nova Express. Such a concept (if that is what it is) is post-critical, while at the same time being almost ludicrously prescient; but then, what precisely would that mean? It would mean, I suppose, that the crazed, prophetic stories of the West have come true; and so, perhaps, they have. Junk vision might be the only vision left, the fate and glory of the dionysiac; according to this reading only the addict can see with the real clarity born of despair – that would be the challenge, and the one in order to prevent the acceptance of which the addict must be continually sacrificed in an agon which is also 'our own'. Afghanistan's poppy fields, to take one of the most obvious examples: no doubt poppies cognate with those with which the West commemorates the dead of two world wars; what kind of symbolism is that, and what relationship does it suppose between junk and war (the military-technological complex, the driver behind cyborgisation, the perfection of creativity in the service of mutually assured destruction)?[19]

## Waste and Perish

In *Nova Express*, one of the most interesting and alarming features is the way in which Burroughs's 'wasted' land parallels and parodies Eliot's 'waste land' at all points:

> 'What thinking, William? – Were his eyes – Hurry up please its half your brain slowly fading – Make yourself a bit smart – It's them couldn't reach flesh – Empty walls – Good night, sweet ladies – Hurry up please it's time – Look any place – Faces in the violet light – Damp gusts bringing rain – '[20]

Cut up, deconstructed, images fragmented in the rapturous and dislocated mind of the addict, but also just, of course, like modern western civilisation, particularly now as seen refracted through the dangerous eyes peeping, for example, through the hijab, eyes which, for all we know, might see right through the coverings, might come to assert that there are different kinds of value to be placed than merely its preservation or prolongation. Like, again, Gothic castles, monasteries, convents cut up, deconstructed, remade in psyche, turned into transcendent, sublime images of themselves which are endlessly irrecuperable in the cold light of day: 'Got up and fixed', as Burroughs repeatedly has it, 'in the sick dusk'.[21] A dusk in which nothing seems quite as it is; or, more worryingly, a dusk in which the machine-induced 'certitudes' of day are forced to reveal themselves as fictions – fictions of enlightenment, as suspect in Burroughs as they are to the Gothics as they pursue, with varying degrees of internalisation and understanding, the project of displaying the limits of enlightenment, the scenarios in which the apparently destroyed forces of the dark continue to assert their supremacy, the validity of a view of life which is, in all senses, 'out of control'.

It is of course obvious that if one wishes to draw a systemic connection between the Gothic and addiction this is easily done. One has only to think of S. T. Coleridge's questionable and questioning uses of laudanum; of Thomas De Quincey's opiated dreams of quasi-imperial magnificence (to which I shall return); of Sherlock Holmes and his needle-sharpness of intellect and body: the outer connections are all neatly laid, in place.[22] Gothic plays dangerously with morality, even with health; the reader enjoys the transient thrill of encountering deeper, less explicable emotions, a momentary anxiety about whether, having succumbed to this 'other' view, one can ever be brought back – from the 'seizure' of rapture, is there or is there not a further 'counter-seizure' which will release one from the clammy addictive grip of fear?

But perhaps there is also a deeper connection, which Burroughs (whose fictions are so often also tracts in the making) is happy to suggest in what one might see as a parody of polemic:

> This virus this ancient parasite is what Freud calls the unconscious spawned in the caves of Europe on flesh already diseased from radiation. Anyone descended from this line is basically different from those who have not had the cave experience and contracted this deadly sickness that lives in your blood and bones and nerves . . . They didn't belong to themselves any more. They belonged to the virus. They had to kill torture conquer enslave degrade as a mad dog has to bite. At Hiroshima all was lost. The mental sickness dormant 30,000 years stirring now in the blood and bones and bleached flesh.[23]

As with, for example, C. R. Maturin when his ranting about despair and the void become most extreme, we might say that this is not easy;[24] this is not simple; this is (probably) not true, in any sense of the word 'truth' we would want to deploy. But the implication is nonetheless all too clear: what we choose (or what happens to us in a realm beyond choice) to know as history – the history of the species, the history of Europe, for example – is at root a *perversion* of history, it is a 'way of putting it' that depends on the dominance of certain interest groups, in whose 'interest' it is that we view history in a particular way which prevents the putting together, the reassemblage of the story. Thus far, this is itself part of an overt intellectual history; it is the entire Marxist theory of ideology, it is Louis Althusser's notion of interpellation.[25] But what Burroughs dwells on is the multitude of ways (which are all, in the end, the same way) in which we become *addicted* to that view, in the senses that, first, we cannot do without it, and second, we want endlessly more of it. '*Timor mortis conturbat me*', perhaps:[26] but this thought would demand its own comforts, its own conformity, and for Burroughs addiction is the paradoxical culmination, the glorious zenith of conformity. What is truly dangerous lies all on the other, occluded side: with the police, with law and order – and of course, quintessentially, with the occluded gender, women. To which I shall return in a moment. After my next fix.

I could suggest, *inter alia*, that this was in part the way in which the early Gothic flourished. People, it would appear, wanted more of it – not necessarily different, but 'more of the same' – this, after all, was the source of William Wordsworth's disquiet in the Preface to *Lyrical Ballads* (1800).[27] The same settings were wanted, in which the same narratives were played out, the same stock of characters whose interactions could be predicted down the same trajectory. What makes Burroughs' texts distinct, it has been sometimes said, is precisely that they are all the same: the same endless boiling of the silver spots during orgasm, the same inevitable eruption of homosexual desire in the midst of apparently 'different' texts. The only suspense in Burroughs is the literal suspense of the hanged man, whose plight, whose susceptibility to interpretation and myth, whose fatal orgasm is always the same, and always without point, without alleviation.

Thus addiction, we might say, is the very mechanics of 'the same'. Under conditions of addiction, the supposedly exciting possibility of every day being a different day, of there being endlessly new things under the sun, is dissolved, resolved, absolved under the condition of sameness: each different morning succumbing to the 'long, empty noon', each hope of a new beginning cancelled by the repetition of the past. Some commentators, some of the practitioners of what is now being called 'drugspeak', posit a terminus for addiction; but the terminus is really, almost literally, beside the point: the point is 'more of the same'.[28] Very few drugs, the medical literature now tells us (although it changes its story from week to week), actually require increasing dosage; 'tolerance', although a topic of debate as I shall mention below, is regarded in some medical (or pharmacological) quarters as a cultural myth; what is at stake is something deeper, the replacement of myths of human progress, of individuation, of development, by the brute facts of the absence of escape, the tying down to the wheel – not, in this case, the 'wheel of desire' with its many, if painful, points and spokes, but the more bitter wheel, which perhaps Saint Catherine knew, the wheel which endlessly reproduces the same point of stasis while the body is being torn apart and demonstrating an endless, but in the end unfriendly, resilience.

## Perversion, the Black Hole, Whispers

I have mentioned perversion on several occasions. That uncanny point at which perversion reveals itself would have in common the otherwise antithetical commentaries of Burroughs and, for example, Lacan and Andrea Dworkin – namely, that heterosexuality is the ultimate perversion, the very *form* of perversion.[29] But it needs to be underlined that the heterosexual, the dealing with the Other, if it figures at all in Burroughs, figures only as a kind of 'black hole', the absent womb, the final figuring of womb envy through deletion, a willed ignoring. There are women in Burroughs, for example in *Cities of the Red Night* (1982), but they are, so to speak, sireniac, and very probably not real in any obvious sense; what they may be, however, are figures for a certain 'beckoning', a certain call, but their call is not to be heeded, it is instead a diversion, a deviation into the 'wrong' kind of life. I shall receive this 'call' more directly below (as Orpheus might have said).

Everything in Burroughs is, obviously and flagrantly, homosexual (although not, in Eve Kosofsky Sedgwick's sense, homosocial[30]); yet of course homosexual relations are, in the most obvious of all senses, 'end-stopped', they are (to use an essential linguistic translation) incapable of *enjambement*. They relate, as does addiction, to the cessation of a 'moving' (in several senses) world. Nothing can go forward – this is fully recognised by Ann Radcliffe, Matthew Lewis, Burroughs – except by permission of the female. And so one comes upon the 'per-version' – the more thoroughgoing version – of Aleister Crowley's famous aphorism, which we may rephrase thus: 'Everything is true, nothing is permitted'.[31]

We can turn to consider two comments by medical theorists of addiction, which show, in some ways unwittingly, the slipperiness of the phenomena with which they are trying to deal. The first explains more or less exactly the inapplicability of conventional rules of accumulation – those very rules of capitalist accumulation which the early Gothic writers found so troubling – to the condition of the addict:

> . . . the economic approach to addiction [assumes] that the potential addict is acting rationally for the purpose of maximising total (discounted) utility. In [this] theory, addictive substances are a special type of commodity whose use can be explained by two specific features. On the one hand, earlier consumption has an impact on the utility of present consumption: The more you have consumed in the past, the lower the utility of consumption in the present (tolerance). On the other hand, the marginal utility of present consumption is very high because it tends to relieve withdrawal symptoms (which include the low utility derived from other goods in a dysphoric state).

> Even a small amount of the substance can relieve or reduce these symptoms.[32]

This comment does, of course, rely on a certain view of 'tolerance'; yet it also suggests that a simple logic of tolerance is incapable of explaining addiction. On the contrary, there is a possibility suggested that addiction might approach to an almost homeopathic condition where 'less' and 'more' are interchangeable (an anti-capitalist and anti-militarist logic, which is also why homeopathy is perceived as such a threat to the pharmacological industry) provided the substance is the same. One might also want to note the concept of the 'dysphoric', the reduction of goals and aspirations which also serves to abject the notion of rapture.

The second quotation is about the 'unspeakable' collusion between drug taking and drug prohibition:

> Like Newspeak, the purpose of Drugspeak is not only to provide a medium of expression for those in power but also *to make all other modes of thought impossible*. It aims to make heretical thought literally unthinkable. This is achieved by inventing new words, eliminating words thought to be undesirable and stripping words of unorthodox and secondary meanings.[33]

Attempts to deal with 'the drug problem', the problem of addiction, are thus also efforts to reduce and minimalise language, to strip it of a certain, perhaps Gothic, floridity, a fake closure of the lesion of the symptom. What is at stake in Burroughs is an attempt to persuade the reader of an endless *proliferation* (of a rhizomatic sort, of course) which flourishes in secret; yet, once we know the key, the addict's key to all mysteries, reveals itself as omnipresent, as the code handed down by all secret societies, as the substrate on which all organisations have built themselves, as the presumed necessity on which they attempt to project themselves into the future.

A further quotation from Burroughs:

> The last word is written lost voice whispering in the living room that night of stale cigarette smoke a moment palpable in the air years later I remember London the grimy stations and the tracks your name remains as the human structure not a word is mine I have no words left breathing old pulp magazines in the living dust of the dead Gods lonely fringes of a remote galaxy a million light-years away the pale skies fall apart T.B. waiting at the next stop spit blood at dawn is it later I remember London grimy pants open I pulled at my face in the mirror my new face agony to remember the words 'Too Late'. Don't you understand overgrown with weeds a long time. Do you

> begin to see there is no face there in the tarnished mirror? I was waiting there pale character in someone else's writing they called me years later your name remains breathing in these trite phrases . . . [34]

Perhaps this could be the start of an entirely different discourse on Burroughs and the Gothic; one which would be centred not only on addiction, but also on ruins, and especially those peculiarly literary ruins signified in the 'pale character in someone else's writing', the ghost which is all that remains of addicted subjectivity, of subjectivity *as* addiction.

However, for the moment we need to stay with addiction (after all, what choice have we?), but to move away from Burroughs. The possible tracks are endless. One would take us into a labyrinth, where we would find ourselves confronted, not by the Gothic of Matthew Lewis, but instead by the 'Lewis rat', a creature of experimentation, a further measure of the subjugation of the animal which we encounter when we try to trace the collisions between the literary and the pharmacological. The Lewis rat, of course, does not speak for itself; instead it traces lines, performs trajectories, scampers across the page at the service of another voice; it obeys the command structure built into the exercise of authority. Here is an example of that voice:

> . . . the Lewis rat generalises this vulnerability to cocaine, heroin, and marijuana, relative to otherwise comparable rat strains. Thus, Lewis rats are more sensitive to the stimulant effects of cocaine; show consistently higher self-administration of cocaine, opiates, and alcohol; show greater degrees of persistent preference for environments in which they have previously received morphine or cocaine; and show unique vulnerability to $\Delta^9$-tetrahydrocannabinol (the psychoactive constituent of marijuana and hashish) in the electrical brain-stimulation reward paradigm . . . [35]

What are we to make of this rat, how shall we try to be companionable to it – is it indeed, to use contemporary euphemistic rhetoric, a 'companion animal'? Well, firstly, it is clearly – in some significant sense – not a rat at all. It would be better considered as an element in a cyborg. When it is said of the various drugs to which it is subjected that they are 'self-administered', this is clearly to be taken, as it were, with a pinch of salt (or maybe a sugar cube). It is true, the reports tell us, that the rat – an individual rat? a subspecies of rat? essence of rat as a punishable symbol? – has been placed in a position whereby it is able, through the flick of a switch, to give itself a high; but at the same time this means that it is simply wired to, or inside, a machine. Under these circumstances, we may fairly wonder, unless we have already been blinded by New Labour rhetoric, what exactly 'choice' may mean. Could it, for example, actually mean a narrowing of vision, like that, for example, of a rat in an experimenter's tunnel or cage?

## Pressed Rat and Warthog

But, again, what *is* an 'element in a cyborg'? For the whole theory of the cyborg, as expounded by Donna Haraway and others, is that in the state, or condition, or 'being' of a cyborg, it has always already become impossible to separate out what might be identified as 'elements'.[36] It would therefore be impossible in a virtually chemical, or chemically virtual, sense to identify the rat; the animal has lost identity, become one of a number of functions of the cyborg which may, however faultily, only be identified as 'rat-with-drugs'.

Or, of course, as 'drugs-with-rat', for here the pre-eminence of the animal, or of the organic, has vanished into a symbiosis. The rat becomes, in a sense, a version of the definition of un-freedom. Wired into the machine, reduced to a set of functions which exist primarily in order to render it the object of an experimental gaze, the Lewis rat is not in a position to return that gaze, or to sense the peculiar kind of order which, from behind the screen, structures its brave new world.[37] It is not my purpose to mount a diatribe against – or in favour of, however perverse that might sound – animal experimentation, but what does appear certain is that here 'preference' and 'vulnerability' are inextricably joined. The rat shows preferences (for an environment-plus-drug over an environment where no drug is on offer) but these preferences are inseparable from a process whereby the rat is considered 'vulnerable', defenceless. Which is, of course, in any case what one might expect of a caged rat, a rat considered as sadly without vision, without a proper investment in its future. We like (or need) to pretend that animals have no vision, even where it is immeasurably superior to ours.[38]

So the addict comes, as we have seen, to demonstrate a certain peculiar condition of subjectivity. The rapture, the ecstasy, the 'high' is not separable from the come-down, from the fact that there will no longer, in some putative, experiment-free future, be the possibility of a return to a state of neutrality. The balance, the pendulum, has been set in motion, and the point of stability on which conventional notions of subjectivity from Descartes onwards have been predicated has been dissolved – into a wider unity, perhaps, but also one where the boundaries of the self no longer hold.

> Drug abuse seems to provide good examples of this predicament. Most

> people do not have sufficient knowledge of the long-term consequences of intake of drug molecules. Their behaviour is characterised by a limited form of rationality, which is then made even more vulnerable by hypofunction in the motivational circuits with a concomitant impact on the ability to make future choices.[39]

What needs immediately to be said about this diagnostic discourse is that it is, perhaps fatally, the wrong way round. There is a supposition that a certain degree of knowledge (whatever that might be) would induce the potential addict (if there is such a thing) to 'think twice' before starting on the inevitable spiral. What this ignores, and what Burroughs's texts make painfully clear, is that such knowledge may itself be, precisely, unbearable. Therefore the (in)ability to make future choices may be precisely the desired outcome: a preference may indeed have been expressed, but for an experience of rapture, because the alternatives appear too bleak, too depressing. Knowledge that this might well shorten one's life would not figure as a problem; rather, it would be part of the desired outcome, and thus again the inseparability of addiction, rapture and death is drawn tight.

What lies behind this thinking is that 'life', however (usually conventionally) it may be defined, is worth living. Yet what is most strange about this assumption is not whether it may be true or untrue, but rather that it sidesteps a major drift of Western culture, at least from the Middle Ages, to the effect that life is not *in itself*, unconditionally, worth living;[40] typically in the course of chivalric love, for example, a test is set up: is life worth living without the presence of the object of desire? The answer to that question, all too often (and as we shall see in more detail later in the emblematic case of Sylvia Plath) is as likely to be 'No' as 'Yes'; furthermore, this profound 'No' to the inadequacies of life is not without a certain attribution of honour, a sense of sacrifice which may be linked back to the whole question of the vulnerability of the addict.[41]

And it needs further to be said that this vulnerability, in Western culture – and as we might expect from a wide variety of mythological sources – is linked to a process of scapegoating and demonisation. The behaviour of the addict, it is claimed, is unpredictable, whereas in fact (and as many a Lewis rat would testify if given the chance) it is the soul, the essence, of predictability. The problem is not one of the unexpected; it is rather, according to Burroughs and many others, that the fate of the addict appears as a humiliating caricature, a cartoon of 'normality'. It is life, as Giorgio Agamben might have it, pared down to the bare bones;[42] what Burroughs and Eric Mottram describe as 'an algebra of need',[43] where all sentiment has vanished and a pure process of cause and effect, a skinned model of desire, is acted out on a stage where all is devoted to the concealment of these embarrassing – humiliating, vulnerable – demonstrations of basic drive. Before such demonstrations, the processes of institutions are in danger of appearing as what they are, as cover stories, as ways of cheering oneself up – in, of course, the always sensed but constantly abjected absence of the rapture.

Rats in a maze, perhaps; but with what quality of inner life? A life from which the exigencies of time are paradoxically banished and at the same time of the utmost, compelling importance; a life in a process of constant abutment upon death. Life, as the heroic myths tell us, as it should be lived: in immediate contact with *danger de mort*, measured in a series of intervals between heights and depths, life from which the prospect of inhabiting an otherwise flat (desert) terrain has been banished. But, of course, we return to the paradox at the heart of rapture: for in Burroughs, as elsewhere, there is no real reporting of these processes. There is, rather, a *translation* of experience into the commonly intelligible: the recounting becomes the boredom, while the essence of the rapture is hidden, sequestered away from the observer. The literature of rapture is, in one sense, a game of hide-and-seek; everything is hidden, occluded, but the trick to this game is that the proffered possibility of final revelation is itself a delusion, a hope held out to be constantly dashed. And thus we sense another root of the demonisation of the addict, which is envy: that which is withheld readily becomes the precious, that which is not available for the discourse of the everyday, that which manifests itself only in hints of the numinous, moments where the gaps between, or beneath, words come to seem more important than the words themselves and where secrecy becomes what Heidegger refers to as the 'ground of Being'.

## Booty Call

This further reference to Heidegger rings bells, perhaps alarm bells. One reason for this is that it reminds me of Ronell's extraordinary text, *The Telephone Book* (1989), which arranges life, seeks a translation of life, into the terms of the telephone, a telephone (a speaking at a distance) in which great voices of the past are always on the other end of the line, coming through a crackling, endlessly misrepresenting ether, within which the rapture is dissolved but at the same time inflects every pronouncement. Here, for example, is Ronell effecting a connection, putting in telephonic contact, Heidegger and the poet Georg Trakl:

> The spirit which will return stone to speech is flaming. It is not ethereal [*sic*], but, giving off something like shock, it is electrically empowered. Trakl's spirit must not be read in the main as *pneuma* nor as a sighing flame that loses its speaking wind; no, it is a generating kind of force, a 'flame that inflames', an electric charge. Can we think of Trakl's poem in this light? The spirit's speaking comes so suddenly that its shock effect can startle or horrify or even shatter the petrified stone which it arouses.[44]

This is shaping up to be a long quotation, a long communication with spirits of various kinds, live, dead and undead. Perhaps it would be best to pause, to 'hold the line'. One of the matters which is at stake in Ronell's book is the question of 'hearing' (to which I shall return in a later chapter): how do we hear the past? How do we hear across even the minute gap in time which attends upon telephonic communication even at this historical moment (later than Ronell's) of the mobile phone, teletext, and all the other spurious signifiers of technological immediacy of contact? What 'comes down the line' is, certainly, a kind of representation, but it is one imbued with a certain element of delay, a postponement which is antithetical to the conveyal of rapture. Let us pick up the phone again:

> The ghost of Heidegger (of Trakl) is **wed to the white abyss cauterised by the schizophrenic probe**. It finds the glowing illumination of an *ek-stasis* which may reduce the stone to white ashes – not dark ashes but the ghostly incineration called forth by excess light, the flaming side of blindness's pain. This spirit beckons forth the ghost as that being which it is, a being beside oneself, projected as the immateriality of its own pain, wandering outside of one self, a more-than-divided self, a thing whose movement is the *ek-static*. Yet the spirit responding to this call is sheltered in the structure of a *bothland*.[45]

Ronell here relates her notion of the 'call' to what I take to be a wider notion, one which I have mentioned before, namely the 'beckoning'. These 'voices from a distance' – the paranoiac's recipience, for example, of thought broadcasting – beckon us: they confront us with the possibility of an inestimable danger, and taunt us with the impossibility of reaching the far shore, of going all the way, 'down the line'. The bold in the passage is Ronell's own; but at the same time it is more than obviously Burroughs's discourse – cauterisation, schizophrenia, the abjection of affect – and here it is – of course – linked to rapture, *ekstasis*. And at the same time what Ronell's discourse effects – in sharp distinction to the technological implications of her argument – is a manifestation of the ghost, an irremediable irruption of the Gothic within the texture of tele-contact. A ghost which is 'projected as the immateriality of its own pain', or perhaps of its own vulnerability: this is not the ghost which threatens and frightens, this is the ghost which, addicted to its own wanderings, prevented from any achievement of freedom, comes to remind us of (its own) fears and to beckon us, with a call which we cannot but resist, to share that pain. The ghost of subjectivity, perhaps: removed now to a realm where the lying has ceased, where 'bare life' (but of course held only in, or after, death) manifests itself, but also (as perhaps is the case with all ghosts) the promise to tell the tale of the future is always subverted, always 'wrapped' back on itself, so that the future continues to recede and become insubstantial; as does the rapture in which that future may be caught.

Another passage from Ronell:

> It wasn't my own addiction, it was yours. My withdrawal symptoms answer to your addiction. I become an answering machine, responding like a thing to your poison. Come here, I want you. I picked up your call, automatically receptive like an addict, structuring myself on the resistant woman who, after a sharp pain, dissolves into submission. That's the way she wrote it. Resistant but wanting. After the sharp pain. Then tranquillised by habit, increasing the dosages.[46]

And so we are now on the terrain of 'crack wars', but perhaps in this involution, this invagination of voices, we are also hearing the suppressed voice of the Lewis rat. Amid the troubled residues of virginity there would be an echo of the condition of 'being before the cyborg', before being hooked up to the sharp machine, the uncontrollable waves of desire. But the wider question Ronell poses is, 'Whose addiction?'. What is it to be addicted to the recounting, to be out of control in the face of an other's addiction, always the addiction of another – what is it we want to hear yet not hear, to *know* but not know, because real knowing (whatever that may be) would remind us of our own vulnerability, of the brink which is right in front of our feet but in the context of which we can only live through a series of acts of unknowing, of ignoring the fate of the repetition, within which is perennially hidden, like the jewel in the heart of the lotus, the unimaginable, the unrecountable rapture?

Thus we might consider in a new light what it might mean to live a 'non-addicted life'. It might be to accustom ourselves to a state of continual exile. After all, the anthropologists tell us that nowhere have they found a tribe (which we may interpret as meaning a condition of being) which does not live its life in the light of the potential for rapture, even if most social rules have been invented and predicated on the abolition, postponement or control of that rapture – without which rules, of course, nothing would ever 'get done', no system of general values could be established which would have the force of law, law as a discursive body which we may now construe as a series of always faulty defences against addiction, always in need of refurbishment lest there be the slightest 'crack' (to coin a phrase) though which the accounts of the habit, the recounting of habit, might seep.[47]

'It wasn't my addiction, it was yours'. The message here (coming down the line) would be that there is nothing 'treatable' in addiction, even as there was no treatment available for Hölderlin's silenced screams; the idea of 'treatment' is an effect of the addiction, a series of guesses as to the shape of an 'other' world. 'As if one could get off the drug', as Ronell puts it, 'by the same paternal injunction that put Hamlet onto it'.[48] Drugged by an injunction, rendered the creature of an always unslakeable habit, haunted by a placeless ghost and by doubts as to the ghost's veracity; haunted also by the possibility that the future is, as it were, 'on tracks' – why not, then, wait and watch it happen, see and hear it as it unfolds before us. Thus, then, Hamlet in the place he always feared, as the audience of his own play, as the observer of his own parade – one from which we, as the 'real' audience, are always excluded, put in an impossible position. Spellbound. Rapt.

> The boundaries of the concept of addiction are in dispute, but the core meaning of the term is evident from its etymology: the term originally meant judicial enslavement, as when a person was sentenced (addicted) to serve another (*OED*), so that as a metaphor it clearly means enslavement by an appetite.[49]

But is this so 'evident'? What, indeed, is the evidence? And what, beyond that, are the meanings of the term 'judicial enslavement' – enslavement as a judicially correct or 'justified' process, or enslavement to and within the body of the law? What concept of law can remove the claims of subjectivity – or would we be correct in saying that the body of the law is precisely that body which forbids subjectivity, which reverses the patterning of the human so as to revise the concept of exile, to remove the addict to the final site of fear, distrust, demonisation?

But let us not forget, as we pursue the defiles, the defilement of rapture, the Lewis rat, or the imagination of animals.

# 4

# Imagining Animals

Where (again) to begin? Or better, perhaps, where to continue along the trajectory of the animal, which bespeaks a hidden rapture which can only be sensed from a distance. A health warning is in order. 'Imagining Animals' is a catchy title for a chapter:[1] it means to suggest, of course, not only the ways in which humans may imagine animals but also the entirely putative distinctness of human beings as the animals which uniquely 'imagine', as well as implying through this trope some attention to the phantomatic, hallucinatory realm through which writing operates, as something which is human yet distanced from the human, as something which participates in the making of marks, the inspection of signs, which places us immediately in close proximity to other animals as we try to emulate their superior senses and to unlock the secrets which, we sometimes think, they are withholding from us.[2] The first part of the chapter will be devoted – one might almost say 'consecrated' – to one of the greatest of all 'animal texts', Books VIII–XI of the *Natural History* (AD 77) of Pliny the Elder. If this classical opus seems a remote and ghostly scene, then I can only say that I hope to cheer you with a few examples of Pliny's more curious beliefs before making my way into a mode of approaching that text which will, I hope, shed some broader light on the questions of 'imagining animals', of secrecy, and, eventually, of rapture.

## Dreaming the Alphabet

But my engagement with Pliny has its own roots; some of them I may refer to much later, but the immediate originating cause of my recent reading of the *Natural History* – which may, for all I know, have been a partial re-reading, since I believe I have a memory of some passages from the book that might derive from my early education in Latin, and yet, of course, might be a screen memory, masking something more deeply hidden – was set off by a brief piece in the selection of Italo Calvino's occasional writings called *The Literature Machine* (1986). The piece is called 'Man, the Sky, and the Elephant', and it was originally published as the Preface to an Italian translation of Pliny. In it, Calvino recommends reading particular volumes of the *Natural History*, and especially Book VIII, on these grounds:

> The natural history of man is extended into that of the animals throughout Book VIII, and this not only because the knowledge recorded is to a large extent concerned with the rearing of domestic animals and the hunting of wild ones, as well as the practical use man makes of the one and the other, but also what Pliny is doing is taking us on a guided tour of the human imagination. An animal, whether real or imaginary, has a place of honour in the sphere of the imagination. As soon as it is named it takes on a dream-like power, becoming an allegory, a symbol, an emblem.[3]

Calvino goes on to say that Book VIII describes 'nature as external to man, but not to be separated from what is most intrinsic to his mind – the alphabet of dreams, the code book of the imagination, without which there is neither thought nor reason'.[4] Of the terms Calvino uses, the ones I would want to save from what otherwise seems to me an overly humanistic, albeit intriguing, account of Pliny have to do with the imagination, 'dreamlike power', 'the alphabet of dreams'; but there are reasons for wondering what precisely is going on in this modern recapitulation of Pliny, for as we look more closely at the project of the *Natural History* it might appear that these tropes are far distant from what the writing of that text suggests to us, and that, as perhaps is always the case, these assertions of the imaginary marvellousness of animals are imposed in the service of specific cultural and literary goals. Calvino might indeed wish to envisage 'invisible cities';[5] but did Pliny? Or was he more concerned with the difficulties of discerning and displaying a secret life, life *as* a question of secrets?

The *Natural History* is the only book of Pliny's to survive (in contrast, we could add, with the rather more voluminous correspondence of his nephew Pliny the Younger). Pliny was born in AD 23, and was during his life a soldier, a friend of emperors, and a man of action; he was not a scientist, but it seems as though writing, for one reason or another, was for him a natural accompaniment to these other professions; certainly he has come down to us partly because of the keenness with which he observed life around him, and it may be well known that he died, as a direct result of his determination to observe first-hand the eruption of Vesuvius in AD 79, from the ingestion of poisonous fumes.[6]

The *Natural History* consists of 37 volumes and constitutes an encyclopaedia of contemporary knowledge of the natural world, from the condition of the universe to human physiognomy. When I came to look at other modern accounts of Pliny, I was struck by the difference between

Calvino's assessment of his importance and that of other twentieth-century commentators, all of whom have seen fit to castigate him on the grounds of style, we might even say of that haunting term 'singularity'; it seems clear that, as far as German, French and English critics are concerned, Pliny could not write a decent Latin sentence; Calvino, an Italian, claims that he could and did, but I do not have any further linguistic means to judge between these views, even were it to the immediate point.[7]

Whatever way one plays it, however, it is difficult to ignore Pliny's views on writing and on reading, with which he immediately confronts us in his Preface. On writing, he makes some interesting points related to the Greeks – on his general relation to Greek culture I shall have more to say in a moment, but in general it was negative, with the following exception. He says:

> so as not to seem a downright adversary of the Greeks, I should like to be accepted on the lines of those founders of painting and sculpture who, as you will find in these volumes, used to inscribe their finished works, even the masterpieces which we can never be tired of admiring, with a provisional title such as *Worked on by Apelles or Polyclitus*, as though art was always a thing in process and not completed [*tamquam inchoata semper arte et imperfecta*] . . . [8]

An encyclopaedia, then, without pretensions to finitude; an 'inchoate' contribution, perhaps, to an ongoing process of discovery; writing as uncertain about its future, its reception, as so – we shall see in a moment – it was about its origins and its past, despite Pliny's claim that his *Natural History* contained 20,000 'facts' or matters of importance and drew upon 100 sources (recent number-crunching has demonstrated that both of these figures are very serious underestimates).[9]

## Is there an Emperor in the Audience?

We might add, if only for the sake of completeness, that this theory of writing was accompanied by an ironically negative theory of reading; in the course of his dedication of the book to the Emperor Titus, he explains his 'table of contents' of the several books as 'very careful precautions to prevent your having to read them' ['*summa cura ne legendos eos haberes operam dedi*'].[10] Whether this comment amounts to an irony against his own authorial role or a rather more dangerous one at the expense of his grand friend the emperor is difficult to discern; but it is perhaps possible to connect it with his later comments on the difficulty of recording the real or imaginary status of the birds called the *sanqualis* and the *immusulus* as being related to the 'general slackness that prevails';[11] they, it would seem, can be allowed to hold their secrets, at least for the time being, as the work of connecting the secret life of the animals to the unavoidable restrictions of the human proceeds – never, Pliny implicitly claims, to be finished, never to achieve a total decoding, always to remain partially lost in the shadows.

On that note, let us immediately move to consider the general reason why we read ancient authorities on the natural world, namely, how many impossible things could they believe before breakfast? I do not want to dwell on these, but it seems unfair to cheat an audience (if that is the right word) of the flavour of them, and so let me try these out:

> Snakes mate by embracing, intertwining so closely that they could be taken to be a single animal with two heads. The male viper inserts its head into the female viper's mouth, and the female is so enraptured with pleasure that she gnaws it off.[12]

Perhaps this is one answer to Freud's infamous question as to what women want. Or:

> The most prolific of all animals whatever is the mouse . . . It is stated that with it impregnation takes place by licking and not by coupling . . . and it is believed that they are made pregnant by tasting salt.[13]

Elsewhere we have speculation as to where insects hide in winter, since the fact that they mostly die was, of course, only to be revealed much later; an alarming assertion that cuttlefish, like certain bottom-dwelling shellfish, under certain conditions fly, which puts a whole new spin on Blake's 'invisible worm/That flies in the night';[14] and a detailed account of the resurrection of bees, to be accomplished most expeditiously, although to no clear purpose, by covering their remains with 'fresh ox-paunches together with mud'.[15]

Yet Pliny is not especially credulous for his time; indeed, the limits of his credulity are expressed in both political and scientific terms. On the political front, the reader is told the story of Hanno the unfortunate Carthaginian, who tamed a lion only to find that this

> supplied a reason for his impeachment, because it was felt that a man of such an artful character might persuade the public to anything, and that their liberty was ill entrusted to one to whom even ferocity had so completely

> submitted [*quoniam nihil non persuasurus vir tam artificis ingenii videbatur, et male credi libertas ei cui in tantum cessisset etiam feritas*].[16]

Scientifically, or perhaps one should rather say pragmatically, Pliny receives with suspicion the story that mice have 'a very discriminating palate', tartly observing that he is 'curious to know how the authorities detected this'.[17] He did not, of course, have the privilege of the company or discourse of the Lewis rat.

But perhaps the location of Pliny in the development of writing about animals is most clearly demonstrated in a tiny sentence at the end of a passage in which he is describing the number of feet that various creatures possess. He has worked his way through creatures with two feet, four, six, eight and ten, but then remarks: 'No kind has an odd number of feet' ['*numerus pedum impar nulli est*'].[18] Leaving aside the issues raised by the starfish, I would suggest that this addition, unnecessary as it surely would be in any more modern natural history, marks out for us at once the immense range of possibilities within which his writing is ambiguously circumscribed.

This circumscription, the delineation of the scene within which Pliny's writing occurs, can also be represented by the themes that he pursues. As a stoic who, at complete odds with the fantastic reading habit I have portrayed as typically modern and, I hope, caricatured above, made little distinction between the factual and the marvellous, he is concerned, first, with species conflict. We can find long lists of the animals who are natural enemies; equally, we can find lists of those who are natural friends, although this often takes the form of their mutual antagonism to a common foe, and thus, without bothering to enumerate these lists, we can clearly see a politics of human alliances and betrayals writ large in his imaging of the animal world; whatever secrets there may be here to be revealed, in the end they can be encoded in terms suitable to the 'modern' reader.

Secondly, we find that animals all perform according to what we might call, following the rhetoric of circumscription, a 'species-script'; it is in the nature of snakes and mongooses, snakes and elephants, and so forth, continually to enact scenes of conflict one with another. In this continuous-present scenario we can find, I suggest, the problem of the unnameable other, of the enemy who has no individual identity, the trace of the problematic animal lack of faciality of which Deleuze and Guattari speak in their analysis of the process of 'becoming-animal',[19] to which I shall return shortly.

## Beaver, Phoenix, Amphisboena

Thirdly, and perhaps most significantly, Pliny is at all points interested in how it is that animals know what they must *hide* from man because, if they do not, it will be seized upon as valuable: to take a rather extreme example, beavers, it would appear, amputate their sexual organ (it appears to be male beavers he is talking about) 'as they know that they are hunted for the sake of its secretion, the medical name for which is beaver-oil'[20]; to take a slightly less alarming instance, hedgehogs (and now it is time to speak for a moment of hedgehogs) in danger are said to urinate over themselves to ruin their spines, which would otherwise be, as Pliny says although without going into detail, 'of particular value'.[21] There is, it would appear, a 'natural' secrecy about animals; they live, in a presumably anthropomorphic translation, in a world where their secrets are constantly in danger, under siege, and large parts of their behaviour have derived from their instinct, which is to protect and guard this secrecy, to become the very unwitting protagonists in a 'secret history' which proceeds alongside the history of the human yet in terms which are not readily accessible; indeed, if we were to absorb ourselves in becoming fully fledged 'inspectors of marks', then we might find ourselves 'rapt' in a *different* world, a world from which return might prove difficult.

And fourthly, Pliny is concerned at all points with problems of reproduction. Some creatures, he claims, are born from dew and from the wind; similarly, when we look at the animal kingdom we have always to cope with the problem of hybridity, since lions and leopards, for example, are capable of mating and producing curious hybrids; these fears, we might suggest, are redolent of those that so frequently beset a colonial power – the Roman Empire, the human race – when trying to observe the apparent yet secret malevolence with which their subjects respond, through disguise, or through so-called animal means, to attempts to understand or thereby control their (unnatural) nature.

What authority does this text, this reanimation of the animal world, claim? Pliny is unusual among his contemporary writers in supplying long lists of older authorities, principally Greek, whose work he has, if you like, consulted or plundered, according to taste; indeed, most of the first volume is devoted to an examination of these authorities. We might, then, think of the text as a compendium, as a collection of facts and opinions, but the role of authority in the text is more complex than this, for Pliny is also at all points concerned to convict the Greeks of excessive credulity. In connection, for example, with the werewolf, a clearly exasperated Pliny, dismissing the legend, records that one Evanthes even goes so far as to claim that, upon resuming human form, the werewolf 'gets back [into] the same clothes!' 'It is astounding', he adds, 'to what lengths Greek credulity will go; there is no lie so shameless as to lack a supporter'.[22]

But when in the world of animals, we are, as Deleuze and Guattari know so well, on tricky territory; perhaps we could put it more clearly in their own terms, and speak of the compulsive deterritorialisations and reterritorialisations forced upon us as a species when we consider our role in the wider context of a 'natural history', whose limits are perennially shading off into the 'unnatural' and the 'supernatural', the hidden possibilities of an unknowable rapture. Indeed these arabesques, these folds and crevices of textual belief, infest the text from beginning to end, and not only in terms of the relation between the writer and his past authorities. The translation I have been using, the most recent authoritative one, is the Loeb version edited by Harris Rackham in 1940. Remaining with the brief and dismissive section on the werewolf, we might be surprised to find the editor, writing a mere seventy years ago and notoriously sparse with his editorial notes, adding a footnote to the werewolf consisting of the one word 'imaginary'.[23]

Good heavens, we might expostulate, he has not seen fit to issue such a clear warning against belief in the phoenix or the amphisboena, presumably because he regards his readership as having already dismissed these fabulous beasts from our modern bestiary; but clearly a doubt lurks in the presumed public mind about the werewolf. But then, perhaps these are wider doubts, doubts as to the points at which the history of nature will merge imperceptibly into a dream-history of monsters, an imaginary and childlike realm where observation is indistinguishable from hearsay, where to 'hear' of something is to place it 'here' in the text, to bring in from the shadows the marvellous, the hallucinatory, the phantomatic forms of creatures who inhabit unknown jungles and deserts. 'Only phantoms fight with the dead!'[24], observes Pliny in his Preface, quoting Plaucus. Admittedly his context is somewhat different, since he is referring to the unpleasant Roman habit of leaving rancorous declamations against intellectual rivals to be published after one's own death; nevertheless, the spectacle of phantomatic battles, in which the weird forms of elephant and snake locked in mortal combat in some sense shadow and exemplify scientific divergences of opinion, looms over the *Natural History* as it painstakingly carves out its space between history and phantasy. We *need*, it would seem, these imaginary *topoi*; they have some kind of relation to our own self-definition. We are, one might fairly say, dependent on them: our symbolisation of the animal is a habit, something we can not do without, because without it we would become unsure of our own boundaries. Could we say that our relation to the animals is an 'addicted' one? We cannot, certainly, do without them. We choose to imagine that they are under our control, that we can liberate ourselves from them any time we want. But we also know that, whether it is in the form of the man-eating tiger, or of the 'companion animal', or of the deadly and life-deforming encroachments of the microscopic, there is no way of leaving the animal behind, no way to kick the habit. 'Cold turkey' indeed.

## Intestinal Lesions

Within the context of these contestations, however, we do need to read Pliny's work as adumbrating a theory of signs, the crucial aspect of which is the relation between the human and the non-human. The most obvious example of this lies in his constant referral to notions of prognostication. Animals, he appears to say, are sign-writers, for example the crocodile, whose place of incubation, year on year, served to predict the level to which the Nile would rise at full flood. Pliny speaks of

> the story handed down by Democritus, who mentions birds from a mixture of whose blood a snake is born, whoever eats which will understand the conversations of birds . . . even without these stories life is involved in enormous uncertainty with respect to auguries [*'immensa vitae ambage circa auguria'*].[25]

How and where are these signs, these auguries, written? How should they be read? They are written on and inside the bodies of animals; in some remarkable cases, principally that of the raven, they are even intelligible to the animals themselves, but mostly they constitute precisely, to use Calvino's term, an 'alphabet', albeit a usually unintelligible one to be deciphered only by the most discerning of human observers. Here, of course, with Latin we immediately encounter further complexities, insofar as Latin can itself be seen to serve as the hidden sign-writer behind the Western languages; it is difficult not to become absorbed in the secret twining etymologies behind, for example, the 'torpor' engendered by the 'torpedo-fish', or the 'calamities' foretold by the octopus, or 'calamary' – both of these latter terms, incidentally, intimately bound up with writing, whether it is the throwing of straws (*calami*) that foretells disaster or the pen-shaped body and ink-like protective substance which have gone together to compose the ancient name of the octopus.

Some animals, of course, are less remarkable than others for their propensity to write legible messages to us, to recount their unnameable experience, and it may be these that Pliny chooses to refer to as 'contemptible',[26] among which are numbered, to take a sad example, the moles. Although this example is not without its own special interest, for there is, of course, a sense in which moles are precisely only known to us by the signs which they 'throw up'; their comings and goings remain 'below the surface', prelinguistic, even while we cannot ignore the manifestations of their presence, their continual secret disturbances of order. 'Old mole', indeed; below the stage of life they continue with a life which is in one sense omenistic, yet when we try to rely on the signs they provide we find that we have not really uncovered their secrets, the chambers and chasms of the mind which their activities represent remain still unplumbed, still held in secret, still unamenable to the putative translation which might indicate to us their hidden sources of rapture.[27]

But that what is valuable in animals is evidenced and confirmed by their ability to write to us, to send us legible messages back from the abyss, is confirmed above all by the treatment of the elephant with which Pliny begins Book VIII. He gives us many facts and anecdotes to support his contention that the elephant is, of all animals, 'the nearest to man in intelligence',[28] including, for example, the spectacle of elephants walking on tight-ropes; elephants, bemused by the length of a gangplank they were to cross to board a ship, managing their consternation by turning around and walking backwards; the charming story of a slow-witted elephant who was discovered during the night practising the skills he had been supposed to demonstrate the previous day. But all this remarkable yet secretive deployment of mind finds its culmination in the elephant discussed by one Mucianus, who was three times consul (Mucianus, that is) and is thus an authority in whom to place implicit trust, and who mentions an elephant who 'actually learnt the shapes of the Greek letters' and was apparently accustomed to writing out the mysteriously self-referential sentence, 'I myself wrote this and dedicated these spoils won from the Celts'.[29]

Pliny, of course, was not familiar with an evolutionary model. The textual consequences of this are, I think, interesting, and in one ethical sense, one might say, beneficial, for there is little apparent hierarchy is his ordering of the animal world. It is true that he tends to work from the largest creatures down to the smallest, but even among these latter he can spend many pages on the social structure of bees or even admiring the, to him utterly mysterious, question of exactly where the flea, almost unobservable without the aid of microscopy, manages to keep the several senses which, to Pliny's mind, it must evidently possess in order to perform its complex natural role.

More broadly, one may say that this absence of a constraining teleological notion is a condition of the space of imagining, the dream space, the space of rapture even while constrained by stern scientific dictates, that the text inhabits. Everywhere in Pliny, one can sense the redoubled trace of an echoing lack. What humans appear to lack is the species-script;[30] compared with the animals we are, both literally and metaphorically, all over the place; the incapacity to read the auguries reliably has mainly not to do with the animals' difficulty or unwillingness in providing them, but with our own lack of a collective organising structure, a master-code, by which the necessary work of interpretation might be performed. The animals know what is really going on; our problem is that we do not have the skills of literacy, the 'literature' in one sense of the term, to understand the secrets which they keep trying – even if not exactly consciously – to impart to us.

## What is Schizophrenia Hiding?

What animals, according to Pliny, lack is at once more easy and more difficult to see. On the surface, we might say that animals, although for Pliny the more advanced ones certainly do not lack self-consciousness, lack the specific kind of intelligence that would allow them to use *their own* signs, to write their own script large upon the world. But the text also hints at other things. For example, much of the material on reproduction and infancy in animals centres on the length of time different species take to grow to maturity, but nonetheless that growth is always envisaged as a straightforward development, predictable in its outcomes: what animals lack, on this reading, is the possibility of a mystery, a kink, in development, and we might thus say that what Pliny's unconscious is hinting to him is something about latency, about the unclarity, the deferral of human development which is the biological and psychological root of that conjunction of delay and individuation we now call 'difference'. And we might well also say, following Freud, that this process of latency is in fact the root of the secret.[31] Latency is a period of time in which we are sequestered away; enduring 'growing pains', perhaps – certainly locked into a process, a quasi-system of secrets of which we believe, against all the odds, that we are the only possessor. Within that secrecy there is, of course, a kind of rapture, in the sense that there is the hypothesis of a set of experiences which cannot be transmitted to the outside world. And here, therefore, we come across the scenario of drugs and addiction again, albeit from a different angle. Insofar as drugs are linked with adolescence – and they are, both in the sense of the factual site of primary addiction, and also in the symbolic sense of drugs being linked with a fear of youth – then they are linked also with a *topos* of generational secrecy. What might s/he be doing in their own room with the door locked and only stray sounds, scents to give them away? Abraham and Torok speak of the 'transgenerational phantom'[32]; but what they do not touch upon is the difficulties we encounter when we try to regard the difficulties of escaping from dependency – the task of adolescence – without finding precisely an alternative dependency. Thus we may speak of the family as the ultimate site of addiction: repetition, habit, predictability – the problem would be of how to elude, or to develop beyond, this 'same dull round', without precisely 'repeating' the addiction to habit. Youth, it is famously said, seeks to assert its individuality through everybody dressing exactly the same as everybody else.

However, to return to the topic at hand, but in a roundabout way: Pliny also wonders at the ways of women. He does so at much greater and odder length in other books of the *Natural History*, in passages we may need to read in conjunction with his resonant claim, made to his nephew, that he wrote best and fastest when seated at his desk with an article of women's clothing tied round his head.[33] This article was known to him as a *fascia*; this has no reference to a car dashboard, but true it is that interpretations of its real meaning have been somewhat mixed. But leaving that to one side: his particular speculations on women in Books VIII to XI concern jewellery and adornment in general, and here we can detect a link with issues of fetishism,[34] which also, of course, has its roots in infancy, in the malign incorporation of ambivalent objects and, often, in our relations to the animals, or at least to their products. I do not, however, wish to propose a conventionally psychoanalytic reading of Pliny, whatever that might be, or indeed of the multiple significances of fur; but rather to move from this scene of writing to some more modern ones which again touch upon the animals and the problematic physical textuality which they represent and the ways in which they challenge the limitations of human experience.

I have already referred on a couple of occasions to Deleuze and Guattari; what I now have had in mind is a formulation of theirs concerning 'becoming-animal' which has now haunted me for years. In exemplary form it occurs in their remarkable book, *Kafka: Toward a Minor Literature* (1975), and we need no reminder of the mice, dogs, apes and cockroaches which infest Franz Kafka's textual world. 'To become animal', Deleuze and Guattari say,

> is to participate in movement, to stake out the path of escape in all its positivity, to cross a threshold, to reach a continuum of intensities that are valuable only in themselves, to find a world of pure intensities where all

> forms come undone, as do all the significations, signifiers, and signifieds, to the benefit of an unformed matter of deterritorialised flux, of nonsignifying signs.[35]

There is a psychoanalytic concept of the 'moment of non-transference', which, I would contend, can occur in contexts of psychotic or non-psychotic withdrawal;[36] I take it that Guattari, at least, may have had this in mind in thinking a space freed from signification, which would amount to rapture, to a 'being seized away' from the constraints of the human. When we put Deleuze and Guattari together with Pliny, at first sight we may appear, perhaps unsurprisingly, to have a discontinuity: on the one hand the notion of an animal realm that is crowded with ambiguous signals, on the other a realm where signifying itself is superseded, relegated, annulled, but above all transcended. I suggest, however, that these form precisely the inseparable, anasemic poles of what Deleuze and Guattari also refer to as a 'map of intensities'.[37] For they are surely wrong when they claim that 'the deterritorialisation of the becoming-animal is absolute; the line of escape is well programmed, the way out is well established'.[38] I feel moved again to quote a line I seem to quote in many contexts, the final line of Bret Easton Ellis's problematically rapturous text *American Psycho* (1991): 'This is not an exit'.[39]

## Inspectors of Marks

Nor is it; the 'recourse' to the animal is only a way out insofar as it is also a way in. We may consider, for example, Pliny's comments on the mullet. 'It is an amusing trait', he observes (or, perhaps better, recounts) 'in the mullet that when frightened it hides its head and thinks it is entirely concealed'.[40] Who here, we might reasonably enquire, is thinking what? Is this simply the story of the *fort/da* game writ large? Has somebody been watching their own children (and, for inexplicable reasons, mistaking them for a smallish and rather pleasantly edible fish)? At all points the recourse to the animal fails to serve us as Deleuze and Guattari's beloved and longed-for route of escape; at all points instead we find ourselves forced into an activity of reading, a reading which can embrace the extremes of passion, from the exorbitant love we lavish on our pets (whom we perceive as enraptured when we stroke them) to the extremity of detestation which runs through our species in connection with the apparent exoticism of the octopus, the crab, the spider, the fear of touch or of being touched, the reverse of emotional exaltation, the fear also that theirs might be a secret, different life on which we indeed cannot 'touch', where our own senses go down before an imaginary which is all too full, all too present, all too rich in misinterpretable signs yet also the harbinger of a life lived more fully in touch with a realm where words always fail us, where we fail in the words we try to use to describe these extreme contingencies of experience.

That Kafka constructed a world from these elements is, of course, incontestable; but neither is it contestable, as I see it, that all these curious forms, the signs of the beast, come already infested with projected human characteristics, so that our very attempt to escape the constructions of allegory – to take the cardinal generic example – are only swings outward on a loop that eventually brings us back to where we began: a minor literature, with its attempted recapitulations of the suppressed, the animal, the otherly languaged, exists only in the context of a major literature, a master-code of signs from which the suppression of which no zoo, no aquarium, can help us to escape; for who is the captive here, the writer or the written? Who has been 'captured', seized within the ambit of the Other – and this would take us back to the curious case of the werewolf, of the fusion of man and beast which, apparently, continues to haunt us even when it would seem that its status has been long exploded, long relegated to the stuff of childish fantasy. But the werewolf will not, does not, go away, even if its avatars make occasional changes among related species; consider the long history, in Western and more particularly Eastern literatures, of alternations between human (and more specifically, usually, woman) and fox.[41] Rapture cannot be achieved, this sequence of myths and quasi-myths appears to indicate to us, without a sinking or rising into the trajectory of the animal – apparently because only there may we delude ourselves that we cannot know where such a trajectory may take us, even though, as with the dialectic of the addict, the trajectory of animals is only too clearly redolent of the script of basic need and satisfaction which human institutions, residing as they do on the terrain of the 'earth people', seek to evade.

I have said that I am not intending to pursue a psychoanalytic investigation; that might be, as Deleuze and Guattari repeatedly emphasise, 'dreary', although this is also what is said of the transgenerational phantom locked in its bedroom enjoying who knows what primal satisfactions, albeit ones which will be incapable of recounting in the morning – or indeed at any other time, even though we may, as adults, live in a continuing hope that the sequestered dreams of adolescence (our own and those of our children, which will regrettably never figure on the same plane of discourse) may release their secrets. But that will not prevent me from adverting to psychoanalytic materials, always under the sign of the animal, and in particular, now, to an exemplary passage from Abraham and Torok's *The Shell and the Kernel* (1994), for here, I suggest not without some surprise, the relation between the human and the animal is precisely reduced to that level of the allegory from which Deleuze and Guattari tried to sever it. In the as always amusingly titled 'A Remembrance of Things Deleted: Between Sigmund Freud and Emmy von N.', Torok speaks of Emmy's 'violent fear of animals', and quotes the familiar dream in which she talks of snakes, of 'a monster with a vulture's beak', of mice and toads and other creatures.[42] Quite uncritically, Torok says that 'the vultures and wild animals tearing at her and her past happiness were her husband's relatives', and goes on to connect the German word for mouse (*Maus*) with Emmy's own husband's name of Moser as a explanation for what she calls Emmy's 'hallucinations'. This remarkable piece of crude analysis culminates in the following set of statements:

> [These] animal phobias seem to me to have sprung from three separate sources, each denoting a different aspect of her situation: (1) her persecutors behaved like wild beasts and she had cause to fear them; (2) she was being slandered and persecuted on account of her husband by his relatives, so she included a resonance of her married name in her hallucinations; (3) she took in the accusation . . .[43]

and so forth, but the third statement does not concern animals. What is remarkable here, I suggest, is the simple and indeed disarming (although always with an even number of arms) *copula* by means of which the animals are robbed of the complexity of their being and forced into the service of a modern bestiary which is not even tested for the remotest accuracy against what we might still, albeit now rather oddly, want to term a 'natural history'. This would be one among many moments when one might want to remind oneself of Heraclitus' founding comment: 'Nature hides itself'.[44] I shall return to that in a moment. What is this, for example, with vultures tearing at the living? It does not appear that they do. And when did the 'wild beasts' become 'persecutory'? This is a literally unrecognisable phrase. And how many people whose name is not Moser are worried about mice? However, one might continue on this note for a long time; which would be dreary.

## Witless

I suggest that in this kind of interpretation we are indeed lost in the wastes of a certain deterritorialisation and an anxiety about the secrecy of the rapture; I suggest, to be brief about it, that there are matters to do with the animal that make us lose our wits. Let me give you another example. In her essay 'Story of Fear: The Symptoms of Phobia', Torok, speaking as so often of the Wolf-Man (who is not, of course, the werewolf, and whose 'magic word', were it to exist, would not permit of shape-changing or any of its many concomitants, which are instead the signs of a different sort of neurosis), comments that 'as soon as the unconscious was willing to provide the image of the father, rising up against the boy's oedipal desire, Sergei was supposed to have been in good enough condition to return to his native steppes'.[45] 'His native steppes' – who or what returns in this extraordinarily racist – or, as Deleuze and Guattari would have it, deterritorialising – comment, analytically, textually? Man or wolf? German or Russian? Eagle or bear? Maybe Rackham's stern reminder on the topic of the imaginary was not so far out of court after all. I suggest that if the continuing saga of the wolf-man indeed reveals a 'magic word', then the word is, of course, displayed where the purloined letter was eventually to be found, in the most obvious place of all: the word is 'wolf', and the very mention of it seems to be enough to turn man's wits to water, to suggest a source of rapture which is beyond human ken.[46] Where are we, after all, on what territory, within the memory, the scenario of the *Steppenwolf*? Or where are we with the she-wolf in Cormac McCarthy's *The Crossing* (1993), where all boundaries and borders, all past and future wars, are as nothing beneath the paws of the padding wolf, distraught with grief, obeying ancient instincts, yet forever hidden from those who attempt to pursue her – not for the always ambiguous and unsatisfactory purpose of killing but for the far more important appropriation of her senses, for the purpose of making not 'men like gods' – we have enough of those – but, even better, 'men like animals', men possessed of the gifts which alone could make a 'stealth bomber' or a lunar probe really work? What did we imagine we would learn from the 'first dog in space'?

And so to a different realm, to an 'abyss of crabs', attacks of *zoopsia* (translated as 'animal hallucinations'[47]), all of this, it would seem, is grist to what we might term a psychoallegoric mill. Consider, on the other hand, Pliny on the topic of physical and psychic incorporation:

> Aviaries with cages containing all kinds of birds were first set up by Marcus Laenius Strabo of the Order of Knighthood at Brindisi. From him began our practice of imprisoning within bars living creatures to which Nature had assigned the open sky. Nevertheless the most remarkable instance in this record is the dish belonging to the tragic actor Clodius Aesop, rated at the value of 100,000 sesterces, in which he served birds that sang some particular song or talked with human speech, which he acquired at the price of

> 6000 sesterces apiece, led by no other attraction except the desire to indulge in a sort of cannibalism in eating these birds . . . [48]

'Nature hides itself'; yes indeed, but that does not preclude humanity from endlessly inventive ways of hiding creatures and then releasing them at our own whim, any more than it precludes us from the utmost cruelty towards those which we alternately claim to be the greatest sources of our (literary) inspiration. 'A sort of cannibalism'; what a remarkable phrase. Is that, perhaps, how it works? That the nearer we can draw the animal realm to the human, then the wider we can open our mouths; not to depict these creatures in text but to eat them, to devour them as mere adjuncts to a scenario in which they have no independent existence of their own but are seen rather as simple analogues for the all-important human passions, so that, presumably, the hidden, secret rapture we envy in them (which is, after all, a rapture of our own discursive invention) can somehow become our own, and we shall be able to sing with all the notes of a harmony which continually evades us as we grapple with the problems brought about by the consciousness of subjectivity?

To consume a song-bird for the properties he or she may confer upon us, or to consume him or her in order to prevent or pre-empt the competition of non-human song; all of this we have already known from the myth of Philomel. But what is so different about the violent incorporation of the vulture or the crab into our own human attempt to reverse the feared, auguric performance of sign-writing; to send a message back to the animals, a message that says, you are here only temporarily and on sufferance? Cockroaches have outlasted humans; perhaps that, indeed, although Deleuze and Guattari do not seem to notice it, is the secret of a new metamorphosis.

How might we get further with this issue – an issue which vexes us, which has us 'foxed', which disturbs us as moles disturb our well-ordered garden and then challenge us with finding 'humane' ways of dealing with this irruption from the underworld, from the nether regions where things go on which we may never understand, where other kinds of 'habit' rule, a chronic, irresolvable addiction to the harmless earthworm? I suggest three ways. First, I think a great deal more has to be recovered about natural history; and being a literary critic, I believe that one way of doing that is literarily, linguistically, etymologically. Animal, anima, animation:[49] to set even these three cognate terms in motion, to give them back the 'breath' that is, of course, their original word-form, would be to look again at a distinctively human animating principle, something which various theological and analytic discourses have referred to as soul. I notice that some of this work is beginning to be done: even in the last couple of years, criticism seems to have been beset by an influx of moles, flies, wolves. Farther back, in 1881, we find the scientist T.H. Huxley declaring that 'the essence of modern, as contrasted with ancient, physiological science, appears to me to lie in its antagonism to animistic hypotheses and animistic phraseology',[50] but we need to ask where these hypotheses and phraseologies have gone, how they continue to haunt a textuality that professes an anthropocentric purism; the points at which those animals, monsters and hybrids that continue to parade through our dreams elude the apparent revelations of the scientific while refracting back to us fragments of the displaced subject. What does not seem to be helpful here is the bland notion of an 'eco-criticism';[51] we need neither to castigate nor applaud our ancestors (any more than we do the moles, although this might well be labour better spent) but rather to consider the relation between our human investments in the law and all that is suppressed, all that might be aspired to and yet considered impossible of attainment, all that habit might bring, a habit, in the sense of the 'unthought known',[52] from which we are permanently exiled and yet which we continually need to recreate through a sense of the rapture.

## Of Eels and Ethics

Second and on a more personal note, for written text is not all, a thought I hope to explore later on. Five years ago I was at a conference in Singapore, and after it my family and I explored the theme-park delights of that country, as far as we could see them beneath the haze of Sumatra's at that time government-induced forest fires. In one insectarium, a kindly assistant showed us a foot-long grasshopper, but did not seem to notice, as he placed it with all due gentleness back in its box, that in closing it he had broken off both of its feelers. Then again: in an aquarium there, I saw a great conger eel, breathing slowly in that way that conger eels seem to do so menacingly while remaining in large part invisibly coiled in what appeared to be a giant underwater flower-pot; on looking more closely I saw that it had a great rip in its back. Pliny speculates endlessly on whether all creatures have blood; whatever had seeped from this eel had been washed away, but not its condition, that condition that anglers are wont to attempt to differentiate, nonsensically, from pain.

And third, springing naturally from what I have just said, there is the question of ethics. As of the moment, the issue of ethics is under much discussion in psychoanalysis;[53] this is, as I understand it, part of a far larger debate, which is occurring in many forms. It is occurring in terms of the law: what, for example, is the nature of individual responsibility (and even in saying that, I am tempted to reverse all of its terms: what is the individual's responsibility for nature, for example, but then the question would flow – and should, even in these post-Marxist days – what *is nature*?). At its most extreme form, this is significantly all around us in the difficulties of mustering a human – or humane – response to contemporary phenomena as apparently widely diverse as paedophilia and the complexities of false memory syndrome; but then again, perversion and fetishism are human matters, foreign to the Lewis rat, the mole or the conger eel, and cannot be allegorised into oblivion through the citing of examples of the 'wild beasts'. But that ethical question has even further ramifications: for our attention, it would seem, and as I have indicated above, is now being more largely directed towards the cyborg, the amalgam of human and machine characteristics.

So perhaps, in the name of pursuing the sources of rapture, we ought to inspect this more closely. The 'organic' in the compound term 'cyborg' is, in fact, largely the human: it is, perhaps, as though now that attention has been taken away from 'natural history', a pseudoscience, we might want to say, that simply filled an evolutionary gap before the emergence of biology, we are free to concentrate on 'higher' transmutations. In terms of disease, of a riot of illnesses, we already know some of the consequences; perhaps there are more to come.

In conclusion, however, we need to turn back to Pliny. In Book X of the *Natural History*, he speaks of various species of birds:

> We have been told of strange kinds of birds in the Hercynian Forest of Germany whose feathers shine like fires at night-time; but in the other forests nothing noteworthy occurs beyond the notoriety caused by remoteness. The most celebrated water-bird in Parthian Seleucia and in Asia is the phalaris-duck, the most celebrated bird in Colchis the pheasant – it droops and raises its two feathered ears – and in the Numidian part of Africa the Numidic fowl; all of these are now found in Italy.[54]

I want to direct your attention, not to the specific mysteries of the phalaris-duck, of which I am quite ignorant; but instead to two phrases: the 'notoriety caused by remoteness', and the fact that 'all of these [species] are now found in Italy'. I take it that in these two phrases we can capture a quite specific tension between the exotic and the familiar, between that which engages our fascination – because its being and 'habits' are founded on hearsay – and that which exhausts our interest because, after all, we can now see it directly, and in so doing its habits and its life are stripped of wonder;

we no longer need to rely on dependence and addiction in order to see it in its full splendour.

What would it be like, this then suggests, to envisage an animal textuality? What would the consequences be of accepting that all texture, textual and physical, flows from our experience of living, breathing, animated bodies, and that it is these textures, half-remembered, half-imagined, which go to comprise the forms of the inner world and which constantly remind us of a rapture which we imagine we have lost? As we look at the animals, the animals look back at us; what would it be like to take on the shape of those endlessly mysterious inner, secret worlds? Perhaps in a way we already know some of the answers; Carl Jung, for example, speaks of the cold, implacable reptile brain[55] which operates like a continuing phantom, a phantom body if you like, and which under the sign of fear can be assimilated to the psychotic parts of our apprehensions and behaviours; the part which binds us to our addictions and refuses to let go of habit. For Pliny, perhaps, it was otherwise; for us, with the ambiguous revelations of evolution to cope with, it can, of course, never be the same again. All this remains though, as Pliny says, a work in progress or, as we might perhaps better put it, the provision of yet more food for the crows.

# 5

# Hearing the Case

Among the side-effects of rapture, we may now say, are discontinuity, a rejection of the linear and the master-narrative, a willingness to engage with fragments and dismemberments. I shall be returning, at least implicitly, to that theme later in this chapter; but my immediate purpose in mentioning it is because I want here to deal with a 'moment' in the history of psychoanalysis, and particularly in terms of the radically discontinuous and inauthentic form which we know as 'hearsay'.[1] One obvious reason for this is that hearsay is, in more than one sense, the mode of psychoanalysis; or perhaps it is the always potentially untruthful ghost of all discourse. Hearsay; hearing the case; having secrets revealed under a sign of interpretative uncertainty, becoming threatened by the potentially addictive nature of reading the case history.

The audience for such enterprises is never, of course, identical with itself; specific reception can never be guaranteed, the call will never be heard, or picked up, by the same person twice. No two acts of hearing, especially of multiple hearing, can replicate each other. However: 'hearing' the case remains an indissoluble part of the gathering of evidence, as it also is of the disclosure of the secret, if such a thing is possible: I want to expand a little on the trope of 'hearing the case'. Hearing is also, always, pre-hearing; hearing in psyche, hearing in advance, a pre-existent ensemble of voices; it is here that the connection between hearing and psychosis is drawn tight. Hearing, we might also say, and the much talked about 'remains' of psychoanalysis:[2] can we hear the remains; do the dead speak; what voices can we hear in the analytic process, to what rapture do they entice, to what potential fullness of body and mind do they appear to pay tribute? Hearing and the symptom: analysis is, among many other things, that process wherein one hears the symptom, where the symptom speaks its own name, from another place, with its own authority, but of course in the *writings* of analysis what we get is still hearsay, the unauthenticated, perhaps the forever inauthentic.[3]

## Hearing Disorder

What could make an account of psychoanalysis authentic, what could induce you to hear voices, recountings, which are trustworthy, what can we make of events, auditory hallucinations no doubt, which go on in the secret, enclosed room from which a third is excluded, how many voices speak within the analytic session, to what hearer do we address ourselves on the couch? A stab at authentication: I have been in analysis myself, and was for seven years. When I went into analysis, it seemed to me necessary to gather about myself the protective armour of a presenting symptom: that symptom was my inability to remember my father, who died when I was eight; my inability, if you like, any longer to *hear* him, or rather to recognise his voice. Obviously my body gave up the attempt some years after his death, because when I was twenty-one, which at that time, in this culture, was the age of attaining majority, the potential rapture of entering onto the domain of the completion of development, the age at which the male is confronted with the dream, the nightmare, of following in father's footsteps, half of my hearing closed down, I became deaf in my left ear. *Sinister*, you might say; fears of an illegitimate birth, common to us all because the father, until recently, has been the parent who can prove nothing; paternity is historically a matter of hearsay, of long-distance and faulty communication. My father, for what it is worth – have you heard this already? – was a radio operator.

But if one is to hear, then *some* tale must be told; and so I shall try to tell the tale of Little Hans; from hearsay – and so, despite my best efforts, the tale will remain a secret, or perhaps a tissue of secrets – secrets, we might say, which are especially withheld from the deaf. Once upon a time, Little Hans was born: in 1903. His father was an adherent of Freud's; a man interested in the then novel science of psychoanalysis.[4] At the time Freud was asking his adherents, his contacts and acquaintances, to gather information on the sexual life of young children. As Freud put it, he had already been gathering evidence from his adult patients and this evidence seemed to him to point in certain directions, to suggest certain assertions one might be able to make about early sexual life, life before latency; what better method to demonstrate the truth of these assertions than by learning – by hearing – about that life at first-hand? No, that will not do; at second-hand, at third-hand, the chains of hearing and textuality, correspondence and hearsay, spin out impossibly – everything remains hidden even as we speak its name, that name which continually slides off the object, which conceals more than it demonstrates.

Little Hans's father took it upon himself to communicate such information about his son's sexual interests as he could; there seems little doubt that he expected that this would provide a model of an undisturbed, successful childhood, for he regarded himself and his wife as good parents, sexually enlightened and analytically aware. But when Hans was four and three-quarters something disturbing occurs, about which his father writes to Freud in the following terms:

> My dear Professor, I am sending you a little more about Hans – but this time, I am sorry to say, material for a case history. As you will see, during the last few days he has developed a nervous disorder, which has made my wife and me most uneasy, because we have not been able to find any means of dissipating it. I shall venture to call upon you tomorrow . . . but in the meantime . . . I enclose a written record of the material available.[5]

There are interesting ellipses in that paragraph, but we shall return to the discursive complexities of the text in a moment. In the meantime, what was this disorder? I can only tell you – you can only *hear* from me, and only that if you are, for your own mysterious reasons, reading this text out loud – one version of it, one redaction: Little Hans, his father, Freud, now myself – a lineage of males hearing or professing to hear males, of course. Let me put it this way. Little Hans developed a phobia. His phobia, like all phobias, was complex, it evolved over time, the tales – or *legends*, as it might be better to call them[6] – Hans could tell about it varied from time to time; but we must find a path through the swamp. Let us say that it had to do, like so many phobias, with animals. In this particular 'case' it had to do with horses; it also had to do with loading and motion; it had to do with staying indoors; it had to do with shit, which Hans calls *lumf*; it had to do with mother, father, and the recent birth of a baby sister, Hanna, to Little Hans. What a strange defile of naming; how curious that Hans might have considered himself to have been potentially buried under a load when his sister had been given substantially the same name as him. But that, of course, would only apply if Freud were giving us their real names; as we shall see, that may not be the case, but if not the question of who 'makes up' the names of Hans and Hanna, who encoded a secret succession in these signs, remains to be (almost certainly fruitlessly) investigated.

Hans found himself unable to go outdoors. He related his fear, under questioning from his parents, to fear of horses. It seems as though at some points he was afraid that a horse might bite him. At other times he was afraid that a horse would fall down, that if it did so it would 'make a row with its legs' in a way which would frighten him. These fears attached themselves particularly to heavy horses, dray horses; outside Hans's front door and across a busy street – we learn this from several diagrams incorporated into the text, which are presumably distillations or translations of hearings – was a Customs House which was visited by horses and carts all day long. Hans was also frightened by various features of horses' faces: by things which, he said, they wore in front of their eyes, by 'black around their mouths'; it took Freud, the professor who was good at hearing, only a moment to interpret these as the spectacles and moustache of his father, but much displacement remained to be unravelled.

## The Motion is Carried

The heaviness of the loading, for example, becomes interpretable as the 'analysis' – if indeed it is an analysis – proceeds in terms of bodily motions, movements, displaced anxieties about shitting, once a pleasurable activity for Hans but now very recently repressed into anxiety by a sequence of events. It has also to do, we hear, with pregnancy, with the knowledge – illicit knowledge from which his enlightened parents nevertheless thought they had protected Hans – of his mother's pregnancy with his sister Hanna and his incommunicable understanding of the connections between shitting, giving birth, dropping a load, lying on one's back . . . and so on.[7] It has to do with Hans's impatience with the pack of lies he has been told about animals, and particularly those favourite – or scapegoated? – animals, the storks, so that the carts become his already ironic equivalent for the birth process, the carriers which conceal their own contents, the womb and its opening of which he is not supposed to know. The gates of the Customs House were clearly orifices of the body for Hans, and he was scared and fascinated by them.

What else can we say about Little Hans, what else do I want you, in this 'authorised' account to hear? For after all, there should be no secrets between us. I should like you to hear Hans's voice, his pain and confusion, his occasional raptures, his short-lived triumphs of feeling and understanding, but we cannot hear that, not any more. We do not really know whether his father could. I should like you to hear about Hans's early experiences of playing 'horsey' with his father, and subsequently with his friends; but this would be to bring an animal voice to life, and this, as we know, we cannot do either without the utmost risk, without challenging the presumed supremacy of the human, the being at whose service the world works and within whose raptures the animal can only be called on to play its subservient role.

Towards the end of the text Freud also asks what it might have been that Little Hans had heard, what it was which he recollected – or reconstructed

– when he saw the fallen horse, on its back, drumming its legs; parental intercourse, Freud wonders, but then he closes down this line of enquiry as insoluble. Some things cannot be heard; what *is* on record is that Freud only 'heard' Hans in an analytic situation once, and then only in diluted form for on that occasion a third was present, Hans's father who, Freud tells us, opened the session by presenting the facts as he then saw them.[8] There would thus be, we are assured, no secrets held between Hans and the professor; there would always be an overhearer, an eavesdropper. And this, of course, is still a deeply contested issue: who is entitled to secrecy when lives may be at stake? Is the young anorexic to be allowed private, secret time with her/his doctor from which the parents are excluded? Or does the fact that the parents may be instrumental in any regime which the doctor (Doctor Benway, perhaps) prescribes mean that on this terrain secrets cannot be allowed, that the addiction must become more public, shared property, a realm from which privacy has been exiled, so that the addict becomes a refugee from his own rapture?[9]

Anyway, to revert to Little Hans: what kind of a story is that? Little Hans had a phobia; he was cured of it; he was cured in the proper way, according to Freud, because the singular good fortune of having a father interested in analysis meant that he could talk about his experiences, about his imaginings, that he could be *heard* and thus was enabled to proceed towards maturity unencumbered with certain repressions which would otherwise have become sedimented, unshiftable, repressions to which he was in danger of becoming addicted.

But what kind of a story, I ask again, is that? Well, in more 'material' terms it is a story distilled from a text – a text which is of course itself a translation, but which also demonstrates many more complexities than that. The text of Little Hans's 'case' is divided into four unequal parts. The first three were written in 1909: Part One is titled 'Introduction', Part Two 'Case History and Analysis', Part Three 'Discussion'. The fourth Part, titled 'Postscript', was added in 1922.

Part One consists of a brief set of statements about Freud's purposes in recounting the tale – these are interestingly varied, and bear as much on Freud's wish for us to hear a vindication of certain aspects of his theories of infant sexuality as on the nature of Hans's childhood. Where, however, they come to bear on the latter it is through detail of the father's communications about Hans during the period which we might want to designate as pre-phobic. It contains some interesting information about Hans's interest in his genitals, and about his mother's perhaps similar – or perhaps not – interest in Hans's genitals – including her famous comment, which occurs on the third page of this 136-page 'case', to the effect that if Little Hans continues to put his hand on his penis she will send for Dr A to cut it off. I am not aware that research has demonstrated the identity of Dr A; but I think we men all know him well, at least the little boys in us do, from the nursery. We may rediscover him in the hospice.

Part Two, which opens with the father's communication of disturbance which I have quoted above, recounts two histories, which Freud takes care to differentiate: the history of Hans's phobia, and the history of Hans's analysis – although we might fairly want to ask who is the 'possessor' of this analysis – the two accounts culminating in a resolution which is said to be mutually satisfactory, although quite who the parties are of this mutual satisfaction remains, we might say, not clear. This occupies the bulk of the text. The oddly-named Part Three, titled 'Discussion' although it is notably less multivocal than its predecessor, offers us Freud's thoughts on the issues raised by the phobia and by its analysis. It also contains a supremely important couple of sentences which describe Freud's interest in the case, which I shall for the moment quote without gloss:

> I have for some time been thinking with pain of the way in which the adherents of 'the normal person' will fall upon poor little Hans [like heavy horses?] as soon as they are told that he can in fact be shown to have had a hereditary taint. His beautiful mother fell ill with a neurosis as a result of a conflict during her girlhood. I was able to be of assistance to her at the time, and this had in fact been the beginning of my connection with Hans's parents.[10]

I can hardly bear to leave aside the extraordinary implications of these sentences for the imbrications of psychoanalysis, literature and rapture; but I assure you (and you have to trust me) that I will come back to them later. In the meantime we must turn to the fourth Part, the 'Postscript', and it is here that we can begin to raise some questions: questions about impossibility; questions about ending; questions about what secret knowledge we have, or perhaps we might better say what secret knowledge, what faulty knowledge of secrets, possesses *us*, when we are *hearing the case*.

## Here Comes the Score

The 'Postscript' tells us that in 1922 a young man came to Freud and told him that he was Little Hans; he was now nineteen (I suppose Freud heard him saying that). Freud is pleased: he describes this apparition, this ghost of the past – whom he accepts as Hans, after all, only on hearsay – as a 'strapping youth', asserts that he is 'evidently' cured and healthy despite the later divorce of his parents; but adds two further comments, one of which is evidently disturbing to him, Freud, the other of which effects, it seems to me, a radical disturbance in the text itself.

First, he says that Hans has read his published case history; has, presumably, read a work of literature which lays bare, or purports to lay bare, or plays with laying bare, the secrets of his early life. He does not explain how or why this came into his hands, and he says that to him, Hans, 'the whole of it came to him as something unknown; he did not recognise himself; he could remember nothing'.[11] Whatever secrets there are at stake here, they are not communicated: but whether this leads us to think of a plenitude of knowledge, such that the unveiling of further secrets has become unnecessary, or alternatively of a further intensification of repression in order to cope with the hidden knowledge that one's life has been 'laid bare' in a public, literary way, is a matter of fine judgement. Freud at any rate, and somewhat elegiacally, says that 'the analysis had not preserved the events from amnesia, but had been overtaken by amnesia itself'.[12] There is, then, an acknowledged technical problem here, about whether we are discussing intensified and further entwined repression or a healthful dismissal of the past, but that is a clinical matter; I am more concerned with the textual crux here, because it suggests the death of a certain facility of hearing, the outgrowing of a sensory apparatus, such that listening in to one's childhood may in fact become impossible under certain conditions (except perhaps over the telephone). I am tempted to say that these conditions may be defined in terms of certain types of over-attention, an excess of presence; but I cannot prove that, and in any case I am now veering into my own analysis, betraying the roots of my addiction to this case history.

Of more general interest, it seems to me, are Freud's final sentences, where he compares Hans's apparent amnesia with what he asserts to be common experience in the following way:

> Any one who is familiar with psychoanalysis may occasionally experience something similar in sleep. He will be woken up by a dream, and will decide to analyse it then and there; he will then go to sleep again feeling quite satisfied with the result of his efforts; and next morning dream and analysis will alike be forgotten.[13]

In order to let the implications of this sentence sink in one would have to listen to it again. And again. Do I need, does anybody need, to spell out the uncanny impossibility of what Freud is saying? If we wake up having forgotten the entire dream/analysis episode, then how can we know that anything of the sort has taken place? And if we do have some curious intimation of such a structure, how can we refer any part of it to the realm of the wakeful rather then the realm of dream itself? What we have here is an aspect of the 'unrecapturable', that which cannot be authentically recounted or transmitted, a night-time rapture which will forever elude our attempt at recall because it has, already, been seized away.

Impossibility of recall, impossibility of rehearing; it is significant that this textual and analytic crux occurs in the last sentences of the text and undercuts all the rest. But there are other impossibles and unnameables in the text and in the 'case'. Naming itself, for example, and renaming: Hans's name in the earliest redaction was not Hans at all but Herbert.[14] Father and mother have no names, and neither does Freud within the body of the text, although otherwise names and especially pet-names abound. We might think back to Novalis's choice of a name;[15] or to Derrida on the association between the 'proper name' and death, which itself is perhaps only a refraction of older beliefs that to have one's name known, to have one's innermost (yet also, in a curious sense, outermost) secret betrayed, implied the imminence of the end, the approach of undifferentiation.[16]

Father also speaks on several occasions of recording on the spot exactly what his four-year-old son was saying; was he really? He tells us that he uses shorthand: do we speak to our children with a shorthand pad in our hands? And the final impossible: for we might say that no analysis happens in this case history at all, no interpretation; for there is no pure analytic situation to be encountered. Never mind: the text, any text, is after all a structure of impossibilities. So is all literature. Let us return to something easier to grasp, the question of hearing, which must fall apart into two elements: who hears whom, and who is not heard. First things first.

Who hears whom? Freud hears the father – they talk together – and reckons on being heard himself as a composite voice; on first publication the paper was interestingly not described as being 'by' Freud but as being 'communicated by' him, and later we learn that this was with the express consent of Little Hans's father.[17] Yet even here there is a question: on the second page of the case Freud tells us that he will 'now proceed to reproduce his father's records of little Hans just as I received them'[18] yet the very first words which succeed these are Freud's own, and as the second Part of the text in particular progresses it becomes increasingly difficult to hear a single voice in the cacophony which confronts us – and which, of course, surrounded Little Hans, rather, perhaps, as thought broadcasting surrounds the patient during a psychotic episode and makes it impossible for him or her to discern a single, individuated voice, makes it also impossible to hold on to one's own 'secret' inner discourse, which is forever on (or beyond) the brink of being drowned out by the insistent drumming of the horse's hooves, for example, by the constant intrusions of the repressed animal, which may of course also at the same time be describing its own rapture (Little Hans certainly thought so) but refusing to communicate its secrets.

## Cutting Off

The threat of castration which I have already mentioned is, interestingly, reported by Freud as mentioned by the parents themselves – an early example of the apparent presence of the mother in this otherwise male account, and one to which I shall return, although the mind boggles at the elision which can have Freud thus commenting if the only evidence is that which we have, which is clearly from the father; in what precise terms – and with what tonality – did Hans's mother report her comment to her husband? How are we to hear this palimpsestic remark?

And then, what does Freud hear of himself? Two quotations, only two pages apart, on the subject of infant analysis: 'It is not in the least our business to 'understand' a case at once: this is only possible at a later stage'; and then, 'no moment of time is so favourable for the understanding of a case as its initial stage'.[19] Awestruck hearing, we might say; not hearing ourselves; drowning, dissolving our beleaguered subjectivity in voices. What *Hans* presumably hears, of course, is the outcome of one of Freud's major instructions to his parents, which is that he, Hans, should be subjected to a gradual process of sexual enlightenment; one of the elements in this strategy, since Hans has shown an apparently unusual interest in his mother's 'widdler', as he calls it, is that he should be informed that 'his mother and all other female beings (as he could see from Hanna) had no widdler at all'.[20]

Freud, as we have already heard, hears Hans only once; his parents hear him a great deal of the time, as for example on the occasion when, as we learn, his mother 'examined him all morning'.[21] But then, perhaps the more important question here is the second one: who, or what, is *not* being heard? What is being held in secret? What hearing is not possible – not possible particularly, perhaps, if we are to try a *case*? The father, still in the letter in which he reports Hans's 'disturbance', mentions in an almost offhand way that 'no doubt the ground [for Hans's phobia] was prepared by sexual over-excitation due to his mother's tenderness';[22] whatever else we may think of this remark it obviously sets the scene for the mother as a suppressed correspondent in these processes of responsive hearing. It is her castration threat which has been reported, without corroboration, as 'heard'; with her we are always in the realm of hearsay; with hearsay, I suspect, we are always in the realm of the mother, which we may alternatively translate as the oceanic, the rapturous, that within which we continue to bear the memories of our prior dissolution and also the traces, the residues of our addiction to such a state, beside which any conceivable present or future seems pallid, shorn of the total involvement, the moment of ecstasy or bliss, which alone makes the interminable processes of time seem bearable.

But then Hans himself, as we might expect, is heard in a peculiar way. For example, there are many occasions on which we are told that he speaks of his phobia as 'this nonsense of mine'; on one occasion his father, reporting such a comment, adds apologetically that 'that is how he speaks of his phobia'.[23] What is remarkable here is that we are also told that Freud and Hans's father have themselves agreed that this is the phrase which *should* be supplied to Hans as a way of talking about things; in hearing this phrase they are hearing, or mishearing, themselves and failing to recognise their own voices. Hans, of course, knows that he cannot be heard; during one of his lengthy conversations with his father (recorded, presumably, by the father himself, notebook in hand), Hans says 'You don't believe me again?' and at another moment 'I'm not joking, you know, Daddy'.[24] Voices drive one mad; madness is signified by the hearing of voices. Voices which are 'disembodied', which speak from the shadows, which come to remind us of a different world, a world to which we are denied access, a world, perhaps, behind the 'green door', which would also be a world of childhood fantasy from which we are now in permanent exile yet also doomed to the re-enactment, to the hope of recalling rapture through whatever means, however faulty, disagreeable or downright addictive, may be to hand.[25]

What are we to make of such moments in the history of Little Hans? How can we imagine the facial expressions, the suppressed elements of dialogue, the ellipses which occasioned these comments, these desperate requests for a serious hearing, for the case to be properly tried without allowance always being made for assumed silences, secrets, misprisions, assumptions, arrogances? What are we to make of the moment when Hans, apparently hopelessly confused in his attempts, at the age of four, to describe the processes of birth and to signify his continued but doubtful adherence to the narrative of the stork (which he *knows*, with uncanny prescience, to be the 'wrong' animal), says, 'I heard so – or didn't I hear it at all? – or did I say it wrong?'[26]

There are many, many other examples: perhaps they are best summarised by Freud himself in his so-called 'Discussion', when he describes the interpretative technique as 'presenting the unconscious complex to [the patient's] consciousness *in our own words*'.[27] Who here is the 'our', or rather the 'we'? Is it inclusive, does it permit the patient at least some participation in the process of hearing, or is it a statement on behalf of the 'enlightened', the loose professionality which, in this *case*, also includes the father who is so much disturbed by the notion of the son as case history, the case history as son, but decisively excludes the patient himself; and also excludes an intriguing panoply of others, to whom we must now turn.

There is a continuing trope Freud uses in this case history and in others, which is to do with 'clearing up'. 'Now that the matter had been cleared up', for example, 'Hans's father attempted to examine the boy a second time upon this important point'; or 'I say no more than that it is possible, because the matter was not cleared up in the analysis'. On the one hand it is evident that this legend of 'clearing up' relates to a collusive activity of Freud and Hans's father; this is made strikingly *clear* in a phrase used near the beginning of the analysis, connected to a sexual dream of Hans's, when Freud notes that 'his father's penetration . . . succeeded in clearing it up'.[28] But 'clearing up' can also be seen in a different light; when trying to deal with the addict – with the mess the addict makes of things, with the mess he or she is making of their life – it is a metaphor which springs to mind. It appears to signify a hope of order; but really it signifies the imposition of a 'different' order, the nullifying of an 'other' version of order which may be quite transparent to the addict but which is not allowed its function because it offends against the moral and temporal law.[29]

Without wanting to get too side-tracked for the moment onto Freud's attitude to Hans's father's potency, we might still legitimately ask about the bodily equivalents of this process of clearing up, about what awful kind of mess Hans makes. We have already been told he is in danger of making a mess of his parents' well-ordered lives, but we will come to see that it may well have been Freud himself who has run that risk, and thus that in attempting to work with the case of Little Hans Freud is in fact performing a substitutive act of self-analysis. Well, we know that children make messes, of various kinds; we know that Hans is preoccupied with *lumf*, we know that a large part of his analysis is concerned with separating out shit from babies. We know also that masturbation can be considered to be a mess, although the connection between the secret and the public in this instance is endlessly complex. In this connection it is perhaps useful to recall that in order to assist young Hans with his professed project – age four, remember – of desisting from masturbation his father says to him, after a prolonged philosophical discourse in which Hans is attempting with extraordinary sophistication to discriminate between incantation, wish and act, 'Well, but to prevent your wanting to, this evening you're going to have a bag to sleep in'.[30] What a privilege; but also, what an example of being 'well wrapped' in order to prevent the exercise of your addiction, in order to torment you with the withholding of a small avatar of rapture, in order to enforce the moral law.

## You Can't Find the Help these Days

But I think the most important question about clearing up the mess is really about exclusion; and about who the suppressed but significant others might be in the hearing of this case. We can find them exactly where you would expect, in adjuvant positions, for around this case, which professes to be clear in terms of presences and influences, of key witnesses, which professes to say that here is Hans, here is Hans's little sister, here are his father and mother, and here, offstage left, is the hearing professor, there is in fact a huge cast of extras: mainly maids, who are notoriously the hearers and bearers of secrets. Hans's early experiences of playing 'horsey', his early immersions in the rapturous realm of the pre-symbolic animal, for example, have to do with maids. When Hans is elaborating a fantasy of how the stork came to deliver Hanna – a fantasy which by now we know he does not believe but through the manipulation of which he is probably mocking his father's attempts to 'enlighten' him about matters of which he already knows more than he can communicate but which he continues to elaborate, in secret – he says that the stork came to the door and rang the door-bell. His father, surprised into a moment of 'normal' communication, asks how the stork did it and Hans says he did it with his beak; his father asks whether he shut the door again and Hans, in a mood clearly difficult for us now to discern because of our lack of hearing, says that a maid shut it for him. As a final example, which also bears upon the unheard secrets of the text, Freud near the end mentions how he entertained a suspicion that 'Hans's repressed wish might now be that he wanted at all costs to see his mother's widdler. As his behaviour to a new maid fitted in with this hypothesis . . . '[31]. But it is unnecessary to continue.

Maids, governesses, ghosts; those people who fill a house but whose word is presumed untrustworthy, those whose thought broadcasting we are always receiving but who play no part in the 'hearing' of a case, those who are supposed to have no hearing at all except for what they are permitted to hear; we are here clearly in the world of *The Turn of the Screw* (1898), but we can go farther than that by wondering about selectivity of evidence, about the paralysing fear of 'hearsay' which conditions this restriction to family positions, which sets up this carapace over a set of experiences which certainly, on Little Hans's part, were richer and more various – more rapturous, perhaps, who can say? – than could be heard.[32]

And here in particular we are at last in a realm of experience of the female, even if unheard; and we can now turn to look at it more closely, and particularly at Hans's mother. For it is around the silent, secret, unheard figure of Hans's mother that the key contradictions of the text operate and it is also, as I shall attempt to show, around the figure of the mother that the desire of the text, Freud's desire, the desire of analysis, the wish and need to be 'rapt' and to deny that rapture, coagulates. I want to deal with the mother here under two headings, first, in terms of 'Legends of Love and Beauty'; second, in terms of 'Legends of Fear' and the 'Mother of Separation'.

Legends of Love and Beauty; and as I talk through this – if that is what I am doing – I want you to recall to mind, to re-hear, the passage I mentioned earlier on. Let me remind you of one or two elements in it. 'Hereditary taint' [of addiction?[33]]; 'beautiful mother'; 'of some assistance to her'. To take the middle one of these first: throughout the text when Freud refers to Hans's mother he refers to her as the 'beautiful mother'. Sometimes he goes further; there is a reference to her as Hans's 'excellent and devoted mother'. He says, in the context of a remark of hers about pigs to which we shall return, that she must be excused such comments because 'she had a predestined part to play, and her position was a hard one'.[34] There is a fantasy here; and it is one in which Freud sees the mother as a paragon of all virtue, and this can hardly be unconnected with the fact, of which he apprises us, that he has in the past been 'of some assistance to her'.

She is, then, the healed product of his own analytic practice, the source of his own professional (if it is fully professional) moment of rapture, and thus she is necessarily beautiful, excellent and devoted; we may go further and say that in this text Freud betrays every sign of love for her. This leaves the 'hereditary taint'; what may we hear in this rueful comment? We must turn here to an extraordinary sentence of Freud's which occurs when he reports on the one session he actually spent with Hans and, of course, his father, when, Freud assures us, he said to Hans the following:

> Long before he was in the world . . . I had known that a little Hans would come who would be so fond of his mother that he would be bound to feel afraid of his father because of it; and I had told his father this.[35]

On the surface, this is presumably Freud's way of explaining the Oedipus complex to a four-year-old; but we may enquire further, especially in the light of the previous comment that Hans's mother's position was 'a hard one'. There is a reference here to a 'primal' event, to Freud himself as Hans's fantasised precursor, indeed his progenitor; this in itself might solve the reference to the 'hereditary taint', for there is no doubt that insofar as Freud considers anybody in the legend to be married to the beautiful, silent, suffering mother, it is he himself; he must suffer the addiction to guilt – or pass it on to Hans – and it is clear too that he considers himself to be the incarnation of Hans's unnamed, acolyte, unmanned father; what we have here is the fantasised record of a love affair which has not ended, from which all prospect of an ending is in recession.

## Professions of Love

But this love, this tension in silence between the hearing professor and the unheard patient, is by no means without its vicissitudes, and the text betrays many of them in its ceaseless attempts to inscribe meanings on the mother's body, to hear a voice which makes and masks itself through the text and through the masculist collusion which forms the peculiar birth scenario of Little Hans as a textual object. Legends of Fear; the Mother of Separation.

For Freud's love for Hans's mother is struggling against some very real alternatives, real blockages – it is in this text, you may remember, that he refers to the clitoris as 'permanently stunted'.[36] We have already seen that, according to the textual account, it is Hans's mother who threatens to send him to Dr A – back to the beginning? back inside the fearsome womb? – to have his penis cut off. It is also Hans's mother, further to unravel a clue I have already mentioned, who, when Hans asks her why she will not touch his penis, responds helpfully with the comment 'Because that'd be piggish'[37] (another maligned animal appears on the scene at a moment of the utmost vexation). It is, by the way, not clear to me to what aspect of the behaviour of pigs this remark refers. Hans's mother it also is who, when little Hans announces that he wants to sleep with an older female child rather than in the company of his parents, says, 'Well, if you really want to go away from Daddy and Mummy, then take your coat and knickers and – good-bye!'[38]

What *is* this sort of evidence? What are we hearing here? What are we to hear when, twice, Hans tells his father that his mother beats his baby sister, and his father receives this information without turning a hair? What are we to think when his father says, with an apparently matter-of-fact air, that his mother frequently threatens to attack Hans with a carpet-beater?

Nineteenth-century practices; a refraction of an age-old history of abuse; patriarchal mysteries; violence and silence interlocked, violosilence, ancient twins of nightmare and enclosure. All that, certainly; but particularly here in the text, it seems to me, a knot at the root of analysis; and, perhaps, of discourse. For we have rapture and hatred here, certainly, inscribed as on a motorpsycho's knuckles; we have a long-suppressed love on Freud's part for his past patient, an unhandled transference trying to seep out in the constant references to 'little Hans', to the complex childing undergone throughout the text by its many 'patients'; but also here we have, I think, the figure of the Mother of Separation.

The Mother of Separation (perhaps myth has known her as Kali or Artemis) is an analytic concept which perhaps needs some explanation.[39] The situation is thus. The primal mother, the mother of undifferentiation, the mother of rapture and fullness, offers everything. We are prone to fall into the Lacanian trap and say that Daddy comes along and spoils all that (Freud falls proleptically into that trap too; so does Hans's father). But this is to underestimate the richness, the rapture of the child's world, in which fullness is already entwined with emptying, *kenosis*. The Mother of Separation is always there; there in the moment of the withheld breast, there in the moment of inattention – there indefatigably, of course, at the moments surrounding the birth of a different baby, and a baby sister at that; she is the mother who is not available and thus she serves as a figure within which all unavailability is collected, the withheld female who attracts all the blame and punishment, one way of looking at the origin of rape fantasies and of addiction and its successor, of a lifetime of withdrawal, of cold turkey.

But Mother of Separation is also there within the analytic session, it is she who hears, she whom you can hear but cannot touch. She sits just behind you, out of sight, in secret, and she whispers back to you your dark thoughts. She is permanently unavailable; her promises to soak up the energy of the transference are hollow; her hollowness is the hollow voice of the grave; in this incarnation she is not the brazen, flashing Artemis but black Hekate, goddess of household garbage and rats.[40] She calls you a pig, and you are a pig; she wields the knife and you put up with it because you know – or think – that she has another face, another set of hands, to embrace, to 'coax', as little Hans expresses his thoughts about the caress. It does not matter in this context whether the analyst is male or female; transference to a wished-for mother will still proceed, and the culmination of those unleashed feelings will still be thwarted; or, of course, sometimes not, if we are to believe the accounts of abuse of therapeutic process which have been for some time current in the media.[41]

## Don't Look Now

Mother of Separation: a presiding deity of this text, I would say, and the secret block against which Freud constantly stubbed his toe, here recapitulating an insufficiency in no way palliated by the long years since he was 'of assistance to' Hans's beautiful mother – in bed, perhaps, or at least in the guise of midwife. I would remind you that we are talking of the realm of fantasy here; or of the undecidable secret line which blocks off the 'truth' of history, the truth of the case. But we must move on (as Hans could not); and also we must leave the scene. And there is so much more to say. More to say about the nature of the 'case', for example; for the case, if we look at it etymologically, betrays its own contradiction. It is that which proves but that which disproves. All existing laws founder on the special case; no number of cases amounts to anything other than case law. What is the case? How can we construct an anomic series of events – for events may be seen as apathetic beyond all control – into a 'case' which will speak with a single interpretable voice? And is it only on that basis that we can conduct a 'hearing', legal or otherwise? Is this where our hearing becomes engaged, in the demonstration of the normal, or in the bringing to attention of the atypical? Was this the dynamic for Hans's father, the search for a 'case' which would interest the hearing professor, which would unconsciously shift the paternity of his problematic child, which would move all responsibility through the web of the Mother of Separation?

Truth and explanation are at stake here in many forms, but emblematised in Little Hans's dealings with all false interpretation, in his sophisticated rejection of simplistic secrets, in his inventive reappropriation of the lies he is told about the stork. Who is 'on trial' here, who is to get a hearing? I want to conclude this chapter with some speculations on hearing, psychoanalysis, criticism, rapture. First, we might bring on stage a notion of a 'refugee reading'.[42] It is becoming clearer to me as I write (speak?) what might be meant by that. For the refugee cannot hear. The refugee's plight is the opposite of rapture. The refugee is stuck, fleeing, amid the gabble of unintelligible voices: scrabbling, perhaps, for some news of home, news which she or he knows from the outset will be a distortion, will perhaps suffer from a 'hereditary taint'.

The refugee hears only from a distance, through the web of the Mother of Separation; the promise of rapture has been emblematically withdrawn; we are here again in the world of *over*hearing, which we have seen also as the alienation of the romantic poets, as the distant echoes of the oft-told tale of the Ancient Mariner. Little Hans had to cope with these distancing problems too; and if Mother of Separation is really Hekate's earthly avatar then we are also in the realm of death, for Hekate represents a more total death than Hades, she stands for humiliation and obliteration, the stuff of very early fantasies, the being eaten up and having our bones thrown on the rubbish heap, extinction without the succour of Hades's crucial *voice,*[43] a realm where there is nothing more to hear, where there is no more 'here', the long come-down of the addict (but which addiction also evades). This, as I have said elsewhere, is the gift of analysis, it deals in the *remains* because it takes its strength from the dark background, which is death, and thus it is that all Freud's recuperative moves necessarily run the risk of ending in contradiction.[44]

Little Hans is death-bound, and knows it; in the darkness around the horse's mouth he sees, not for God's sake only his father's moustache but the darkness of all *destination*, a destination which precedes articulacy; and thus it is that he prefers not to move, he prefers (wrapped in a different skin, like a cyborg) the alien animation of his own phobia (or perhaps he is the phobia's own possession, for possession is an emblematic trope here) for he senses that overloading is the substance of which psyche is made, that he will soon be embarked on the black coach with its terrible freight – the best realisation of this is one of the earliest fantasies in Iain Banks's *The Bridge* (1986), which is also *in toto* a fantasy about the problem of movement, as Freud says in this text that all of our motive phobias will eventually cathect onto the railway.[45] God help Network Rail.

Perhaps that is a distraction (or, at least, can gain no traction). This is probably right, because when we are thinking about hearing we are automatically thinking also about tuning ('my father was a radio operator') and we are tuned to different spans. In analysis there is the analytic hour, which lasts fifty minutes, no more and no less. Does 'reading time' transgress such laws of order? Of course it does. But it remains necessary to posit a few questions. One is the obvious one in terms of the location of analytic practice: are we dealing in recollection or in a new dealing of the cards, are we hearing ancestral voices prophesying war or the rumbling of our own hungry refugee bellies, memory or desire, rapture or addiction? Another is, what of the symptom, what of the fact that while trying to prepare the presentation on which this chapter is based, and having a poisoned foot, I inevitably stubbed my toe on the door of my own office, thus conclusively preventing myself from moving? The last (perhaps) is about real refugees, about those who surround us on all sides, about those who are disenfranchised at birth, about 'foreign bodies' in the most extreme sense. And so a double parting gesture. First: if you really want to know something about the foreign body, about its fragments and dismemberments, about its refugee 'difference' from the possibility of the rapture, I recommend that you read alongside the legend of Little Hans an entirely different text, a text by a South African called Bloke Modisane, called *Blame Me on History* (1963), which has a different way of conjuring the primal scene;[46] but second, of course, because even in the line of flight, as Deleuze and Guattari call it, of the scapegoat or, as I for the moment prefer to call it, the refugee, there still must be points of recognition, border controls, thus my effort at securing the presence of what would be the next stage of this presentation were it to be part of a true dialogue (which literature, by definition, never is) would be to ask you to let *me* hear something else about this curious *case*, a case which calls all possession, all naming, all secrets, all signification, all possibility for rapture into question.

# 6

# The Well of Life

Rapture, then again, is cross-cultural; rapture is that which abnegates cultural distinction. Well, that at least is a hypothesis; how could we ever know? Are the raptures, the ecstasies of mystics the world over, the same? Is ecstasy a transcending category, a crossing, a passing into another realm where quotidian distinctions cease to have a meaning? Perhaps; but regrettably it does not matter, because all we have are reports, accounts, discursive artefacts which are the survivors of experience, the 'memoirs of a survivor', as Doris Lessing, in her Sufi phase, put it.[1] But this does not allow us to avoid the task of considering rapture in the light (or shadow) of cultural difference; rather, it enjoins us to a more strenuous attempt to see the rapture from a variety of perspectives.

And yet rapture is perhaps that which denies the multiplicity of perspective. This, after all, is what the psychotic lacks: a sense of perspective. The psychotic moment marks the time when it is above all difficult to 'pull oneself together', when the disparate strands of experience can no longer be brought within a single controlling vision.[2] Cubism and psychosis: there is a book to be written about that, but this is not it. We may, however, touch on cubism's materials: on the conjunction of impossible perspectives, on the rivalrous occupancy of space, on the difficulty of achieving a unitary point from which to view. When we are 'carried away', we sense a lack of the ground beneath our feet: we are the victims of a shifting of tectonic plates, helpless before a series of incompatible perceptions which appear actively to resist symbiosis. We are, in short, precisely on the terrain which post-structuralism heralds as the absence of master-narratives, but whereas the post-structuralists attempt to populate this vacated space with a host of local phenomena, we may sense that this too is a translation, that what we become in touch with as sublimity self-destructs is instead an untranslateable plethora – a moment of *jouissance*, no doubt, but also not without its terrors as we discover that the points of the compass are endlessly malleable, flowing, as in a Salvador Dali painting, or in some of Plath's poems, from one solid into another.[3]

## Deep Thought

The secret of rapture, then, is that of what happens when the ground beneath our feet opens up and we are confronted with the abyss, with risk, with vertigo; and these are the materials I want to explore in this chapter. Initially I shall want to do so in the context of a story from the *Mahabharata* often known as 'The Well of Life',[4] but before doing that I need to say something about the whole question, now already broached, of depth imageries. James Hillman has a great deal to say about them: crucially that in his practice as a Jungian analyst and trainer he uses, and implies that 'we' use, such imageries in order to relay metaphorically the significant fact that, as he puts it, 'soul' moves in a different dimension from matter.[5] Since matter relates at all points, in our experience, to the surface of the planet on which we live, the notion of depth, which in turn and necessarily carries with it the connotation of impenetrability, stands for the 'other', the realm through which we cannot *move*; and this in turn reflects one, at least, of what Hillman takes to be the essential qualities of the world of soul – or, as we might tentatively put it, of rapture – namely that it is static.

It would be foolish to ignore the fact that 'that which goes on below the surface' is also related (as it was for little Hans) to female genitalia; and thus, as well as for other reasons, depth is associated with birth and the granting of life, the origin of life-giving forces, and also, and for precisely this reason, with the possibility of those life-giving forces being withheld through, as we have seen, the power of the Mother of Separation. Life, thus, becomes *that which happens* on the surface; but the *conditions* of life, Heidegger's category (which is also a non-category) of Being, that which gives it ground and being, that which surrounds it from every direction, that is depth.[6] And from this we can play out whole strings of dream imagery, particularly, as I have mentioned, to do with vertigo, which we oddly name as the fear of heights although it is at least as overtly the depths we fear, the falling rather than the climbing; or perhaps the being stuck between stasis and collapse, which is a feature we shall notice in the *Mahabharata* story, but which is also the opposition we face when the natural, or at least normative, operations of gravity are suspended, in either the material sphere or in the sphere of soul.[7]

It is gravity which makes the 'journey to the centre of the earth' untenable; we already know that it is easier to get to the moon than to the centre of the planet we stand on, and we can be sure that, resources permitting, we will find it easier to inhabit the farthest reaches of the solar system than to live one hundred miles inside our own 'home', a home from which we are therefore in fact in permanent exile, refugees from the very material from which we claim to derive our origins, separated from the rapture and the fire. We crawl around, so writers and philosophers of many a stripe tell us, and also according to one compelling account of psyche, outside it looking for a door, finding caves in which to worship, imagining entrances to the forbidden realm inside (a state of mind familiar to us from, among others, Little Hans); and since it *is* forbidden, then we demonise it and instead of the domestic warmth of a return to the maternal home we imagine the flames of hell-fire licking out from these quasi-organic folds and crevices. All of this is to do with depth, and it is also to do with otherness: because we also know, to our often suppressed anguish, that what is forbidden to our material bodies is given to us every night in dream, where we penetrate the most absurd depths, hang suspended in the milkiest of caves, are shot or rushed through the most violent and exhilarating of underground rivers, make our very home, the home of instability, in 'caverns measureless to man'.[8]

From depth psychology there would seem, provisionally, to be little 'recourse': from the dead earth, from Hades and the chthonic depths, it is but a short step to the crypt. Secrets hidden under the earth have greater imagistic resonance, we might suggest according to the withheld logic of secrets which I am trying to elaborate – against much inevitable resistance, against all the forces which claim that what is secret must remain secret, that what has been hidden must not be brought to the surface – than other secrets written, say, in the clouds:[9] because by being there placed they simultaneously assert a union between birth and death, they are secrets which 'know' (in some sense) that they have preceded our conscious knowledge and they are also secrets which will await us in our coming tomb when we shall at last know whether or not they have meanwhile – that is, during the time of our lives but simultaneously and inseparably 'on another scene' – been decrypted for our inspection. We shall know, we might say as an example, the origins of that quintessentially enigmatic tomb, the *kaba* of Mecca. For it is on that site, more than most others, that the great struggle (one meaning of *jihad*) between polytheism and monotheism is emblematised; it is here, we are told, that Mohammad overthrew the 360 tribal idols of the Arabian deserts, and it is thus the burying ground of many gods.[10]

We need to continue with this image. For in the reformist terms of many religions, that last sentence would have continued 'and replaced them with . . . ', but of course the story and destiny of Islam is different: we have here the deconstruction of all images, for there is only one unforgiveable sin against Allah and that is the sin of association, the sin whereby any characteristic or trait comes to be 'associated' with the oneness, the unity of God, an association which detracts from his unapproachable, transcendent, rapturous divinity. Thus the fullness of polytheism is replaced by what we might refer to as the perfection of the blank: the richness and diversity of a realm of differing and overlapping powers, representing the diversity of the natural and human worlds, is superseded by a white light in which all is bathed but nothing can be 'seen' because the very act of perception, the ground of all perspective, caught up as it is in the always hovering threat of *representation*, is the essence of blasphemy and detracts from the hovering possibility, if always and endlessly deferred, of the rapture.

Instead of the potentially overweening presence of the lesser gods – or indeed of those who might be dangerous beyond the point of all belief – there is placed a 'deferred idol', the mark which indicates the very direction of Mecca, a singular compass point which will keep us alert and grounded even as different geographies rise and fall on the surface of the earth; although, of course, not in the *kaba* itself, which is the shrine towards which all the invisible – and indeed blindfolded – sightlines point. We may see this as one form of an enigma of origin; another is encoded, or perhaps encrypted, in the paradox of the 'birth' of Islam, which is the newest of monotheistic religions but is *also* the oldest in its claim to signify a return to a truth which antedates the distortions which, so it is said, came to beset the Judaic and Christian revelations. Here lies a myth of origin as restoration, of construction as recollection: it is perhaps not irrelevant that the only monotheistic sect in the world to believe in reincarnation is that forgotten – and secretive – branch of Islam, the Druze, who accept 'the transmigration of souls until perfected souls cease to be reborn and ascend to the stars'.[11] In, no doubt, rapture.

## Heraclitus' Adventures in Tibet

What do these myths of succession mean? Were the many gods an attempt to hide from the sight of the one true god whose gaze was more than we could bear; or was the imposition of the one true god a manufacture of later date designed to draw the gods away from us? The sociological evidence would probably support the latter interpretation, and would focus on the perceptible need for a greater and more transcendental power in the increasingly highly organised and settled society Arabia was becoming in the time of Mohammad, a society which after all under the rule of Islam went on to some eight hundred years of expansionist civilisation at a time, at least to begin with, when Christian Europe was experiencing the Dark Ages, that curious historical equivalent to the latency period of childhood between the age of early, easy knowledge and the coming lifetime of adult recapitulation under the sign of death – an equation surely not unknown, at least at some level, to the classical scholar Freud.

To return, and to recast the question in its original Heraclitean form: which lies further in the depths, the many or the one?[12] Will the decrypting which we shall know, perhaps, in the crucial few days after our death, the days which are as firmly enshrined in Balinese ritual as they are in Tibetan Buddhism[13], the days also which survive in displaced form in the Christian myth of the resurrection, reveal to us concentration or dispersal, the apotheosis of the selfhood or a retroactive knowledge of the non-linearity of consciousness? What shall we *bring back* from this unavoidable journey to the depths, and how shall we manage to recount it?

This, at any rate, is one form of question hidden in the depths; but the depths we have to deal with when we think of the 'well' are perhaps different from those of the crypt. The well and the crypt share a thanatic burden. There is death in the well, death by falling, drowning or poison. There is death in the crypt, death by cold, starvation or suffocation. But what of the erotic counterpart? There is life in the well, and it is the life of water, nurture, liquid clarity, the potential slaking of otherwise eternal thirst. Is there life in the crypt? To put the question is immediately to alter its meaning, to conjure up images of what kind of life this might be: the life we attribute, as the reverse of the anthropomorphic, to the rat and the spider, the life of monstrous things 'bred in the depths', a crawling, slavering, desperate kind of life, drawing the most minute kind of sustenance from the dripping rock, waiting for the next victim . . . None of this is to deny a manifestation of Eros, but it is of a peculiar kind: a highly Christianised Eros, perhaps – Gothic, hanging in chains from the walls, bricked up in caverns and behind walls, tortured? Is this what is encrypted within the 'crypt', within, for example, the root metaphors of cryptonymy, the myth of the tomb that will reopen, the rolling away of the stone, the attendant question of whether such an event will even be believed, no matter how carefully or rapturously it may be recounted?[14]

At any rate, it seems to me that the image of the crypt cannot claim the double-sidedness, the vitality of the image of the well; and we might go on from this to an analysis of these twinned images of depth in Western and Eastern myth and psyche. Among other things, of course, the well is cyclical, with the seasons and with the turning of the slow handle, as the controlling myths of Hinduism and Buddhism are also cyclical, the almost silent flickering of the prayer wheel, the necessity of turning with *dharma* the wheel of life. The crypt is endstopped, it is the point of no return where the only way out has to be through total transformation and the abandonment of the body to add to the array of skeletons locked into the tomb; as

Western myths also tend to be endstopped, lacking in *enjambement*, to give way in the end to the total transformation of Doomsday, beyond which is a world not open to inspection. But there is no space to pursue this further: the plight of the brahman in the well of life, hanging on a curious brink between a story told (many, many times, for the *Mahabharata* is a living myth, a constant guide to actions and behaviours[15]) and a story not told, becomes urgent.

And so to 'The Well of Life'. There are many versions of this story; the one I shall quote is adapted from the translation of the *Mahabharata* by Roy C. Amore and Larry D. Shinn. The first paragraph reads thus:

> A certain brahman who lived in this world wandered into a deep dark forest that was filled with ferocious wild animals. The forest was populated with lions, bull elephants, and other animals that roared incessantly. It was so terrifying that even the god of death, Yama, would cringe at entering this malevolent realm. Realising that he was lost, the brahman became very alarmed and began to run in circles hoping to find the way out. Attempting to elude the frightening creatures which were all around, the panicked man ran deeper into the forest. Still, he could not rid himself of his pursuers.[16]

We are here, of course, on terrain familiar from a myriad of fairy stories which can be replicated across an enormously wide swathe of cultures. The essential point is this: if you lose yourself in a deep, dark forest, if you lose the thread of where you are, or indeed where you were in the story (or if you fall asleep while the story is being told, which is part of the paradoxical point of such stories, although they are also concerned, at another level, with the warding off of sleep and with the ever-present questions posed, for example, by the Balinese demons who may be one avatar of the coming nightmare), then inevitably you find yourself – or rather, you do not 'find' yourself – going deeper and deeper, farther and farther in, ever more distant from the possibility of recounting an unrecapturable experience.[17] It is interesting how C.S. Lewis's heavily Christianised children's 'myths' in *The Chronicles of Narnia* (1949–54) sidestep this depth problem by having the direction of progress designated as 'farther *up* and farther in', not a scenario we will frequently find in the Brothers Grimm.

## Of Running, Struggling and Giving In

So: confronted with (and pursued by) this scenario, what do you do? You run. And as you run you inevitably penetrate deeper into the forest, even as you re-encounter (or think you do) your own footprints in the deepening circles, mazes, labyrinths; and in this running there is always dream, there are the unseen malevolent pursuers who we know will catch us in the end, because that is the fate of all addiction, of all the running in circles, of the deepening repetition. In terms of pathology, we might look at how these pursuers are constructed, decrypted, brought up from the tomb, in the many forms of (drug-induced) paranoia. A shrine to Kali, for example, exists to defy vision: we are not enjoined to look straight and clear at the image of the goddess, but instead are jostled, are lost in the rush and shouting, so that the point of the encounter is to render us uncertain of what we may or may not have seen, to perpetuate the rapture, the mystery. But the pathological explanation would also miss the deeper level of the passional, where the pursuers perform a different function, which is *precisely* to chase you into and through this deep dark forest; because there you may encounter something, something which you need to know, or which you delude yourself to be a necessary knowledge, even if it can never be brought back.[18] And if you are not chased there (drug users talk obsessively of being pursued by their demons) you may never go, and then the learning, what Hillman refers to as the 'cooking of soulstuff', would not occur.[19] Are they passionate or passionless, these pursuers? Do they chase us because they *want* us to have this essential but impossible experience, or do they chase us because chasing is their role, they are the hounds of heaven, the hunters of the dark lord, Hern the hermetic, and they know no other form of life, no other pattern with which we might resist inevitable self-destructive behaviour? Certainly the brahman does not know; but then, in the world into which he is penetrating the emphasis is less on knowledge than on – as we might by now imagine – on hearing, but now also, above all, on 'seeing':

> The brahman looked up and saw that the forest was surrounded by a net held by a huge woman with outstretched arms. Serpents with five heads also encompassed the forest and were so tall that their heads reached nearly up to the heavens. In a clearing, there was a deep pit covered with creeping vines and underbrush. As the brahman ran frantically through the forest pursued by a wild elephant, he stumbled into the open pit and became lodged halfway down the hole in the vines that grew over it.[20]

The brahman may not know the purposes of his pursuers, but what he comes to *see* is a vision of difference, coded as we might expect in the imagery of height and depth which precisely signifies a different dimension and thus the possibility of entry into a world of soul, into the rapture. For what the brahman does is to fall off the edge of the world. His pursuers have chased him as far as it is possible to chase anybody without some kind of liminal change taking place, and this change is possessed of that odd half-symmetry which we encounter in dreams, especially on the threshold of dream and waking, for as is becoming increasingly clear it is on this threshold, where the rapture awaits but cannot become immanent, where the recounting of drug-induced travellers' tales beckons but cannot be accomplished, that the realms of order and chaos meet and thus the stories of symmetry and disorder fuse and shift. As they do in, for example, Balinese concepts of narrative and as of course, to move back (with relief) onto more 'familiar' – yet nonetheless, naturally, uncanny – terrain they do in the solid yet evanescent form of Blake's 'tyger'.[21]

We need to remind ourselves – and this lies at the heart of the problem of rapture, of being 'enrapt' or 'wrapped' – that it is impossible simply to *cross* a threshold: rather, the act of moving to cross it places one immediately in precisely the 'realm of the liminal', wherein values and assumptions are automatically transformed, changed according to a pre-existent script which we neither know nor understand. Thus after an encounter with, or upon, a threshold the remainder of the tale – the tale of the remainder – will take place in some overarching sense *within* that threshold; and this is exactly what happens to the brahman.

The 'huge woman with outstretched arms' (the inner life and support of the world, the great overarching mother, the destination of all our running, chasing and being chased) and the 'deep pit covered with twining vines and undergrowth' (the opening onto a new world or onto one so archaic that we fail to recognise it as our deferred home, the trap in which we always caught, the giving of ground beneath our feet in vertigo, which is also the destination of all our running and chasing), these are phenomena or experiences which cannot be comprehended within the still recognisable world of the forest and the wild elephant, and so the brahman plunges 'halfway'. He cannot get directly through this knot of experience, this encounter with a realm of impossible visions, this tangle or cross-hatching[22] of contradictions symbolised in the 'twining vines', but neither can he return: he is stuck halfway down the pit,[23] perhaps in that place where latent and manifest meaning fuse together in the hypnagogic image, perhaps on that spot where one still believes one can 'speak back' to the phantomatic 'other world' of the real, where one believes one can deliver the message of hallucination, but where one also knows that a veil of some kind separates one from this possibility, renders the 'real' world a constantly vanishing chimera. Another experience associated with the liminal, with being strung between the psychotic inner and the beckoning but always evasive outer – and it is one which Blake associated with the mythically complex world of the spider in *The Marriage of Heaven and Hell* (c. 1790–3) – is of being upside down:[24]

> As the brahman hung upside down, tangled in the vines, he saw a huge serpent at the bottom of the hole. Looking up, he saw an elephant at the top of the hole. The dark-skinned elephant had six faces and twelve feet and seemed intent on maintaining its vigil at the mouth of the hole. In the vines that held the brahman, bees had built hives filled with honey. These hives dripped honey near him, and he reached out to catch the sweet nectar in his mouth as he hung there. The more honey the brahman ate, the more he wanted; his thirst could not be quenched. Meanwhile, black and white rats gnawed away at the roots of the vines which held him. With elephant above, serpent below, bees buzzing all around, and rats gnawing at his life-support, the brahman continued to reach out for more honey.[25]

The life-threatening yet curiously satisfying terrors of addiction, certainly – addiction, perhaps, to life – yet I suppose the first thing to strike one about this part of the story – and this, remarkably, is its final paragraph – is the enormity of its proliferation. There is the proliferation of symbolism, and perhaps it is not worth spending time dilating on the huge woman, the many serpents, the hole into which the brahman is cast and so forth, or on their relation to the notion of the brahman as representative of social and sexual purity; and perhaps we can also leave aside the honey from this essential but somewhat reductive sexual perspective. There is also the proliferation of creatures, the complex multiplication of the animal and its body parts: elephants, snakes, rats, bees – a cast of thousands which seeps up from this world of the threshold, all the forms which can inhabit two worlds without apparently suffering the fate of their own gravity-defying contradictions, this (other) elephant, for example, with 'six faces and twelve feet'. There is, in one sense, nothing surprising in these manifestations; as it is said, one feature of the dreamworld, or of the hallucinatory sequence, which never ceases to astound our waking (or recovering, or recuperating) senses is that in that world itself the element of surprise is totally missing. The dreamworld is not a matter suitable for crime fiction. For there can be no surprise *in* a world where there are no norms and no expectations, no social rules and no conventions to be observed: surprise is reserved for the continually revealed yet also continually hidden discrepancy *between* such a world and the conscious realm, the realm of the moral law, where everything either conforms or does not conform to a set of expectations which provide the limiting horizon according to which our experience is taken to *mean*.

## The Hanged Man

The next thing we can say comes in the form of a question. What is the form, the genre, with which we are dealing here, especially given the mode of the ending of the narrative? For we are here in the presence of that 'curiosity of literature'[26], a formal structure without resolution; or rather, perhaps we should say, with a resolution which occupies a temporally *continuous* space rather than marking a point of transition. Insofar as the ending seems to demarcate a space at all, it is a space of changelessness, of stasis – and thus, we might say, a space in the world of soul, but also a space within which time is (virtually literally) suspended, the time of the addict, the time of the rapture which is nevertheless marked in its intensity by the extremity of the surrounding dangers, the ever-presence of the brink of death – over which we have already, in some sense, tumbled, but *within* which we still hover, neither dead nor alive, experiencing a last-minute fulfilment which, we know all too well, is merely inviting the precipitation of its own doom.

There are many more points we could make, but before doing so I should note the textual situation. For the next sentence in Amore and Shinn reads: 'The story of the brahman in the pit is explained by the story-teller as an allegory of life itself'.[27] In other words this 'story' is itself an element in a multiple text: it is recuperated in the *Mahabharata* itself through a critical account, here referred to by Amore and Shinn under the crucially tendentious sign 'allegory'. They then give their own version of this 're-version':

> The inaccessible forest is really the limited sphere of one's life. The woman who holds a net over the forest is likened to the aging process which takes youth and vigour from the body. The beasts of the forest are the diseases that threaten every life, and the serpent at the bottom of the well is Time, the destroyer of all living beings. The creeping vines are the desires that entangle every person. The six-faced elephant with twelve feet represents the months of the year, and the black and white rats symbolise the days and nights. The honey represents the pleasures of life . . . [28]

The 'text', quite clearly, is becoming too complicated, proliferating in every direction like the creatures themselves, searching for a 'common ground' which continually undercuts itself and threatens to deposit us as readers precisely into the space that opens up, beyond our own wits, under the threshold. I want for the moment to attempt to take only one path through this repeating forest, which itself is strewn with innumerable pitfalls, although it is a path which is itself in a sense pathless, for it is the path of representation: the Amore and Shinn account constitutes in itself a bewildering repertoire of rhetorical strategies for the recuperation of other-worldly, hallucinated experience. 'Allegory'; 'is really'; 'is likened to'; 'represents'; 'symbolise': this is a spreading compendium of textual relationships; it is such a compendium, such a hybrid, as we encounter in dream or hallucination, where every act of recuperation, every attempt to relay, decode or explain the secret signals its own insufficiency, its own partiality, its own quailing before the multifariousness of the phenomena.

Let us, though, try again. Within this world of stasis, we might say, this world which is stuck and has ceased to spin, which is now consumed by the mere buzzing, by the very static on the wires, by the sound that underpins all sound and prevents us from hearing any sound, every device must be used – so the story of the story goes – in order to try to seize back, to lay hold of, that which cannot be grasped, that which is in constant danger of being 'rapt', of being seized away from our understanding. Thus the strategies themselves re-present the ambiguity of the story's virtually unbearable final gesture – of defiance? of shame? of complicity? – 'continued to reach out for'. Does this signify the seizing, or the endlessness of non-consummation? Does the brahman hold or fail to hold, does desire, especially perhaps a desire which has moved over its own threshold into the world of addiction, reach or not reach its intended goal, its chosen but ultimately meaningless object? All, we could say, slips through our fingers: as the substance of, for example, this unimaginable elephant eludes its own allegorical force. Holding, holding to, withholding: this is perhaps a series of terms which emerges from the story, the world held by the huge woman, the brahman held by this inverted set of vines, the creatures held in place by their presumed functions, which define them yet beyond which they are in the process of continually escaping, suggesting the ghostly presence of other half-seen and half-heard forms in the forest, whose depths have, of course, not yet – never yet – been fully penetrated.

What we have here is a soft trap, a soft machine, certainly,[29] and we can trace its surface lines as ones about attachment. If the pit is a well (although oddly yet emblematically nothing we have seen, or heard, so far makes this clear), then it certainly has the dialectical quality of the well of myth: it enacts, or permits the enacting of, a poised image of falling and being prevented from falling, of the rapture and all that comes to menace rapture and to 're-mind' us of risk, but at the same time it takes us into an amoral realm where the passions are themselves re-presented in the dread form of addiction, where pointful action has been succeeded by activity in the shadow of oblivion, where the body of the brahman is reduced to the body of the dependent child, where all the complex considerations of pain, fear and hope are reduced to an inarticulate cry of 'I want', or perhaps 'I need', as a sick child may crave the food or drink which will cause it harm.

We may talk here about the passion of greed, the pain of addiction, or about the pathology of the repetition, about the attainment of rapture and the endless deferral of rapture: in the face of the imminent change, even unto death, threatened by the proliferative and the monstrous, only the repeated action driven by something which is equally beyond human control, even if it pertains to the inner world of needs and desires, can provide recourse. The brahman, we might say, is abandoned to endlessly realised longing. What, we might ask again, is the all-embracing buzzing of the bees – is it that which eludes allegorical recuperation? Interference on the line? A sign of danger? White noise which blanks out meaning and interpretation? A reminder of a fertility which moves beyond and against the human? A warning against eco-trespass? The noise of *différance* in the night which reminds us that, even when our dream actions seem comparable with our waking ones, they take place against a different, darkened background?

## On the Wire

In general, 'The Well of Life' seems to me to occupy a curious and interesting position in relation to rapture in that it calls our attention to issues of the intertwining, or cross-hatching, of the central and the marginal. The image of the well of life, and especially as recuperated in the internal critique, might seem – or be made – to stand for a fund of common experience, for the central wellspring, the heart from which emerge our feelings and passions. Yet at this core, within this threshold, we also encounter the roots of derangement. The brahman in this tale is clearly also, in an 'other' sense, at the very outer edge of experience. He is in a situation where the presences and voices of the outer are growing louder and louder all the time and he is under constant threat of disappearing from the view of common experience altogether, as his own view is drastically curtailed by the many encumbrances around him. As we cross the threshold, or as we fall down the well, something important obviously happens to our notions of margin and centre. Is the heart of the real a realm of madness, hallucination, do we approach most closely to the sense of life when we abandon all hope of understanding or recounting what is going on? Or to put it in a different rhetoric, is the only way of eluding the Thought Police to approach and inhabit a state of mindlessness where all sense of progression, relapse, trajectory are abandoned, a 'loss of thought' which is the nearest we can come to rapture? We may indeed sense (at least to begin with, and before the lineaments of a new 'habit' take over) that we are upside down; we may not be able to penetrate to the centre of the earth but perhaps in some curious way we can go *through* it and emerge on our heads, suspended in a web or net, still seeing the world, or *a* world, but through some kind of grille which prohibits the social contact which alone could confer meaning on our experiences – until we realise that the conferral of meaning is not a feature of the state in which we now find ourselves.

We can view this as an inner or deeper interpretative level of decentring; and in some way it seems, as here, to 'hollow us out' so that having passed over or through the threshold of fear we find ourselves reduced to simple mechanical gestures, dehumanised, under the control of the drug, lost in the honey-trap, 'living on' as suspended evidence that the heart of the human is the not-human, the secret of the moral law is one of dependence and addiction. This listening to the noise of the bees (and of course the 'listening to' comes only as we are absorbed over and above the simpler, less controllable act of hearing), this sense of an impending doom which nevertheless cannot be avoided and thus evokes no emotion, these things too are part of our 'central' experience; although in our normative assessments of centrality we try to eschew these pathological moments, these times when all there is is the buzzing of the bees and the endlessly unsatisfying, but endlessly engrossing to the exclusion of all else, search for honey.

And this is, at least partly, the work of the body. It is the body only which attends to the bees, for there is no sustenance there for the psyche's surfaçe; it is only the body, with its unslakeable and unintelligible desires, which reaches out for the honey and which is beyond fear or the evaluation of relative goods and dangers even though, seen from a different perspective, this is precisely the body's sphere of operation – to attain the repetition of patterns which lead us inevitably towards both the moment of rapture and the moment of death. But whether it is the body which experiences vertigo is perhaps less clear, for vertigo appears to imply a certain prognostication, of a disastrous form, of the future, a certain movement beyond the moment of being stuck, a certain embracing of a destiny, and all this might, or should, be beyond the body's remit, whether or not it is beyond the remit of the animal, however real or dreamlike that animal might be.[30] What vertigo perhaps *does* represent, however – and I am writing here symbolically rather than medically – is an extreme point of questioning about the relations between body and mind and what might be sacrificed for what, those relations which can be characterised as crucial to the structure of soul or rapture. On the more medical front, indeed, it would be relevant to add that vertigo is intimately associated with diseases of the inner ear, with conditions where the buzzing of many bees is a constant accompaniment to life, where what one hears internally may be more commanding, even if more repetitive, than anything one can hope to hear over and above the constant background, so that one may never be warned of a *specific* 'falling' if 'falling' itself has become a condition, the very ground, of the apprehension of life itself; just as the constant background hum of the drug cannot be separated out from its symbiotic relation to the addict, suspended between life and death, between the serpent and the elephant, yet constantly seduced by the pleasures of the honey.

So on the one hand one might say that in the experience of vertigo we find a collusion *between* mind and body such that the body is willing to accede to, or is overwhelmed by, the mind's preposterous fears. Why? Because, presumably, in certain circumstances the body will choose to err on the side of safety, for it is imprinted in the genes that such erring is evolutionarily productive, that it might at some point in the future save us from some more genuine danger: thus, at least, would go the normative, centralist argument. But on the other hand, we might say that vertigo represents an extreme *struggle* between mind and body, although even this struggle has complicated contours which are relevant to the problematics of addiction and the death wish. What is it that is trying to throw itself off the cliff? Is it the body, 'seized away', enrapt by the thanatic urges which lie buried at the bottom of the heaps of code, reminded by something 'outer' of the eventuality of fate and stirred to emulate or prefigure it, stirred to pre-form its own reactions, to imitate its own script; and if so what is the connection between this 'something outer' – the white cliffs, the bright blue sea below, the yawing sky overhead, the wheeling, screaming gulls – and the rapturous slide down the birth canal, even if in the context of a radically unwished birth, the separation from those comforting sounds, those buzzings which have been the substance of our being and the continuous and assumed denial of this gap between inner and outer, the separation which the body now wants violently to heal?

Or is it on the other hand psyche, up to its old tricks of domination, persuading the body of what is not the case, causing the appearance of sway – *of course* the body knows that it is vertical, and two feet from the brink, but such is the power of psyche that the gyroscope can become unfixed, the compass unhinged, the slanting and inclination can be 'induced', with a mutually cataclysmic result which is perhaps the effect only of the cynical voice of psyche saying yes, I have proved I can do without you, I can float free in an addicted space where your concerns are nothing to me, I can live without the dark encumbering other, and at least *you*, the body which 'holds me back', will not survive; *I* may, who knows, but at any rate I am on the path to perfect freedom, lost in the space below the threshold, moving on out to the white light where the sky is a perfect blank . . .

Over against the struggle, the undecidability emblematised in the rapture of vertigo stand, however, the bees and the honey; against the ambivalent world of free fall the realm of total attachment, dependence, addiction to the point of an alternative death. The well of life becomes, it is not too much to say, the web of life, free flow and clarity become the net, the liquid gives way to the sticky, we find ourselves in fact far from the open air and in a world precisely of *secretions*, a world where sight is blinded, where only the hidden has validity; as the story itself encrypts its meanings down through the levels but laughingly prohibits us from following its own narrative path down to the depths.

## Sway

We might consider in this connection some remarks by the thirteenth-century Sufi mystic Jalaluddin Rūmī. For example:

> The nature of absorption is that the one absorbed is no longer there; he can make no more effort; he ceases to act and to move; he is immersed in the water. Any action that proceeds from him is not his action, it is the action of the water. But now if he strikes out in the water with his hands and feet he is not said to be submerged; if he utters a cry, 'Ah, I am drowning', this too is not called absorption.[31]

What seems to be crucial here, as it is in 'The Well of Life', is that we come into a position where we can no longer usefully separate the actor and the acted upon: rather, what is necessary is to observe the symbiosis, what we are by now more customarily referring to as the cyborg, the further unity within which individual elements can no longer be resolved or dissolved. And what this calls into question is all syntax, all genre. As Rūmī also says, 'when a fly flies upwards it moves its wings, its head and all its parts; but when it is immersed in honey, all its parts are alike and not one makes any movement'.[32] However, I do not mean to succumb to mysticism; I am more concerned to try to elucidate the structure of rapture, if that is not too flagrant a contradiction. We can speak of it, certainly, as being lost in the object, as the *Mahabharata* and Rūmī both do from their radically different perspectives; we can therefore speak of it, as Russell Hoban does, in terms of the 'moment under the moment',[33] the point at which temporal flow ceases and the world in which that flow operates becomes seen, as through a veil or a grille, as a world of constant pointless movement which seeks only to efface the ground of its own being. 'The nature of absorption is that the one absorbed is no longer there': what would this mean when translated into a dialectic of reading? We speak, all too glibly, of 'identification' with this and that 'character'; but what is really happening in the reading act may instead be a species of dissolution – as Plato and others have long suspected, reading may always be 'dissolute', a threat to the stability of 'character' and trajectory, it may represent a different kind of time, a time which may flow but may also not be subject to the moments within which we demarcate a conventional chronology.

The addict can no longer make any effort; s/he ceases to act and to move; there is here delineated the marking of a sacred space, the space, for example, of the shaman; the cry of 'I am drowning' figures only as an interruption of the buzzing of the bees, as a momentary relapse into the world of the living, such that the possibility of imminent death can be recognised as what it is, as a breach in the all-encompassing.

We can perhaps conclude our discussion of the well of life by turning to a contemporary English poem, part of a sequence called 'You Can't Get There From Here':

> The secret, the secret is this
> we make ourselves scarce.
>
> the only thing scarce is us.
>
> & at this point breaks off
>
> slack fingers fall from the keys
>
> what does it all mean
> what indeed we cannot help
> but wander
> as the tracks break off
> no particular place to go
>
> my heart too full to speak
> & have no singing voice
>
> o hear the song
>                     of the nomads:
>             *don't settle for less*
> *than love*
> *(& love keeps moving on)*[34]

Back again on the terrain of the secret – and Derrida too remarks, if in a rather cursory fashion, that the realm of the secret is also the realm of the sacred[35] – we here come across a certain mingling of the commonplace and the enraptured: the pop quotation (and pop too is perhaps a variety of poppy) 'no particular place to go' merging with, or set off against the 'heart too full to speak'. What is certain is that the attempt to gather these forces together effects a double movement: on the one hand, there is the ever-present danger of 'breaking off', of being unable to complete the line, of not being able to 'move on', of being stuck, like the brahman, in the well of life in which all waters mingle and conjoin and yet are reduced to the buzzing of many bees; on the other there is the enduring sense that, in any case, the thought of ending (like the thought of death) is prohibited (*'& love keeps moving on'*) – on what we might ask? On, perhaps, the face of the waters, or on the ever-shifting waters of the face, the face which is the *soi-disant* mark of the human.

Yet, this poem seems to ask, what is the human? Is it human to 'make tracks', or is this the mark of the beast? Or is it instead the mark of an intermediate realm, here categorised, as it is also thus classified by Deleuze and Guattari, as the realm of the nomad,[36] of the mode of 'human being' which is not separable from its surroundings, a being which is beyond reserve, beyond reservation, and therefore needs to be consigned, condemned, to the reservation, so that an inversion, necessary to all statist thought, must be enacted, that which is 'excluded' from the reservation is regarded as free by precisely the token which 'moves' the life beyond reserve into a set of territorial confines, which would here also be an image of poetry, or at least of writing, as an act which limits in exactly the terms in which it strives to press beyond limits, to incarnate the rapture.

'[W]hat does it all mean'? A lifeless phrase in itself, and thus the question comes of how such adolescent meanderings, maunderings, can be set in motion, how would it be possible to move from a listless, addicted staring at the abyss where meaning hangs suspended? '[W]hat indeed we cannot help', a line which is also not a line, a line which is fractured, a line before which we as readers flinch as we try to impose an order on a set of words which flicker, which beckon us to break them apart, 'what indeed? We cannot help/but wander', 'wander' for 'wonder', the marvellous reduced to – or perhaps emblematised in – a pointlessness, a lack of fixed points, wandering, perhaps, lonely as a cloud or, as the group relations analysts would have it, 'as a crowd',[37] a crowd of ambiguous, perhaps animal, signs which mark our tracks, which provide the ground for the series of 'signs' for which native American 'trackers' were hired, suborned, brought over from the 'other side' in the form of, for example, Apache police forces, in which 'marks' of rank were not worn on clothing but inscribed on the body, a re-translation of badges of rank, markers of esteem, into the more primitive forms of body art.[38]

Sign language, of course: who knows how the 'marks' which survive in the forms of Palaeolithic cave art may have related, at some irrecuperable period of the past, to a now vanished mode of body art, of signs marked on the skin, because all flesh is grass and vanishes. But then, to whom may these signs, then or now, be addressed? In the Neolithic period, we know, many of the marks inscribed on graves were written, not on the outside, where they might have been decipherable by the living, but on the inside, designed, or de-signed, only to be read by the dead, a reading by ghosts – for reassurance, as a warning, as a set of injunctions as to how we are supposed to behave when we are dead?[39] With, perhaps, the utmost decorum, quiet, respectful, 'slack' as the fingers which here fall from the keys, because in this enraptured realm what we have to do, as with the brahman, is listen, to still our minds from the noises of the world, to remain even as we know we are simultaneously flowing on. Like writing, like poetry, where we are, as it were, never sure when to stop, when an ending might be appearing in sight. Like addiction, where the 'sense of an ending' is always brought too close, too close for comfort, yet provides its own source of comfort as we give up the 'many things' which might otherwise impede our vision, our hearing. Under such circumstances, how could we – why should we – 'settle for less' than rapture?

# 7

# A Body of Alabaster

A pioneering collection of Arabic Abbasid poets, translated by Abdullah al-Udhari and George Wightman, is called *Birds through a Ceiling of Alabaster* (1975), in honour of the Caliph who arranged for the topmost room of his palace to be roofed in alabaster so that he could see the birds flying from inside. The collection enables us, I think, to engage with some important issues about rapture on several fronts, partly in terms of orientalism and the exotic, partly in terms of the concept of the 'interstice', the lattice or grille through which rapture may be glimpsed, and partly in terms of a problematisation of the relations between the body and the feelings.

The first of these issues is raised by one of the most beautiful and probably the best-known poem in the collection, by Abdullah Ibn al-Mu'tazz:

> Thank God, the new moon,
> Ramadan has gone.
> Quick, lash out the wine;
> The moon's a silver dhow
> Laden with chunks with amber.[1]

It may be that there is almost nothing to say about this poem-in-itself, if there can be such a thing; I do not read Arabic, but then by definition neither do the majority of the people who are reading, have read, will have read this translation, *this* poem; Wightman goes into considerable detail about his translation principles in his introduction to the collection,[2] but the only point I need to mention here is that he says he is – and he clearly *is* – interested in using contemporary western terms ('lash out') to diminish cultural distance, even if, as we sense, such terms are themselves inevitably subject to a certain chronological distance, a certain downhill flow of meaning and intensity, a kind of wasting disease of language.

## Tainted Love

What I do want to say, *from* the poem as it were, is that it immediately confronts us with the problem of cultural difference in one of its most difficult forms, a form to which I have referred elsewhere in connection with key concepts of Søren Kierkegaard's, namely the form of fascination,[3] which is an aspect of the addictive moment and thus by definition always lost in the recounting, only sensed, we might say, from behind a veil; or through a ceiling of alabaster. 'Dhow' and 'amber' are terms which cannot be read in the west without an immediate plethora of associations; the poem almost reads like an Arab incarnation of Roland Barthes' 'second order of myths', the myth, to remember the example Barthes himself uses, of 'sininess', within which a whole spectrum of western attitudes to Chinese culture and history is summarised, embedded, cheapened and reproduced for a readerly 'mass market';[4] and this throws us into an interpretative impasse. It looks probable that this is, in some sense, a romantic lyric, and all we know about the Abbasid poets, particularly when they are working in this particular genre (if, as Derrida questions, 'genre' can *ever* be the right word[5]), would suggest that this is a correct interpretation; but what we in fact have here might better be looked at as an interlocking of several romanticisms. There is the romanticisation which may be intrinsic to the poet's approach to his subject; but it is overlaid – almost literally in the sense derived from midwifery – by the romanticism of distance with which we as Western readers might read the poem. These two specifically culturally located romanticisms which the reader might experience are, however, themselves further entangled with a third romanticism which is more hovering, perhaps less culturally bound, especially complicating in its dealings with intensity and rapture. For as in a large number of Chinese love poems and related lyrics, what is I think initially captivating (fascinating) about the poem is a certain quality of the throwaway.[6] We might even say that the 'throwaway' is its theme: there is an enormously powerful contrast between the conversational tone of the first three lines and the imagistic solidity of the last two, and it is a contrast which is susceptible to a multiplicity of readings, which may or may not be compatible. Three are obvious. First, we might say that the 'image' is carried on the same continuum as the conversation: all of this is *subjected* to a unitary apprehension by virtue precisely of its formal enclosure, its apparent submission to rules, its participation in a world within which there is at least some level on which we might sense the possibility of a shared understanding. Second, we might say that the image serves to rebuke the offhand comments, and that we as readers – and perhaps also the narrator, who can say – emerge, albeit perhaps ironically, chastened by the recognition of the beauty which subsists in the world alongside our petty diurnal emotions of relief. Third, we might say that the image is itself in some sense 'undercut' by the remaining presence, the ineradicable partial framing, of the first three lines; revealed as, although beautiful, nevertheless equally probably the outcome of a drunken distortion, or at least a distortion enforced by a prevailing mood within which, as in the terms of the rapture, *anything* might be translated into anything else. In this sense the concept of the rule-bound goes through a reversal: questions of appropriateness, of register, of the validation of symbolic equivalence, are placed in suspension or abeyance. After all, following this third line of thought, this particular set of marks on the trackless, what does this image signify visually? To what do these 'chunks', for example, correspond? If amber is the colouring and weight of the chunks, then what is the silver? And so forth, as the inner discourse continues (beyond the end of the poem, as we gaze enraptured at its aftermath, at the trail of birds only half-glimpsed through an alabaster ceiling).

The impassibility of this 'lock' (on the river perhaps, the river of night down which the dhow continues to sail) is further locked – up and away – by the translation issue and by the phenomenon we might refer to as 'cultural interstitiality': how shall we translate the intraculturally exotic across cultures in such a way as to maintain or equivalate a sense of, precisely, the exotic uncontaminated by the further layer of exoticism which attends upon all acts of translation?[7] Distances abound and multiply; at worst we might – and frequently do – end up prevented from pleasure by the introjected notion that such pleasure even when *experienced* by the reader can be invalidated by the afterwork – a procedure we keep seeing in the context of the impossibility of 'translation' of the drug experience, perhaps here merely the effects of wine on an empty stomach. As soon as we see this set of processes psychically, though, I suspect that we entertain doubts, and these doubts are always and necessarily in some sense political ones encased in the carapace of an institutionalised *différance*. I would like to try to cut through this knot in the context of considering two further poems from the collection. The first is by Abbas Ibn al-Ahnaf:

When I visit you and the moon
    Isn't around to show me the way,
Comets of longing set my heart
    So much ablaze, the earth is lit
By the holocaust under my ribs.[8]

And the second is again by al-Mu'tazz:

Let the man who brings you to me be given
    What he wants. Why are you angry?

Guards protect you from my approaches. I dream,

Perfect as a branch, and your face the sun
  That shines all day through your body.[9]

What I am principally interested in here are the two controlling images: 'lit/By the holocaust under your ribs', and 'your face the sun/That shines all day through your body'.

These are images of partial transparency. They have to do with a version of omnipotence, which psychoanalysis would refer to as infantile but which I would prefer to see as part of the psycho-dialectics of growth and health. Melanie Klein, for example, might say (were she alive, and were we to listen to her, but here we are back on the terrain of that which is inscribed on the inside of the grave-door, or on the all too solid ceiling of the crypt) that from time to time, as artists go about their work of effecting recuperative work on the body (the body politic, the body of the state as well as the physical body, and very much a spatchcock repair it often is, even if not openly or covertly treasonous) they come to a point where, even while the work is uncompleted, some emergent sense of wholeness shines out from it, a light of rapture, and illuminates other and unexpected landscapes;[10] perhaps after all this is the maximal point of vantage to which the artist, the poet might hope to come – or indeed the lover, the subject and 'operator', as we shall see Graham refer to it, of the 'lover's discourse'.[11] But after all, love poetry is primarily elegy:[12] the fruit of the poet, the after-writer, the endlessly delayed post-man, rather than of the lover, who has, we might hope, suspect or dread, quite other things to occupy her/his time, fantasies and engagement with the ever-fleeting remains of the rapture.

## Masts of Crimson

What we might suggest in the context of these poems, these images, is that the body itself 'remains' an 'outer' (only in psychosis is this disavowed) but not necessarily an opaque one. There is a sense in which to say this is simply to reword what was particularly revealing in the development of European phenomenology from Edmund Husserl to Max Scheler;[13] but in these poems I find the suggested image much more precise. For the image is perhaps partly of alabaster (referring to alabaster, made from alabaster), but alabaster is itself, of course, striated; and thus we are brought to an imagining of the body, a visualisation of the body-imago, as a kind of trellis or latticework (the Arabic cultural connections remain strong here), and through that we have an essential image of the relation of mind to body – I have referred to it elsewhere as the *nature of soul* – as having within itself the appearance of a vantage-point, a well-protected fastness which is also, as we grieve over the non-recuperability of the actual, a prison. We look out, as best we may (we may be assisted here by the body of imagery which asserts the soul as a lighthouse). Love 'shines out', we are told; it effects, alternatively, a beckoning, which may be a beckoning to the other, but may as well be a beckoning to the self; perhaps we might, even with the utmost embarrassment, remember Edward Lear's tragic image of that inhabitant of the 'great Gromboolian plain', forever searching by his own light (according to his own lights) for the vanished object of his desires; never seeing, perhaps (for he is blinded by the light) what is right in front of his nose.[14] The passions, we might say, glow and speak of their own volition, but between bars, or seen from the far side of bars, or endlessly subjected to a misinterpretation which is associated with a misprision, a mis-vision, a mishearing. There is, it would appear, no crossing this terrain (this trackless waste, where nomads roam according to their own indecipherable rules), and yet in the 'outer real' *everything* is transformed by this sense of a source of illumination, which is also fearsomely akin to the after-image, the after-effects of a possible irradiation. And perhaps that is the source of so much of the problematically positive imagery of the 'radioactive', namely that it provides an image of the means by which the soul could notionally, in a realm of phantasy, negate its own self-prisoning, throw off the 'mind-forg'd manacles';[15] provides evidence, however faulty and striated by impurities, that the light which shadows the bars can also fall across the world in such a way that it burns into it, even if the cost of this (for which the lover professes to care not a whit) is from time to time mass death and destruction.

In Western terms this is also, of course, a key image, and we might think for example of the crimson latticework of masts in Coleridge's *The Rime of the Ancient Mariner* (1797), which has to so with the same general equivalences across 'life-in-death';[16] or of Turner's ships endlessly burning in the night and throwing up (or off) images of past conflicts which are all too mistily redolent of present-day struggles against the tyranny of the state, or the tyranny of the institutions of religion and politics, as Blake put it.[17] And probably within this same body of imagery there are cultural matchings to be discerned between seafaring nations around the deathly potency of the unseaworthy boat, of the boat of Eliot's 'Marina', a boat made of spars and spaces but where 'the garboard strake leaks'.[18] But the particular connection, among so many, which I want to move on to is with a specific sequence of visual imagery. It is documented for us in Marion Milner's remarkable book *The Hands of the Living God* (1969), which recounts the therapeutic treatment of a patient, referred to as Susan, through analysis of her created images. I want to quote Milner's descriptions of two items in this image sequence. The first is a picture

> painted in brown, showing a completely self-contained and symmetrical shape that looks half like a face and half like a plate, full of holes but intensely alive. In fact it made me think of some very primitive organism, perhaps one which eats and expels through the same organ. Thus it looked to me almost like a primitive kind of independent body-image, far more primitive than anything based on possible organs of the body.[19]

Somewhat later Susan brings to the therapeutic session

> a very subtle picture. . . . It is a head in which the central form is a mixture between a brown jug with handles and a broad animal-like snout. The rest of the head is made up of holes, by multiplying the handles of the jug-face . . . What strikes me most about it is the intensity of complex feeling conveyed: part sorry, part humorous, part rueful, part resigned.[20]

In what kind of a world are we here? Perhaps in one which is precisely the reverse of the self-sufficient surfaces through which Deleuze and Guattari attempt to gesture towards the hovering possibility of rapture when they speak of the curious joys of the body-without-organs.[21] Through these latticeworks, through these bars of thick paint or bodily matter, something, it would seem – at least to Milner and also, I suggest, to the reader of these words of hers (which are never mine) or the viewer of these images – is shining through; but how to categorise the mood of this shining (which is perhaps also in another way the telepathic sense of the 'shining' to which Stephen King alludes in *The Shining* [1977] and elsewhere[22]) or what the constitution is of this imprisoned passion is difficult to ascertain – partly, perhaps, because it confronts us with an unabashed notion of the 'primitive', with the resonance and redolence of the animal, with a feeling without reservation or reserve, and for this very reason resists the attempt to separate out passions and emotions which – in the rapture, certainly, but only thus in the sense that the rapture is an ever-present transformation of the 'reality' of human emotions – demonstrate the impossibility of such separation, thus again underscoring the presence of the Mother of Separation at the heart of experience.

To start again. In a holocaust, we might say – aware all the time that here we are treading on very dangerous territory indeed, that there is a possibility that the ground might open up beneath our feet and deliver its graves as it delivers us from gravity – no single passion really predominates; there is a thanatic will towards the fiery consumption of the world, but there is also an enforced holding back: in the 'expression of an expression', to use a phrase I have coined elsewhere but which seems peculiarly apposite to the discourse composed of Susan and Milner, nothing can be fully endowed with freedom, even though a certain corrosive version of freedom can never be fully repressed.[23] What shines all day through the body may be beautiful, alluring, fascinating, but it may nonetheless also be imprisoned, impotent, severed from action; or, indeed, it may not be willing to engage with the problems or potentialities of escape; or it may be kept inside precisely by the person, by the artist, by the poet, by the child who fears the catastrophe which would or could ensue if the essential ambivalence of soul is let loose on the world in a whirlwind of passion, or if rapture were ever to find and become capable of using its true symbols; or if the world were to be allowed into its sanctum to perform a ritual passion of suffering on its soft matter, on that soft machine, the 'wetware' which is also the ground of all addiction.[24]

## Delicacy/Deliquescence

The relationship, then, within the components of soul which respect the soft matter within and the latticework which serves as defence and as imprisoning grille seems to be imagistically crucial across a range of contexts; but I will move on to my final example from this collection of poems, which is by Abu al-Ala al-Ma'arri:

> Some people are like an open grave:
> You give it the thing you love most
> And then get nothing in return.
>
> A man hard done by, yet generous,
> Is rock on which light rain falls;
> Tufts of moss grow, but flowers won't bloom.
>
> Tear down every dwelling on earth.
> Each houses creatures who'll destroy
> The untamed soul of a good man.
>
> Hold tight to what is most yourself,
> Don't squander it, don't let your life

Be governed by what disturbs you.
You're given the fruit of one palm tree;
Bear it in a basin of clear water.
Don't trouble with the plight of other palms.[25]

Here we come at the heart of the matter, the matter of the heart, the clear limpid centre; yet what surely is extraordinary is that this is in the context of that astonishing first line, 'Some people are like an open grave'. It is almost as if, as we open the poem, we are already, like the brahman, falling, in a state of suspension, where all anchorage has been removed, where the abhuman has become terrifyingly 'open' for inspection, where the ground has shifted beneath our feet – always already shifted – so that the space between us and the rapture is already impossible to cross; we are in a world of traps and reverses, a world where only the utmost effort, the most extreme of exercises of the will, can effect a traverse across the danger. Or: we might say that in the context of the three previous poems which I have mentioned (and this of course is not the only context within which this poem might be read, has been read) it would appear that we are enjoined to deal with an exact dialectic of openness and closure. The openness is horrifying, because it is equated with the all-consuming, with the irrecoverable ceaseless consumption of soul-stuff; yet perhaps, we might further think, this is itself a displacement, and what is truly horrifying about this openness, about the groove down which all things may inevitably travel, about the cleft in the earth which might lead us to the 'heart's deep core',[26] about the open symbol which is also the open wound of faciality, is that it exposes one beyond the grille; and so we might read the first stanza as in itself a monodrama, if we are again to succumb to the lure of the generic, and one which approaches the same material as, for example, Oscar Wilde's 'Ballad of Reading Gaol' (1898) (which would also, of course, according to one much-traversed critical path, be the gaol – whether or not that also be the 'goal' – of 'reading', whether that be the reading of a book, or of a poem, or of a face – a title which obviously invites endless deconstruction, but from as it were the opposite end).[27]

The second stanza takes up the hardness, the jaggedness, the unyielding quality of the encased soul in its separation from the possibility of rapture. Here we have what we might equate with the Blakean notion of the selfhood, reminiscent also of his dialogue between the pebble and the clod of clay, yet inflected in such a way as to show how the 'hardening of the soul' should not be considered as an emanation of the pure inner.[28] There is nothing inside (nobody here at home, we might say) which will automatically, as in, for example, a process of the extrusion of plastic, harden and roughen the carapace, prevent the vision, seal the gaps through which the safe creature may peer; instead this process, summarised in the dialectic of 'hard done by,/Yet generous', is seen as essentially bound to the confrontation of inner *and* outer, experience and the recounting (and in this case we might indeed be in the position of demanding a recount), the bars of the grille welded together by some force of fusion in which the prison (Jean Genet's prison, as we shall later suggest) and the pressure-of-imprisoning become as one.

In the third stanza the dialectic is, however, further twisted, in the sense that we become even less sure of what is inhabiting what, or where the soul's home might be. These dwellings, it would appear, house 'creatures', but these are not the soft creatures which we devote ourselves to protecting, not only because they are in need of our devotion but also, and perhaps principally, because they represent our own exposure to forces which we fear we shall not be able to withstand; they are also the destroyers precisely *of* soul, eaters of the heart, drinkers of blood, vampires. To continue to keep the image of Milner's Susan in mind confronts us with horrifying possibilities, and indeed they are also precisely the possibilities from which so many horror stories are made: namely that the very thing we think we have devoted ourselves to protecting, the spark of life, the residue of innocence, the principle of deep continuity, this very 'precious' inside its golden cage, may come to be seen, when we finally turn our attention away from the dangers of the outer and inspect it more closely, as already infected, as already glaring at us malevolently from between bars which we now no longer *dare* to contemplate breaking. For we now know that we harbour the great destroyer tigerishly deep within ourselves and that it may always be too late for the soul's work of reconstruction to begin; and we also abject that realisation, we locate it deep within the extruded figure of the addict, the subject for whom it is always already too late, who has embarked on a course of danger from which there must be no salvation: because were the addict to be saved, then our own sacrifices would have been worthless, our compromises with a rapture-less world would have brought no boon, no benefit, and we would find ourselves inhabiting a land as bare and deserted as the come-down from which, we assume, the addict constantly suffers on our behalf.

## Of Wreckage and Cotton Reels

The fourth stanza continues from this motif in the dialectic between 'yourself' and 'what most disturbs you'; for here is the source of disturbance installed at the very heart, inescapable, and competing for control with some lingering sense of whatever preceding self we may be able to salvage from the wreckage (which is also the exposure of the secret, the defamation of the sacred). When we look closely at this phrase, 'don't let your life/Be governed by what disturbs you', a whole gallery opens up before us. At one level we could be talking here directly about Alfred Adler's notion of myelodisplasia, organ inferiority[29] (and not, therefore, about fantasies of the body without organs) – the way in which our personalities form by a process of coagulation around the wound, around the knot of weakness in the biological makeup (deafness or vertigo, for example), and this process itself is obviously dual: on the one hand we are talking about engaging the forces of soul to protect the weakest point, safely placing our inferiority inside our strongest hold, down in the deepest well, as Susan places hers – but shiningly – within the human and non-human complexities of the jug (which is also the container, but one which is full of holes, 'holy' in both senses of the word); on the other we are hugging our weakness like a viper to the bosom, placing the 'source of disturbance' unwittingly (or witlessly) in the very place where it can infect everything around it, contaminate the swathes of the unconscious even while we believe ourselves to be at our most safe.

But that 'point of inferiority' can also be referred to in other terms: as, for example, one's besetting vice (or addiction); as one's cardinal sin; as the taint of character (the 'bad seed') which motivates through and through. Insofar as it is this, then the distinction al-Ma'ari is making might remind us of one of the crucial ambiguities at the heart of the rapture; or, to put it another way, might remind us of the terrain on which the passions are always in the process of engagement, of merging or disentangling, according to an *other* law, the law of obsession or addiction.

The final stanza is centred around the image of the 'basin of clear water' and the fusion of activities in this highly particular act of 'bearing'; what we have here, it would appear, is a process which *unites* the physical, the material, the nurturing of the body of, for example, the palm tree, which is also our own body, and the spiritual, the passional, the rapturous, the activity of 'bearing' as a votive offering, an offering in which what is presented is the only homage there truly is, the absolutely clear and pure reflection, beyond image, which one offers as the highest gift to the object of one's love, the offering which removes all *need* for imagery-in-itself – as we see, for example, in other, Islamic contexts – and in which the very act of self-love is in a situation of continual transformation into something quite 'different from itself', sacralised, consecrated and turned into the thoroughgoing humanisation which is centred on the hallucinatory recognition of the divine spark flickering at the heart's core.

We are dealing here, in all these forms, with the 'one light', the light of rapture, and its material framing: with the complications and twists in our attempts to deal with what lies 'within' and how, or whether, it can or should be exposed – beyond the grille, in some form of recounting which will be forever inadequate, insufficient – with the lamp behind our eyes, as the myths have it, which illuminates that on which we gaze, and yet is in some other sense not of 'our' own making, which is always, in a different location, shining from behind our shoulder; and thus indeed with the very metaphors and tropes of the 'within' itself. And we are finding images here for a kind of 'therapy of soul', as a long tradition refers to it,[30] and indeed as Milner's Susan, through pain and tears and who knows with what eventual outcome, found for herself.

But then pain, of course, is part of the point, part of the addictive dialectic, and here we may recall that when Derrida named one of his major essays 'To Speculate – on "Freud"' (1987), he did so in order to involve, as Maud Ellmann puts it, 'not only the primary meaning of speculation [as] hypothesis, but secondary innuendoes of betting, risking, gambling, as well as those of watching or spectatorship'.[31] Speculation always involves risk, whether it be speculation on the stock market or what we refer to as philosophical speculation. In this latter sense, it involves a transition from one state of being to another; it involves the formulation of hypotheses which, at least in the first instance, may or not be true, or demonstrable, or whatever term is used to signify the 'end-point of speculation'. But, of course the 'point' is that there is no end-point to speculation. Speculation is a habit. In the case of Freud, as Derrida also recounts, the nature of speculation is summarised in the *fort/da* game, the throwing away and recovery of a cotton reel by a small child; what Freud notices – and here again I am following Ellmann's wording – is, however, that the apparently act of 'throwing away' is repeated more often than the act of recall; and this might lead us into some further speculation on the nature of addiction – indeed, Ellmann's phrasing of Freud's insight is that it refers to an 'addictive gambling with loss'.[32]

It is not therefore the case that damage, whether financial, physical or mental, is a kind of by-product of the addictive process; it is not that, as the conventional accounts of, to take the present example, addiction to gambling would have it, the gambler cheers him- or herself up under the guise of believing that they are on the eve of the next big win. What Freud would have us believe is that this kind, at least, of addiction has a double goal: the wish to win is there, but it serves as a cover story – behind it there lies another, entirely different, even opposite wish, which has to do with the death drive, with urges '"inherent in organic life to restore an earlier state of things", the earliest of which is non-existence'.[33] The narrative within the narrative, then, would be to do with a wish for close encounters with death, with risk taken to the utmost, with, certainly, a pleasure in the mere act of survival after continual abuse, of the body or of the wallet, but also with the sheer thrill of risk – as we see also, for example, in the case of extreme sports or even of fairground rides.

It is interesting to note the different valorisations at stake here: they are already evident in Ellmann's use of the term 'innuendoes'. Mountaineering, for example, involves the possibility of oxygen starvation; proximity to certain death by fall and avalanche; and the final achievement (which is only final in the perverse sense that it leads on to further, and escalating, repetition) of a place, or state, of rapture which can never – so the mountaineers tell us – be fully recounted to the 'spectating' public.[34] Drug addiction, including alcoholism, on the other hand involves the possibility of poisoning the bloodstream; proximity to certain death by infection or overdose; and the final achievement (only, again, in the same perverse sense linked to the repetition) of a state of rapture which (again – of course, for we are here in the presence of the repetition) cannot be recounted to any kind of 'audience'. As an aside, we might say that if this is indeed the 'narrative of narrative', then it is so only in the sense that it ceases to be narrative at all: there is, after all, little more boring, little less engaging, than being told a story which keeps saying (as, indeed, Conrad among other does) that it cannot, actually, be told. Perhaps *Heart of Darkness* (1902) continues to be a text of apparently endless cultural fascination precisely for that reason: because the tale itself, Marlow assures us, cannot be told[35] – just as to revert to the example of cave art, the fascination there lies in the way in which it can figure as an endless topic of speculation because the evidence, whatever that might be, is ultimately irrecuperable.

However, to return to the question of valorisation: mountaineering is regarded as a splendid example of man pitting his wits against external forces; drug addiction as a terrible instance of man succumbing to base instincts. There is, as always, an economic question here: drug addiction, we are told, costs the state huge sums of money in crime, health care, lost days of work, and so forth. Mountaineering, on the other hand, costs the state large (although admittedly smaller) sums of money in mountain rescue and, again, health care: but here the money is considered well spent because the wish to 'conquer' the world's highest places (or indeed its deepest ones if we turn to speleology) is regarded as a worthy, indeed admirable goal.

And not, of course, only for the individual (who also has to raise large sums of money, although in this case from willing private donors), for in the case of mountaineering the narrative appears to run that what the individual (or rather the team) is doing is being done 'on behalf of' others: that we are supposed to applaud, even to share a little in the compulsive excitement of the climb, the reaching out and up, the grandeur of risk. Yet one might argue that the issue of who is doing what 'on behalf of' whom is also relevant to addiction: here again we see a proximity to death, an engagement with extreme states (of consciousness – but then, the records of mountaineers, as of polar explorers, also demonstrate that the achievement of extreme states of consciousness is part of the story); yet the addict is the subject of an apparently limitless excoriation. The scenario is one of strength and weakness: the mountaineer achieves, the addict succumbs. Yet the drive to encounter death – perhaps in a prophylactic, or virtually homeopathic, way – is present in both formations, just as both depend, in the end, on surplus wealth, on the ability to spend money on that which goes beyond the necessities of life. One could as easily see mountaineering as a product of capitalism as addiction: certainly it holds little interest for those who in any case spend their lives on mountains and have to endure, year in and year out, the hostility which such conditions can convey.

## Sugar Cube

To return, however, to Freud, one might wish to challenge one particular aspect of what he says: he says that the urges he describes are 'inherent in organic life'. It would seem to me that a better way to put this would be in terms of what the limits of 'organic life' actually are. In its approach to death, in its ever-hovering proximity to an ending, what the addict explores – whether knowingly or not – is the point at which 'organic life' is on the verge of returning to the inorganic, the point at which the narrative of the human runs out. Drugs are, I suppose, 'organic' in themselves; but they are also a 'foreign body', perhaps the definitive foreign body, the 'embodiment' of Derrida's re-vision of Plato's *pharmakon* as both poison and cure;[36] they do not participate in the developmental, evolutionary process which we take to be typical of organic life, rather they serve as inhibitors, as reflectors of the repetition, as signifiers of all that holds us back from the illusory goal which we characterise as the 'fulfilment of our potential'.

And it is here that we may return to the notion of abjection, of the ways in which these ingrained 'habits' of repetition must be continually 'thrown off', 'thrown down', in order precisely to free the body politic from the taint of those drives which are better not acknowledged. The narrative of a narrative: what is a narrative, what is a permissible critical narrative? A narrative, it is often said, which eschews the self, which entails a ceaseless probity in the area of objectivity. We have only to read a few pages of Luce Irigaray or Hélène Cixous to gather enough courage to admit that this is untrue.[37]

And so I shall dare to venture to recount (but briefly, because otherwise you, the ghostly audience, might become bored) the story, the narrative of my Aunt Joyce. During the Second World War, she was a nurse; she saw and endured (I am told, because she died before I was born) many horrific things – physical injuries, mental torment. As a result of this (or not, who knows) she availed herself of the available *pharmakon* (as have many nurses and doctors before and since) and died; addicted. But the story itself is nothing, it is commonplace, it is the fate, we might say, of the English patient, at the mercy of a foreign body. The question is of valorisation. Was she a saint or a demon? Did she demonstrate inordinate strength or fatal weakness? Both of the above, of course; but not, as it were, in sequence, but as the essential elements in a single story, a single life (because of the war, she was also single – the story is hardly a new one).

Can addicts have, or write, autobiographies? In one sense, of course they can: Crowley, Malcolm Lowry, Burroughs (again), a succession of rock'n'roll stars.[38] But in another sense not: the story can only be told in an interstitial way, as an account full of blanks, 'holed' by memory loss – or, we might say, freed from the bizarre hypotheses of coherence which afflict and indeed structure most autobiographies. What the autobiography of an addict does is to tell a tale of which the kernel is finally held in secret; as with the mystic, there can be a set of signs, there can be a 'beckoning' towards a higher, a secret, even a sacred truth, but that truth cannot itself be recounted, it is held suspended in a different realm (like the brahman), threatening to overwhelm with the magnitude of its distress yet, like Susan, offering only holey symbols of the pain – or of the rapture.

A remarkable short story by Michael Gardiner is called 'Jidohanbaiki'. It comes from a set of stories based in Japan, and it is unusual because it is the only story I know which is narrated by a drinks vending machine. This being Japan, the machine sells not only soft drinks but also beer and *sake*. The machine (and here, although I am talking of this specific machine, we may want to broaden the scenario into a set of thoughts on machines in general) has only limited senses: 'when you're lacking sight, hearing, smell, and taste, and only have touch left, this single sense develops to a degree beyond the imagination of others',[39] and through this sense the machine identifies a particular customer and notes the escalating (the collection of stories is called *Escalator* [2006]) amount of drink the customer is buying. Things get bad in December but, as the machine observes, 'it's a good season for pharmacies'.[40]

The next paragraph is probably as good an account of addiction as it is possible to find, when you consider that it is told in the only way (probably) that it can; namely, by a machine imagining what it might be like to be an addicted human (which may also be the only condition in which a human is recognisable to a machine):

> And the next day is that bit more filled with the anxiety you thought you'd lost, and you feel that bit more relieved to take the edge off in the evening, and the first can's opened a minute earlier and downed a minute quicker, and then the same the next night, until you've reached that citadel of soggy cardboard and tired regrets called Drinking. Each day you set forth from a point more sunken, and each day you have less chance of getting back to where you started, for whether or not there ever was a problem in the first place, well there's a problem now. You're in a spiral of debt, like credit cards, or loan sharks, except it comes packaged in time and mood instead of money. And the loan shark: that's me. But I don't have to come and find you and beat the debt from your carcass: you'll come and find me. And I, God help me, I will give you more debt. They say we all have to make a living somehow, by putting someone else in debt: fucking capitalism.[41]

The machine senses (with its machine senses) that the client's drinking is getting more and more problematic, until one day after an event in which he appears to fall against the machine he never returns. About this the vending machine is in some sense philosophical (after all, all it has been doing is speculating):

> It's not that I wanted to stop selling: this is my only reason to be amongst people instead of melted down. All I wanted to do was explain that drinking's a great relief at first but if you keep going, bitterness and loneliness come in disguise, while you tell yourself you're coping better. Your only way of coping is drinking more. And then you've really got problems.
>
> But I was the last one on earth to explain that.[42]

A recuperative ending, then, in a way: the voice of the machine stands aside from the processes of addiction, speaks as a kind of machinic health warning; but this it to underestimate the machine's own bitterness. Earlier it has compared itself to a drug dealer ('which I am').

And so the story – the never-ending story, we might say – gets told; but not through the addict, instead by a blind, deaf and dumb teller, a cyborg endowed with human thought (but not speech, only, it would appear, writing – who or what is writing this story, and to what purpose?)

who/which (there is as yet no proper pronominal form for the cyborg) 'senses' the cycle, and yet is also imbued with a strange nostalgia. It is only this, it says, which keeps me amongst the human, only this machinic 'dealing' in matters of risk, matters of life and death, which prevented me from meltdown. Can a machine feel guilt? Can an addict feel guilt? There is here a weird kind of parallelism: the machine feels (or constructs) the human's pain but is powerless to do anything about it; it is built into the system, hard-wired to the extraction of surplus profit, a passive speculator on a process of speculation which can only end in death (or meltdown). 'Death of a salariman', we might call it; but of course there will be other buyers, other vendors, other escalations and escalators, other ways of building up the odds in the knowledge that they will always stack against you; but then, as J. G. Ballard (repetitively) points out, one might handle the trauma well but still die in a car crash.[43]

## High

To return, however, to the question which we may put as the question of the mountaineer and the addict – or the climber and the faller, that which achieves and that which succumbs, bound as both are to the repetition, which is also the dream of escape, of being bound to Ixion's wheel and freed from the wheel, of redefining the contours of the human. It would be fair to say that here we might come upon a secret definition of the 'literary', and here again we find that Derrida has been here before us, discussing, as he does in 'The Rhetoric of Drugs' (1995) that singular condition, that condition of apparent singularity, which has attached to a certain version of the nature of the writer, or artist:

> In certain always singular circumstances, the recourse to dangerous experimentation with what we call drugs may be guided by the desire to think the alleged boundary from both sides at once. . . . This experience (one to which artists and thinkers occasionally devote themselves, but which is by no means the unique privilege of those who claim or to whom we grant such status), this experience may be sought with or without 'drugs', at least without any 'narcotic', 'classified' as such by the Law. We will always have unclassified or unclassifiable supplements of drugs or narcotics.[44]

'To think the alleged boundary from both sides at once': it does not matter what particular (singular) alleged boundary, 'real' or fictive, Derrida is addressing here, the question is one of 'boundary' or limit itself; it is of an ingress, however temporary or fraught, across a boundary or threshold, and as such it signifies a relaxation of the edges of the human, a putting of one's self on the brink, above the precipice (or indeed, considered from a public viewpoint, above the parapet). The context within which Derrida is making these remarks, however, is one which is all too familiar to students of literature, whether it is explicit or not: it is the idea of 'experimentation', it is the question of the doors of perception, and here again, at these very doors or gates (of heaven and hell), we might consider that we emblematically find the figures of mountaineer and the addict – we can perhaps even give them (proper) names, even if these names are merely suggestive of wider fields: on the side of the angels, taking drugs for purposes presumed to be for the good of mankind, experimentally expanding the definitions of consciousness, Aldous Huxley, scientist, moralist, a figure for bringing that which is out of control within control; of the devil's party, whether or not 'knowing' it, selfishly indulging his self, running pointless risks which end, inevitably, in his downfall and exile, Timothy Leary, exemplar of the 'fake' scientist, the bad doctor, misuser of the *pharmakon*, forerunner of the more violent deaths of, say, Hunter S. Thompson, whose suicide uncannily mirrors Burroughs's own 'mirrored' shooting of his wife, under, of course, the influence.[45]

Yet Derrida knows, and we know, that this is a simplification, a necessary and homeopathic reduction of a complex field into a black-and-white struggle; because only by effecting such a struggle can we rid the scenario of the uncanny doubling, the troubling of the boundaries of vision, the sense that, in either or any event, on whatever horizon, things might have 'turned out' differently, the attribution of the heroic and the satanic could have been reversed; experimentation and indulgence, as we also know from the 'legendary' body of Frankenstein, are bound together, the need to 'speculate' in the philosophical sense and the need to 'speculate' in terms of investing the body in risky endeavours. The 'speculations' of Leary and Thompson, we might say, caused or enacted a crash; they are the ones, it would appear, who 'crashed out', who did not live to tell the tale – except of course that, under the sign of the repetition, of the accumulation of fear and loathing, they did in fact tell the tale; or rather, perhaps, the tale was told through them, it unwound itself as the tapeworm winds itself through the body of the corrupt, addicted policeman, embodiment of the carnality of the law, in Irvine Welsh's *Filth* (1998), a tapeworm which is also a tape-recorder, unwinding from spool to spool, the semi-organic creature which inhabits the bowels of the organic, the voice which is the opposite of the voice of conscience, which has a kind of intimate knowledge, a knowledge of intimacy, which is denied to the machinic organs of Gardiner's drug-dealing vending machine.[46]

Or we might see it in terms of the logic of the virus. David Boothroyd, speaking of this passage from Derrida, has also in mind the textual body of Henri Michaux, for whom, says Boothroyd, 'the drug is a technology for switching *off* the machinery which keeps "normality" and normal thinking going'.[47] The virus, in other words, is already there: the poison is not introduced by the drug, rather the drug, the choice from the available *pharmakon*, comes to provide a moment of relief from control. And so Derrida is right to raise the question of 'classification', which he does, we may presume, in a sense which conjoins and confronts the relation between what we might term the Linnaean notion of 'classification', the presence and construction of a taxonomy, and the legal apparatus of 'classification', the series of faulty attempts to classify danger, as though each drug-in-itself can be 'marked', inspected and have a kind of essence discerned aside from the symbiosis of user and used which alone comprises the terrain on which we may truly speculate on the drug experience.

> The human body is not a thing or substance, given, but a continuous creation . . . . The human body is an energy system . . . which is never a complete structure, never static; it is in perpetual inner self-construction and self-destruction; we destroy in order to make new . . . [48]

Possibly (for we have heard this, or almost all of this, before): but to say that it *is* such a system remains inaccurate and inadequate. The question, rather (as in the cases of the mountaineer and the addict, of the twinned routes to rapture) is of the systems *within which* the body participates, the cyborgic assemblages which at every moment threaten to undermine our attempts to assert the singularity of the human. It is this which renders classification in the end impossible, as a refraction of the rage for order, of the need to find some way, however violent, of obstructing the ceaseless flow, the leakage of humanity, which is symbolised equally in the death drive and in the irresoluble plight of the brahman. If only, as the philosopher might equally bemoan, everything were soluble: if only what dissolves into the bloodstream could also be 'resolved' out of it, but this of course is not the nature of the dialectic, either of philosophy or of drugs: everything, instead, is what Hegel referred to as *Aufhebung*, and the result, the resolution, the re-solution, is always different from what we might wish to 'classify' as the sum of its parts. We are moved, whether we wish to be or not, on to a new synthesis, even as we learn (whether we wish to or not) to synthesise new things.

Or: the difficulty is the difficulty of purity, of how to find, and to continue to find, a pure substance. And this brings us back to the question of rapture. Would we be talking here about the achievement of a state of purity, of the possibility of a purgation which would take us beyond the realm of the human, or of a synthesis, a higher state which yet continues to betray, in both senses of that vexed verb, the traces of its own past, much as the dream is inescapably linked back to the day's residues? Who can say? On what flawed accounts can we possibly rely?

# 8

# Death, Story and the Preservation of the Soul

> Demons possess souls during the vulnerable period immediately after a death, but stories keep them out. Like Chinese boxes or English hedges, the stories contain tales within tales, so that as you enter one you run into another, passing from plot to plot every time you turn a corner, until at last you reach the core of the narrative space, which corresponds to the place occupied by the corpse within the inner courtyard of the household. Demons cannot penetrate this space because they cannot turn corners. They beat there heads helplessly against the narrative maze that the readers have built, and so reading provides a kind of defence fortification . . . It creates a wall of words, which operates like the jamming of radio broadcasts. It does not amuse, instruct, improve or help to while away the time: by the imbrication of narrative and the cacophony of sound, it protects souls.

This passage first occurred, for me, in a curious set of contexts. It is drawn from an essay called 'Readers respond to Rousseau', in a book called *The Great Cat Massacre* (1985) by Robert Darnton; it refers to Balinese customs to do with death, reading and the soul; but I first read it quoted by the late Angela Carter in an article in *The Independent* in 1992, which was itself a reproduction of the introduction to a volume of her criticism which was just being published – posthumously, for Carter had died the previous month.[1] Even in its original setting, Darnton's commentary on a specific purpose of reading is necessarily a kind of translation, as all anthropology must be, a translation from one set of practices into a foreign discourse; and translation itself, as we might already have sensed, is akin to the process of psychological transference as we seek to relocate our subject position amid a maze of different parents, different cultures, different versions of the dismembered self. Here, all is secrecy: we may find, or seek to construct, a version of Balinese belief, but, as is so evident here, we can only do so by trying to *align* it alongside assumed points of reference – which, of course, also have their own secrets, perhaps especially, as we have hinted before, around scenarios of death.

I want to read the text in detail; I want to 'attend' to it, but in the process of doing so I am bound to fall into the trap of interpretation.[2] It is not possible, it can never be possible, to attend to a text in all its singularity; one is inevitably, as a reader, on a line of flight, moving away from the object as one seeks to be moving closer to it, finding deafening cacophonies interrupting the slow, patient work of the inner ear.[3] As I read, I inevitably sever most of the connecting filaments which hold the text together; for what no commentary, no ritual, can do is resurrect the dead. Carter's death, for example, curiously reinscribed (for me) on this text: it remains an event, as it were, inscribed in the Real, which is also to say that it is inscribed in the margins of *this* text – whichever text, by now, *this* text might be, Darnton's, Carter's, my own, that of the Balinese – as an ever-prevailing mark that even the work of art in the age of mechanical reproduction is not reduced to a simulacrum but inevitably incarnates, makes manifest, something larger than itself.[4]

## Of Singularity, Protection and the Machine

That specific 'something larger' here could be related to Jungian notions of coincidence; we have the undecidability of what we are to do with a posthumous quotation which speaks of the force of words themselves in protecting the souls of, not only the dead, but those who have died recently, those who are in the most vulnerable stage of their evolution; as, by implication, Carter was, within the inner courtyard of this complicated house of language. A house of language also, of course, constantly changing in shape and even in building materials, such that even as I write 'mechanical reproduction' I am aware that all has changed since Benjamin's day, that the very notion of the 'mechanical' is now arranged against quite different terms – 'machinic', 'electronic' and so forth – which turn the 'mechanical' on its head, from its associations with the futuristic fantasies of the Italians and Russians between the wars to a relegation to an old-fashioned regime of heavy engineering, repetitive manual work, all the features of social and economic life which are now seen as opposed to (inferior to, abjected by) 'liquid modernity'.[5]

Language plays its part too, obviously, in any discourse which dares to use the term 'soul': and what I have meant by it over the years when I have been writing about it, trying to save it for critical purposes, trying to breathe into it a new lease of life and let the old ghost live, has also changed: beyond, one might say, all recognition. It now seems to take its place alongside discourses of 'singularity' and 'natality'[6]: to reference a point at which categories, histories and interpretations run out, a point at which we can no longer speak of the 'mechanical reproduction' of the generations without being aware of the aggressivity, the instrumental inflections, which attend on any discourse which does not attempt to recognise the singular irreducible. I shall (usually) continue to refer to this singular irreducible (which we have come across before) as soul.

But we need a space in which more can be said about soul. Historically it has often been spoken of as that which has to do with the union, actual or virtual, even-handed or under the sign of domination, of mind and body; but clearly this is hardly appropriate in the context of, reading alongside, the secrets of this passage, because it brings us into the presence of that which survives mortality. Yet perhaps this is only an added perspective on the same thing: perhaps what we are looking at here is the *principle* of union – and thus implicitly disunion – between psychic and material, between the imagination and the body. The *severance* of that central intimacy (Mother of Separation), the image of all other intimacies real and desired, would be no less decisive an event for soul, and for the making of soulstuff, than events which occur within the realm of union. The vulnerability of soul would then derive from a mistiness around this very boundary; are there secrets here, hidden in the fog, or is there really no more to it than imbrication and cacophony, arrangement and noise?

On the Bardo plane of Tibetan mythology, souls cannot be seized by demons but they can make the wrong decision about rebirth.[7] Yet, we might ask, what is the difference? In the story of the downfall of King Nala from the *Mahabharata* the king makes numerous mistakes, from gambling (yes, another addiction) with the evil king Pushkara to abandoning his wife Damayanti in the forest of terrors, yet his plea to the queen at the end of the tale is no less reverberant:

> Oh frail one, neither the loss of my kingdom nor my abandonment of you were my acts. Both were due to Kali. I was possessed by that evil one and forced by him to do all those evil acts which led to your discomfort. That evil one has now left me, and I am here to reclaim your hand.[8]

I was not here; somebody was here in my place; there was a mistake about who was inhabiting whose body; but now I am back, I have returned. A discourse of possession (addiction), familiar from many stories and myths of demons, within which authority passes from the self and there is a suspension of the moral law. What has occurred has occurred on the wrong scenario, according to the wrong script; now there is a chance to put things right, to assert that the fractured subject has been reunited and is once more responsible for its own actions.

In these terms, vulnerability to demons and the making of wrong decisions may be seen as analogous figures: a further related figure would be the taking of a wrong turning, yet here we sense a peculiarity in the text, or, for all we know, in the practice it does or does not recount, for in it the 'wrong turning', the perennial threat of being lost in the maze, 'turns' miraculously and ceaselessly into the 'right' turning; for it is the demons themselves who seem surprisingly incapable of the deviousness required if we are to thread the passageways which open before us immediately after our death; as of course they also do every night in dream, when we penetrate in a different way this 'wall of words' and peer into the crypt with a mixture of pleasure and unease which is in no way clarified as we hear voices calling what *might* be, if only we could remember clearly enough, our proper name.

## Demon in the Box

By what secret power do words deflect these seeking demons? We might surmise from the first sentence of the text that it is through a power which has something to do with non-possession. If demons stand for possession, for taking over the soul and removing it from its usual state of spin, dragging it down to fixity, negating and destroying singularity, then there is something in words which prevents this from occurring, some power of movement, some lightness of being. We are not speaking here in terms of the moral law, as later parts of the passage make very clear: if these demons are tricky and delusive (although, it would appear, not tricky or delusive *enough*) then we must fight them with weapons which are equally tricky and delusive. Deceit, indeed, is one of the kingly qualities advocated in the story of the Wise Old Crow in the *Panchatantra*, which concludes with Longlived the Crow reminding the reader that

> Prowess alone will not bring the supreme desire [defeat of one's enemies] to fruition. Foes that are killed with weapons are not killed, but those that are killed by wit are really killed and never appear again. A weapon only kills a man's body, while wit destroys his tribe, his power, and his renown.[9]

Death by ridicule; death by the exercise of superior intelligence; death by the erasure of the proper name – all these and more could be conveyed by the term translated as 'wit'; furthermore there can be no general rule as to how this killing is to be accomplished, each singular circumstance, with its attendant secrets, will call forth its singular response. The revelation of secrets alone may be sufficient to achieve the 'supreme desire'.

Here as in our 'Balinese text' (if that is what it is) there is a murder which lies behind the murder: as the demons threaten us with a capture and a disintegration which goes beyond physical death, so we must use in return – to return, as it were, this very impulse to its source – the only weapons we have which transcend the merely material, the weapons which are capable of effecting destruction over space and time, the long-distance weapons, if you like, which are at stake in the armoury of telepathy, telephony, all that might fall under the heading of what we could call a 'telepathology',[10] for in order to rebut the demons we have to threaten like with like, to enter into a knot of contamination, to counter secrets with other secrets (or at least with the simulacra of secrets, for who can tell 'what will out'?); and they are vulnerable, as are our wrong decisions (made, it would seem, before we were born, before the origins of subjectivity), to words.

Chinese boxes are multiple containers, one within another; English hedges are not usually arranged thus, unless the motif of the maze has already invaded the text, has become the generator of the text's images, whirring away in the darkness beneath the text, or in the text's inner courtyard. Let us accept that, in fact, it has; in which case we sense once again a curious reversal. Would it not be safer to defeat the demons by inviting them *into* the maze? For there two things might happen to them. They might become lost (lost secrets), never to re-emerge, and have to endure, presumably, a permanent subjection to words, to voices intoning – perhaps meaninglessly – on the other side of the high hedges; or they might reach the centre (if they can do something about the handicap of corners) and meet the Minotaur. What would occur then? What happens when demon meets monster? A kind of cancelling out, perhaps: a moment of recognition, and then a bright flash, the controlling delusions of the outer meeting direct with the source of error, the blindness at and of the heart; a meeting which should not, cannot be allowed to occur, the tabooed encounter in which all sense of purchase on the world – which derives from an ability to make at least *some* judgement of scale between inner and outer error – would dissolve in a second of rapture followed by an unimaginable future, a bleak landscape devoid of demons and monsters alike, devoid of any forms by which to measure, a universe of cold turkey. The maze itself, it is true, would still remain, but it would now have a different kind of secret to protect and incarnate, the endlessly reverberating secret of its own emptiness, the ultimate secret of lack of meaning – the dark encroaching horror so ably and obsessively, addictively described by H. P. Lovecraft, the passion of absence.[11]

So perhaps it is wise after all to 'keep these demons out' (or, as W. B. Yeats would have it, to 'keep those children out', at any rate to resist the principle of interference[12]); and yet the imagery of our text, the imagery which is filling the empty space where the text might be (because it has not yet been constructed, because it has always already gone away, vacated the maze, bellowing to us in the pain of the centre, chanting to us from the agony of the margin) keeps shifting before our eyes, menacing our pleasing and somnolent blindness. Chinese boxes may contain one another; but they certainly do not do so in the relatively disorderly fashion suggested by 'run into another' (unless one is already suffering from a certain delusional perception, a persistence of vision within which shapes are no longer separable – or reveal the secret which is that they have never been separable, that they achieve their singularity *only* through inseparability), and neither does this image of disorder 'fit' with the neat textually labyrinthine encapsulations of the complex and (therefore) death-oriented Gothics of, say, *Melmoth the Wanderer* (1820) or *The Manuscript found in Saragossa* (1805–15?).[13] But these, of course, are tales which include a return to the surface, a telling of the secret, as are most of their modern and postmodern equivalents, the most obvious one being, again, Iain Banks's *The Bridge*.[14] To be *left* in the depths, to be without 'recourse', to know that the Minotaur is bellowing and that you have lost the thread (of the story, of the maze, of the Minotaur's discourse, of the remains or relic of the animal at the heart of the story), these are strategies of risk which would go beyond the boundaries of commonplace ego-psychology. They would also destroy our sense of the future-in-the-mind.

Rapture; where is rapture here? Well, 'running into' is, at the very least, a doubled phrase, a gladsome escape which is at the same time a collision: it is not clear whether these 'tales' are the empty spaces of the maze or material objects which cannon through the pathways, containers or that which is contained: in the image-world conjured up here, perhaps container and contained become increasingly inseparable and we find ourselves in a place where boundaries flicker and warp.[15] And so we have to imagine that, as in a dream or in a state of rapture, when we near the centre of the labyrinth, the threshold of the inner, changes occur. Our fear, perhaps, is of meeting the monster; but at the same time something inside us is telling us that no, it will no longer be like that, for by the time the encounter takes place (the encounter endlessly deferred by addiction) everything will have altered, you, the monster, those green lanes where you have been so lonely for so long; and so the hedges start to shimmer and at one moment you feel that you *are* those hedges, absorbed in the rapture, vibrating to an inner plan which is almost coming into being before your eyes; and then you are yourself again (you are again within the alternative delusion of a unified subjectivity), but what is this? It is you who is lumbering down the paths, growing larger, knocking against overhanging branches, for the maze has grown mysteriously wilder now; and then as you turn the last corner you see him with your one eye, with your unified but blinkered vision, with your alternative perception, this small human coming towards you, you see him with the sight of a bull in terminal agony . . .

So. What then, we might ask, re-collecting ourselves, trying again to read with attention, trying not to wander off on the byways of the maze, would there be in this 'core of narrative space', this emptiness, this stone-cold tomb, which seems to be simultaneously filled with something crucial, something we have temporarily forgotten but from which universes wait to be born – or resurrected? And the text tells us, with the utmost clarity, stark against the mist, a revealed but absolutely concealed secret: a corpse, recently dead, vulnerable. We are perhaps accustomed to thinking of corpses, cadavers, dead bodies in terms of closure, but I suspect that to assume that here would merely constitute another act of bad translation, another attempt on the ascent of the unnameable. It seems more as though this recency of life, this temporary vulnerability, constitutes a rare kind of openness; indeed, it must do so because otherwise the demons could not threaten to get in. This length of time between death and whatever is to succeed death is a chink of light: it *is* the threshold, the *limen*, the moment when the barriers are down and we are exposed to all manner of trickery; according to a different mythology, we could say that we are made over into the world of Hermes, a world of glittering lies and half-truths, a world of winged shoes and paths of flight. Most significantly, it is the time when people make up stories about us; a dangerous time for our memories, because recollections, re-collections of the dead invented in this hallowed space/time which is also the period of the 'wake' (and also the period when we dead awaken) may become inscribed in stone, may become the rewritten personal history, or the case history, by which we shall be known for ever – as, for example, are those other textual 'monsters' – in the original sense of that which is to be shown or displayed – the rat-man and the wolf-man.[16] It is the time when textuality solidifies, when the distance that can be measured between a life and its remembered aftermath collapses and everything is up for grabs, when old singularities are destroyed and reformed, when the subject turns into the relic and all we are left with is that which remains.

## Worrying about the Fuzz

It is therefore of crucial importance that we take care with what is said *here*, that we attend with the utmost care, that we protect the inner ear, in the inner courtyard, *now*, in the passage from death onwards. It is crucially important because everything, for this brief time, is open: the locks are unsealed, the body lies in the open coffin, the vestiges of life hover and float above, secrets evaporate or bury themselves in the sacred ground. All the weight of coins and goods in the world, all the pyramids and catafalques, however much we seal the organic against decay, against the machinic reproductions we call 'nature', through for example mummification or cryogenesis, none of this can fully seal the soul against its leaching away into the outer as the day's residues are re-cooked, firmed up into different narratives, the deceased is remade into the required images, her or his life stripped down and rebuilt. Here in this inner space there is indeed the greatest need for attentive care, for the attentive care which can be bestowed only by the best kind of reading.

We may begin now (again) to see how it is that demons cannot enter this space: it is not, it would appear, because it is a space of deviousness, although that is one of the things it is, one of the convoluted shapes it takes; neither is it that demons are notably straightforward, although in some cultures that is true too. It is simpler than that, it is because this space is a human space, it is the space which is precisely *opened* by the apparent closure signified by mortality. Seen from one perspective (according to one perception, through one single eye, the monovision of the Minotaur[17]) the maze is the body itself, but to say that is to say very little, to speak too quietly even within a space where discretion is at a premium: it is the body transformed by soulstuff, informed by an awareness of singularity, the awareness of making matter into something which *matters*, and in this realm a demon can do very little for he has no understanding of the urgencies which follow from the foreknowledge of death, the foreknowledge which is our doom but also, and necessarily, our salvation.

Here, then, the familiar trope of the journey takes stark form. It is not the journey as quest, for that would imply all the apparatus of the moral law, the journey in the sense implied in the notion of *Bildung*, a rhetoric of development and improvement, education virtually inseparable from its conjoined twin, induction. We are not here in a realm where experience makes us better: instead we are in the realm of the addict, where experience serves instead to remind us of all that we are always on the brink of losing. There are here no grand mountains to be climbed, no raging torrents to be crossed; instead there is a transfixed foreknowledge of a space between life and death, a space within which, for example, the tale of the ancient mariner is endlessly repeated. We are bewitched.

To turn again to our text, a text to which we are trying to attend with the utmost care but which nonetheless seems to be dissolving before our eyes, seems to be 'making a secret' of itself, seems to be hiding itself behind yet another 'wall of words', to be remaining visible only as we sense its passing over the tops of the high hedges: the outstanding word in the next sentence, the generative term from which others flow, is surely 'readers'. So accustomed have we become, under the influence of a certain regime of instrumentality, to associating the creative act primarily with writing, and thus identifying reading as a comparatively passive process, that we may be in danger of forgetting that here we are in the presence, albeit hidden, secreted, of a 'live' reading, a reading that can be heard – a performance, an enactment – although it is one, as perhaps all readings are, which is to and for the dead, a 'performance narrative' where the audience hears everything and nothing, where we need to imagine a full house of nodding corpses, an auditorium within which every seat is occupied by a ghost; much as, for example, we may imagine happening to us when we seek to articulate the words which will bring back, reproduce, the lost experience of rapture.

Let us consider in a little more detail the posture of these readers. We may imagine them, perhaps, sitting around the corpse, the baffling proof (which cannot articulate itself) of singularity. These spirits, we might hazard a guess, are a hundred percent proof. We may also imagine (but we could be wrong) that the definition of 'reading' here is itself a metaphorical one, for it seems improbable that they are sitting there with books in their hands (if that is one description of what reading might be, 'reading aloud' with all the paradoxes that implies around the secrecy, the hiddenness of the reading process). These watchers of the dead, we might prefer to say, are declaiming *as though* they are reading; 'reading' is, as it were, the technical term for what this activity *is*, and it is an activity for which we can find no exact translation for there is no precise equivalent in the English-speaking (English-reading) cultures.

Yet again: surely everything in the description of reading is in some sense metaphoric. We may take the presumed dimensionality of the reading act. We (in the West) read, we are told, 'down' the page, and indeed sometimes we do, if only when we are holding a book vertically in front of us (or if, now, we are reading off a screen, reassembling pixels in an active creation, albeit an approximate one, of meaning). But when, perhaps equally frequently, we are reading a book which is flat on a horizontal surface the 'down' becomes an empty signifier, or rather it is a metaphor which we understand because we internalise a normative, although culturally specific, concept of reading and its attendant physical postures. Reading is thus, as much as anything else, a question of the arrangement of the body; within the reading act what is created is a type of cyborg, the becoming of a symbiosis between reader and text, what Deleuze and Guattari might refer to as a 'becoming-book'; much as the 'readers' who become the only real survivors of holocaust in Ray Bradbury's *Fahrenheit 451* (1953) 'become' the books they wish to preserve – from the fire, from the burning, from the loss of memory, a loss which can only be retrieved – or defended against – through a process of endless repetition, a cultural reaffirmation of meaning from which, we also fear, all meaning may be becoming progressively drained.[18]

But the metaphors here – in this text, in this book, in this enjoined task of protecting the dead – or is it really protecting ourselves *from* the dead? – are even more complex; for while these readers are reading they might also be building, building with words but probably without books, building within the soul of evanescence, even though it might be tempting, and satisfying, to see these imagined book covers, jackets covered with dust, meeting, extending into a solid carapace, rather like, perhaps, a Roman *testudo*, a protective shield built from many shields, a signifier of a collaborative community which can come together in times of threat, death or war.

Or perhaps, again, as we seek to exert leverage on the interstices of the text (as we look for a place from which to prise apart the protective cover which is also the soul and acme of concealment, beneath which all the soldiers, the 'many men so beautiful', have already died, have become as ghosts, are even now applauding as one final reading, a last celebratory gift to the dead, avers against all the evidence that they still have ears to hear, perhaps even eyes to see), it is not that they *are building*, but that they *have built*; but at all events there is a close connection here between reading and building, varieties of construction work which Blake also conjoins in his recurring trope of the 'golden builders',[19] such that we might infer that it is now the reading which keeps the (nominalised) building in place, which provides the continuous stiffening, the strengthening, the scaffolding without which it would collapse again into a heap of rubble, an upturned *testudo*, an empty and shattered carapace, into the unformed matter which would too closely, too resonantly, too menacingly reproduce the condition of the body unconstructed according to the lineaments of the evolving exoskeleton, the jacket of the book.

## Fortified Wine

Via this 'defence fortification', along these battlements and parapets, we could, as usual, 'return to Freud'; or perhaps better to Anna Freud's still potent analysis (and who had a better need for defences?) of the defence mechanisms.[20] If that connection is useful, then we would need to touch on the double function of the ego and return our enquiry to the question of the desires of the body and here, specifically, of the corpse. Perhaps it is not just that demons wish to penetrate the willing or unwilling flesh, to reproduce on its surfaces and in its interstices a shape of non-human rapture within which all is lost; perhaps it is also that the flesh wishes to leap into the wild outer, so that constant reading (the incarnation and reproduction of the 'constant reader') is necessary to drown out the siren voices from the wings of the stage (or the heckling from the all too spirited audience in the 'theatre of sleep'); we might glimpse, for example, highly vocal and, as it were, dressed to kill, the Tantric gods who come endlessly to disturb the order of the domestic Vedic deities,[21] and thus to threaten the convenience of the separation of the living from the dead and to offer a different perspective on those locations where life and death, loss and rapture, meet and interfuse despite the efforts of the myths of unified subjectivity.

For the corpse, we need to note (and we are now, despite all warnings, turning back around another corner of the text, reading not down but up, doubling back in, presumably, the hope of evading the sense of an ending or of meeting whatever is at the centre of the maze, even if this means adopting a convenient fiction about the domesticity of 'households'), is at the centre of the 'household'. It is through respect for this corpse that the household, the central space, the major building block is held together and thus that family continuity is ensured, violent discontinuity set in place as the cornerstone of the hearth. It is thus also that the old stories are rehearsed and kept up and that the dissolution into rapture (the rapture of the dissolute) is kept at bay. What threatens this would be the call of the wild, the howling of the demon, the intrusion of different, unregulated voices. What would really disturb the fabric of this building? One thing might be a voice coming from another, undefinable place, an articulation with no source. For some cultures the fear has been shaped as the terror of ventriloquism, the voice which comes from a different part, the *wrong* part, of the body, an intestinal rumbling which announces the possibility of a shaking of the foundations, however deeply they may have been dug. This, certainly, has terrified Western writers from the nineteenth century on, from Charles Brockden Brown, unconsciously articulating fears as to whether America would ever prove capable of finding its own voice, to *The Exorcist* (1973), with its clustering of images around the question of whether the voice of the demon might issue from human lips, out of the mouths of babes and sucklings, whether dead or not.[22]

And we could pursue this line of enquiry further, for behind this fear of ventriloquism there lies also an anxiety about the dead speaking out in response to the wild in a secret discourse – which nonetheless would be far from hidden, a loudly spoken open secret if ever there was one – which would further 'open' us to the ambivalence of disintegration, and thus to a conflict within the passional structure of the soul. The building, the architectonics of meaning, the never-ending continuity of the reading, the defences and fortifications, all these are in some sense in the service of the mythos of integration, of holding together some semblance of order despite the overwhelming evidence of the prevalence of chaos.

Yet that too cannot be the 'whole story' (no story, we have by now been convincingly told, can ever be whole). There is also, as the worm in the bud, the longing for disintegration, a longing which the vulnerable soul, partially freed from its moorings and with all in readiness to set sail (we shall see Graham describing this sailing in painful and painstaking detail a little later) might now feel sufficiently free to satisfy; in which case we too, as constant readers, might find ourselves with our moorings broken and embarked on a night-sea journey where our perceptions, our perspectives, even our visions of the potential for rapture, no longer retain credence. Indeed, perhaps it is the satisfaction of this *unspeakable* lust on the part of the dead (and in this respect they 'un-speak' on the un-willing behalf of the rest of us, stranded in the wilderness of the near shore) which cannot be avoided; perhaps it is going on all the while all around us – but at least we can try to prevent its incursions, try for a suspect act of exorcism, or at least a quasi-medical process of decontamination. Even if we do so hopelessly, in the light of the decease of hope, we can *say* that we tried, can speak something against the rise of the unspeakable, that we attempted to bring order to the dark, to arrange something of hierarchy, responsibility, even hospitality amid the shifting shadows of the watch-fire, amid the unknowable soundings of the night.

At all events. At, indeed, all events, in the process of every event[23], in order even for the concept of an 'event' to remain within the horizon, the possibility of this 'broadcast', so our text tells us (or so we read from our script, which is always a faulty script, a mere prompt-book when an 'authorised version' would be so much more satisfying, would reassure us of a primal, original authority behind our reproductions and untrustworthy replicas) has to be jammed. Just as is the case with the thought broadcasting of the psychotic or the terminal addict, there is something too fertile, too promiscuous, in this intercourse between the dead and the demon. We suspect that if this kind of thing is allowed to go on (and especially, as it were, in our own back yard, or at the centre of the household) it will not submit itself to the rules we have so painstakingly laid down for civilised commerce for it will be, of course, a free play (one, perhaps, for entrance to which the ghosts have not paid for their tickets), the consummation of a tabooed polymorphous perversity, for there is no reproductive constraint on pale, ghostly dealings between demonic phallus and dead womb.

## Waking the Dead

But yet again we sense here a contradiction, or perhaps the phantom of a contradiction, a slippage of vision: for what can the connection be between this mindless and meaningless jamming and the care for the souls of the dead to which our text has introduced us earlier, introduced us with the utmost courtesy, generosity, hospitality? If, indeed, we imagine the dead, the rapture of those who sleep more easily beneath the roots of the yew,[24] as Hardy imagined it, to be very like ourselves, if we accept the conventional quasi-equation of death and sleep, then the problem seems incapable of resolution. There is no care, no order, no subtlety in white noise, any more than there is in the blaring, greedy craving of the addict.[25] But the crucial point is that the dead are not like the living: they are, in fact, the soul of difference, the soil in which all thought of difference is grounded. We cannot discourse directly with them, any more than we can respond directly to the concrete thinking of the psychotic. The extent of the respect we can show them, we may surmise, will be coterminous with the extent of the freedom we can allow them; the realms of death and the addict are no places for a police force, however well versed (like the critical interpreter) in the dark arts of posthumous detection.

With regard to the dead (in respect of the dead) we may be judged by the multiplicity of choices we can offer, our resistance to foreclosing the issue on the grounds of the commonest of all accidents; a multiplicity which in its very *indifference* bespeaks not a lack of care but a necessarily recessive unwillingness to place limitations on the dead or on those others for whom the moral law has ceased to operate. And for this purpose we might say, as we loop back towards our text, *any story* will do; even if we also sense that within the 'cacophony' there will still be a hidden, a secret order which it is not our province to interpret. These texts embedded within text, these read-out (white-out) memories of other texts are, after all, still narratives, and they will not be blinded out (the Minotaur still has one eye) by the many voices recounting them. So we have here a model of order and disorder, imbrication and cacophony; we have also a model – a working model, it might be reasonable to suppose – for the reunion of the written and the spoken, of those narratives which have historically inscribed, and have been historically inscribed *upon*, the culture and have attained to the power of signs, and these words which, heard in the context of an apparent randomness, from many lips and with many voices, provide evidence of relish for the sheer power of orality, its muddle, its regressiveness, its naked power, its violent rebuttal of demons.

For the addict, and perhaps this is obvious by now, is not so much engaged in illicit commerce with demons; rather, he or she is in the vanguard of identifying those demons and erecting fortifications against them. Here, then, a heresy or blasphemy: just as monastic orders are engaged upon a practice seen as providing benefit to humanity by maintaining a prayerful vigilance, by respecting the reality of the constantly intrusive other, so the addict maintains a kind of vigilance, constantly open to death, constantly aware of the proximity of the demon and the limitations of the flesh. Such a thought is, of course, intolerable: anybody engaged in such a battle must surely have gone native: we need only to think of the treatment of returning soldiers from the crusades to the tragic remnants of the invasion of Iraq. The risk, the danger, is of contamination: no prison can be too strong to hold those who have had dealings with the devil, those who have fought the good fight but who have carried home with them – into our own back yard, into the centre of the household – relics, even if they are holy relics, of disease and who knows what other foreign bodies. The leper is always with us.[26]

Back, however, from contamination to protection: 'It protects souls'. What exactly is the 'it' here, what (or where) is the subject of the sentence? The 'it' must, presumably, be 'reading'; but not, perhaps, the reading of words on the page, not reading held in and restrained by silence, but reading which is full of blood and passion, a kind of reading which rehumanises the word even as it reveals the hidden depths which are the obverse side of the human. This kind of reading would open entry points in the folds of language, would transcend the words on the page, the jacket on the book, and would aspire to the condition of the word as world-maker, while asserting that such a rapturous creativity can only occur in the closest of proximity to death, only when the soul is at its most vulnerable, in its direst of needs for protection.

'It protects souls'. Yet this reading would not be a 'right' reading, the culmination of some demonstrable process of interpretation. It might, indeed, always and necessarily be a 'wrong' reading, a reading against the grain: certainly it would be 'wrong' in the sense that these reconstituted voices are not 'original', have nothing to do with originality. Yet this is no devaluation: this is remaking, what Hillman refers to as 're-cooking', a recombination of residues (perhaps especially of worthless Hekatean residues, the sad remains of life, the relics of the addicts' party), and thus a symbolic conferral of new value, a transvaluation which goes beyond the easy tropes of meaning and invests these human voices which are now, in at least two senses, post-human voices with a power which has nothing to do with morality and which yet can, in some sense, 'call the world to order', even if this version of order is not the one we thought we knew before we started the irreversible process of 'hearing the voices' – or of, indeed, 'hearing the case', albeit now differently put. The force of this new vocal field has to be such that the pettinesses of after-death gossip, wrong decisions, the rewriting of history, can find no opportunity for purchase, no space in which to unloose their demonic effects: the jamming must be total, the thought-broadcasting must occur on all channels simultaneously, there must be no chink in the carapace.

And yet; and yet. And yet I have a nagging doubt as to whether I have been talking about this passage, this text, *our* text (for, as readers, we are sharing it, are we not?) at all. There is something here which appears to 'glance off', both in the sense of a blow being repelled from a protected space, and also in the sense of a watching of what may be occurring 'in the wings', in other parts of the labyrinth which is the text. The focus, the vision of the single eye is constantly distracted. Is this itself the work of demons, or is it that it is the demons themselves who are trying to 'talk sense', advising us to move in straight lines, not to cut corners, especially at too high a speed? What is being protected, against what or whom?

## Bodily Fluids

What we see as protected we can also see as a version of openness, of that which is not secret, not hidden; we might, in a different register of discourse, refer to it as a necessary *fluidity* of psyche which allows it to move between different states, different self-images. The white noise, then, could be inspected more closely: within it, we might say, psyche can hear (as the addict can hear, even if what s/he hears are 'noises off' within the depths of the rapture or against the darkened grain of the symptoms of withdrawal) and what it can hear are fragments, bits and pieces of narrative, self-images at a stage of partial construction, and this, we might again say, is psyche's food, its nourishment, the substance from which it weaves (as a text, any text, *our* text, is 'woven', for that what is what 'text' means). It is through the absorption of this multiplicity that substance can be achieved, that the soul can be continually made and remade during the course of a life – unless, of course, the hard reign of the repetition comes to end that process of transmutation, to freeze the subject in a position of fear and joy, to render pointless any further attempts on meaning and to settle instead for the half-heard sounds amid the noise, the ceaseless fragments of reminder of *another* life, a different kind of life which is, of course, no less impossible to conceive than it is to live.[27]

But at the same time there is, in the text, something 'preventative'; and we may hazard a guess that what is to be prevented is undue attachment. Am I, for example, too much attached to the text, to *my* text? Even as I claim, with generosity, with hospitality, to be sharing it with you, dear reader, is there irony? Would I really share the object of my love and attachment so willingly, unnecessarily create siblings who would then vie with me for parental affection, causing no doubt endless problems in later life (whatever 'later life' might be[28])? It seems improbable, does it not? Yet perhaps what is being said here is slightly different; for there is within psyche always the temptation to rest, to settle for a singleness of self-image, to abandon the search and to relapse towards stasis, the stasis of the addict, the stasis of the death drive. Yet this carries within it, of course, its own fate: for whatever this self-image might be the act of 'settling for it' at the expense of all others is simultaneously to transform it into a narcissistic ego-ideal, what Blake refers to (resonantly when we think back to the ghostly audience before whom we appear now to be performing, the phantomatic reader in the shadows with his faulty hearing and his single eye) as the 'Spectre':[29] it is then to grant it power over us, and the risk then is that psyche itself will shrink and dry up before the conferred might of its own simulacrum.

We could move from this to Buddhist ideas on attachment, and how those ideas themselves could be seen as constituting a depth psychology designed to maintain the freedom and fluidity of psyche, that freedom and fluidity without which we cannot cross barriers but *with* which even death can be relocated within the care of the soul.[30] But this would be to take us into a field in which the prospect of freedom from all attachment is present, even as a liminal possibility; and this is not the trajectory of the Balinese text, which is instead towards a certain promiscuity, a promiscuity which belongs to the desire of the soul but is also the lust of psyche for the rapture of being lost in experience; as such it is also the centrifugal force which resists closure, resists the drawing in on the self which we know also by the ambiguous name of suicide, and with which we shall come into closer proximity in a later chapter. It would appear that it is only in the tension represented by 'these readers' (the readers of the text, the readers in the text, the most astute readers of all, the readers who are lost in the rapture of having no idea what it is that they are reading) that these forces can be kept in balance. What is thus prevented is, on the one hand, the seizing up of the inner (the secreted concretisation of the psychotic) and, on the other, the threat of total dissolution into the outer (loss in the rapture, the ecstasy).

Between these twin possibilities, then, stands the wall of words. Between the fixity of false memory and the threat of total forgetting lies the activity (an activity of humans which is nevertheless constantly reminding us of its abhuman origins), ever variable, which *underlies* writing and reading, and gives writing and reading their sense and their power. Let us inspect (if we have time) this wall more closely: we have already observed it in terms of fortifications, battlements, parapets; we have examined something of the blocks from which it is built, and the significance of building at all, especially *in this place* where the status of all construction is under immediate threat, where there are only shifting sands on which to build and within which no corridor, passageway or path can run straight. But now, if we look more closely, we can see that there is movement *on* the wall; that along the wall there is a continuous wake in progress, a continuous inscription and reinscription of memories, even perhaps the maintenance of a flickering flame. Narrative is thus never without homage: the anxiety of influence dissolves also into its own opposite as we (readers) are strung between remembering and forgetting the dead, drowning in the lethal ambiguity of mourning, the wish for the dead to rise up before us and the terror which we know would follow if they were to obey (or even to dream of obeying) our summons.[31]

Which returns me to Angela Carter's own death. Is it (was it) recent? What constitutes recency in this liminal world? It is, we are told, the 'recently dead' who have, peculiarly and despite – or perhaps because of – their vulnerability, this power: it fades like all things, but as it does so it becomes part of the patchwork, the *bricolage*, the tapestry of narrative, the very dead themselves kept alive by the activity of constant reading, by the repetition of a rapturous reincarnation.

There is then here a passional wish to protect, and a passion to overcome danger; accompanying these is the possibility of an encounter with humiliation, a possibility which needs to be warded off at all costs, for it would be intolerable for the recently dead to be glimpsed when they are at their most vulnerable and it would also, of course, threaten us (readers) with the possibility that the same thing might happen to us (in later life; in the earliest, most childlike, most 'attached' moments of the after-life, at the very inauguration of the longed-for realm of the post-human). That possibility of humiliation, the possibility that our raptures might be exposed to ridicule, that the superhuman powers which we attribute to ourselves in episodes of drug-induced psychosis, that the boasts we make under the influence of alcohol, amphetamines, mescal, might – indeed, we fear, inevitably will – come to seem the nadir of the ludicrous, this occurs to psyche in all its forms and produces many desperate and partial remedies; *in extremis* it has also to do with an abandonment to abjection, the ever-presence of the ashes in which we must roll in order to proceed to a new stage. But it also has to do with the wound, the aporia, the hiatus; which, perhaps all too obviously, has, all along, been at the centre of our text . . . but must remain there.

# 9

# Some Tales of Erythron

That rapture is linked with loss, therefore, seems a thesis not likely to be disputed, and this for the most obvious of reasons. On the one hand, we might say that loss is generally recognised as the most fundamental of existential categories, whether we are to think it in the terms offered by Heidegger, Jean-Paul Sartre or Derrida;[1] on the other, we indeed need to say that many of the passions, most of the outbursts from the primal which deeply score our lives and 'carry us away' emanate from a sense of loss, from a residual feeling of a better state in which we could be: whether this figures as the rage of impotent resistance at not-being-there, or as the lust to possess and destroy another so that we too shall be present (even as survivors or refugees) on the final scene, or as the envy we feel towards those whose apparently greater purity or understanding of motive appears to give them a hotline to a future in which, according to our fantasies, the loss will be recuperated and all things will be judged by a criterion which will be the acme of fulfilment, before which any evidence of loss will be taken as an element in a personal failing rather than as a symptom of *la condition humaine*.

## On the Nod

My contention in this chapter, perhaps banal in itself, is that there might be more to be said about loss in relation to rapture; but that to say that which is 'more' will involve tracing the nature of loss through a number of levels. Deleuze and Guattari might call them strata; the important hovering question is as to whether in pursuing this matter through such levels one is acting upon the promise, or danger, or warning, of increasing 'depth'. Here, however, I will try to leave that question on one side, although it is not clear to me what the reading mind will do with a number of 'unfixed levels'; and neither is it to me apparent what will 'succeed' if a notion of levels is eschewed. What is however entirely clear is that the notion of loss points us at a gap, a gap between a something and a nothing; and it is this gap into which I intend to fall, hoping to keep one eye open, as it were, for the textual implications of this gap, wherever they may be found.

Erythron was a game youth. He was clad in sable and gold; his tabard bore curious inscriptions, at which he looked from time to time, not so much in the hope that he might understand as on the assumption that repeated glancing, 'glancing blows', might eventually enable him to get a fix on their presence (or at least to get some kind of a fix), so that he would be able to reproduce them if the occasion arose. What occasion that might be he could not imagine.

To have claimed that he was happy with the three of them sitting opposite him would have been an exaggeration; on the other hand, the dance hall was crowded, and at least he was not compelled to look at them all of the time. He had noticed them, of course: the length of one half-exposed thigh, the swaying cut of a white neckline . . . what was a young god to do?

But, all things considered (and there were many things to consider) he didn't really think so. How could they possibly have the answer, or indeed any answer? So young (perhaps; although not one of them; for a second he caught sight, the merest glimpse, of a quite different face), so kitschy svelte, so North London gauche . . .

Later, when they had agreed to come back with him (there are some advantages to being a god), he pointed up the problem. 'If', through the exhalations and fumes, 'it were to be about seeking the treasure, what would you have to say?'

Girly trembling, mild shrieking, shifting of nylon, 'Well . . . '.

It came down, as always, to the possibility of a treasure chest. 'Really', said Erythron, tired and wondering where the next day's high was going to come from. But they were not so bad, they had caught the illusion: they were sitting on it suddenly, this treasure chest conjured, hallucinated from nowhere; then they were giggling, lifting their fine legs. And it remained. There. Somewhere. On some level.

'A question', said the brunette with the longest legs; she was the one about whom he had doubts. Her features flickered and flowed; there was a curious double-jointedness to her arms. 'What is the question?'

Although the other two fell about laughing in an unseemly way, Erythron pursed his elegant lips. He knew he had to. There were invisible claws at the window, as usual.

'The question is', he said, struggling for air, his hands tangled in satin, lace, 'whether there is truth to be found at the bottom of a treasure chest'.

A great sigh. The lid yawns upward. He fumbles with what might be inside (if inside is the right word). There is a paper, a scroll. It is

> inscribed, in azure and silver. For a moment, he hopes. He lifts it out. It reads: 'Here is truth, found at the bottom of a treasure chest'. He fumbles again; again he fumbles. There is nothing else. Looking around, sweeping back a lock of hair, there is nobody at all.

The problem of deconstruction, the problem which it addresses and yet which continues to beset it, its glamour and its nemesis, is twofold. It supposes that text is all-important; but it is in constant danger of going on to proclaim that the human consequences of textuality are trivial, because textuality has no access to the 'other' of experience. It might be interesting to entertain the hypothesis that the reverse is true: namely that text is trivial in itself and that to analyse it in grand etymological detail is a tedious and evasive pursuit, but that its human import is immense and without parallel.

There are paradoxes, or at least contradictions, or at the *very* least 'undecidables' in those statements. Of course there are. In the relations between word, event and rapture, between the recountable and the unrecountable, those relations which, I hope, we have been pursuing, all is purveyed, all is open to the process of transaction. What lies here before us as we inspect these categories would be the possibility of a fidelity beyond fidelity, a truth beyond truth, a faith beyond faith. Deleuze and Guattari speak in this context about schizoanalysis and about the 'schizo'[2], but one response to their discourse would be to ask how they dare. Seen from one point of view there is not, cannot be, any kind of schizoanalysis; the notion of the schizoid is a standing rebuttal of the notion of analysis, unless one grants it the critical distance which classical psychoanalysis, whose equivocal will is not to be infected by madness, does. What the notion of schizoanalysis, I would suggest, tries to do is to pretend that there is no loss: that the experience of severance and the experience of drawing together can be engineered into a seamless whole. There is a classical name for this, and it is the spark of tragedy: *hubris*. With this return to *hubris* via schizoanalysis we encounter again the endlessly awkward not-to-be-wished-away experience of loss.

The most significant event in classical, let us say Sophoclean or Shakespearean, tragedy is not frequently commented, because it happens at or rather slightly beyond the threshold and it is not at all accounted for by the comforting theory of *catharsis*: it is about the experience of loss as the audience (we, the spectral readers, those addicted to an experience which cannot be shared and which resists narrative form) go out into the still and reverberating night. We have lost the thread, we have lost the sense of potential meaning, we have lost all our identifications, we are lost indeed in the 'outer'. The absence of tragedy is loss, the imminent forgetting of the rapture, the return to the quotidian, the ebbing of dignity, the revived prospect of humiliation – have we been 'carried away' or 'taken in'?

Classical psychoanalysis has a great deal to say about loss.[3] For example, it talks about early experiences of union and omnipotence and about the slide away from this ambiguous plenitude. I call it ambiguous because, of course, it unites in a single symbolic whole stances which the world will teach us to be incompatible, namely absolute dependence and absolute power. There is probably more to be learned from this conjunction: when we turn this into a wish – in other words, when we consider it not as a condition-left-behind but as the haunting presence which shadows our current state, our actions – then we see several more things. First, at a general level, we begin to grasp the peculiarities of time. For according to this schema, there is *no past*: I do not mean here to advert to Freud's model of the unconscious in *Civilisation and its Discontents* (1930), as all the cities that have been Rome become visible and on display at the same (impossible) time[4], but rather to point out *how* the 'past' figures in psyche, which is as a *presence*, a reminder, and in a very real sense a whiff from the future, in other words, as an element in our decisions on future actions, the conditioning ground for our projects. But second, at a more specific level, we are here in a position to begin an analysis of the will to power as precisely a wish to re-achieve absolute dependency.

On what would this 'dependency' depend? On a new mother, and here perhaps we get another glimpse of, another glance at what goes on 'behind the curtain', in the realm of the secret. Picture the temple, the shrine, the synagogue, the board room. The man of power sits before the curtain; he is enthroned, but only on sufferance. He is chief, but also guardian and intercessor: behind the curtain lies a greater power still. And the measure of the gap between this hidden goddess, the treasure at the bottom of the chest, and her human avatar is also the measure of the gap, held in the priest's imagination, between himself and the remainder of his congregation, class, race. In this matching of distances there is, of course, precisely the danger of an *immeasurability*; that by standing so determinedly *between*, it may come to be impossible for him to see to which realm he belongs. Here all is liminal: the rapture is present, but in the form of a promise, a deferred contract between the hierophant and the people, such that what is promised is never 'on the scene' but always on another scene, waiting in the wings, about to carry us away yet never quite descending.

## Pure, Undiluted, Uncut

Besides, there is always the danger of being outflanked; there will always be groups, sects who want a direct hotline behind the curtain, puritans, antinomians, disrobers of all sorts; they have to be kept at bay as well, and so the presence of loss multiplies. The great exposers of mystery, the debunkers of myth threaten to remove us from our addictions, our dependencies, our attachments: they nail words of clarity, defiance and courage to church doors.[5] But what they offer is too open: there is no real stage without a curtain, without a drawing apart and a drawing together to mark a delimited passage of time; without this nothing can be celebrated, we are lost in flat time, shivering without the squalid and ceremonious warmth of the sacred circle with its attendant drugs, hallucinations, conjurations.

The loss is in the dependence; but it is equally in the absence of dependence. When the loss is felt too intensively in the dependence, when dependence is experienced as loss, then we are in the impending presence of the military, of the jackboot in the night, of macho, of a world where the curtain has to be kept closed tight over whatever supernatural softnesses, whatever soft machine, might threaten the men of steel. When the loss is felt too intensively in the absence of dependence, when absence of dependence is experienced as loss, then we are in, for example, Blake's Beulah, or in a Satyricon, an orgy, running with Dionysos, welcoming revolution with no thought for the morrow, down on our knees worshipping the anarchs and all the old foul gods behind them, whom we thought we had forgotten but who now come stealing out from behind the curtain and will commence to roam the streets with us, interchangeably, so that all hierarchies and all orders are commingled.[6] We would find, if we had time to look, that these twin images summarise each other's fears: they are twinned inseparables, always haunting and stalking each other. We could pin to them also – perhaps it is more than that; perhaps we *should* – the mutual paranoias of the centrally planned and the market economy. But time is (already) running out.

Let us consider textuality again under this heading of loss; let us try to see what is written not in terms of construction or even of deconstruction, but instead in relation to a system from which everything is continually seeping, which is sliding gently down to death. We may start by saying that what comes out of the writer, the fruit of the creative rapture, the result of having been carried away, is conditioned by loss. It *comes out*, of course; it is therefore in a sense excreted; whatever it is or was, it has passed decisively *away* from the author, it has been moved outward to take up a station in the outer world; it has been lost. Whether it has ever reached the reader is, to say the very least, a moot point: if it has, then in any case one could say that it has been 'lost in translation', the peculiar conditions of its creation have been shed as it passes across the 'space between', the potential matching of two raptures appears only after the fantasised possibility of real communication has accepted its own demise.

This suggests, of course, that everything in the outer world has been lost. Literally, that nothing in the outer world is 'in the right place'; that the outer world *is* the wrong place. And also that in it nothing can be 'found' for, to put it at its simplest, we have no idea where anything is; or indeed, as Bishop Berkeley was not alone in suspecting, whether anything is there at all. Each act of 'finding' is indeed a surprise; but it is also a prelude to further loss in that nothing in the outer world can be 'held', only the inner goods – those of which, for example, Salman Rushdie's Sufiya Zenobia was so proud, those well-stocked inner shelves[7] – only those can be held in reality to us, although this is not to say that loss does not figure in the inner world as well, only in a different guise, as the loss of memory of the rapture, as the construction and deconstruction of the secret as a protected space to prevent (again) the danger that it may be taken from us, obliterated, so that only reading can protect us, can ensure that we retain the mobility to avoid the troops coming down, all the time, on our inadequately fortified position.

So we can at least be clear as to precisely what gets lost in the act of writing. It is rapture; or perhaps it might be better to put it, bearing in mind the enormous complexities of the term 'passion', as the 'passion of rapture'. It is that passion which is with us, *in* us as we write, and which we are trying to 'enwrap' as we write. Writing is an activity of incarnation, of enrobing; or if you like (as if any writer really cared what a reader might like) of cross-hatching, interweaving, knitting clothes so that our baby will not have to go forth into the world naked. We call these clothes words. We might say, following Blake, that they are the clothing of lamentation.[8] Each intricately-made christening gown will double as a grave-clout: we know it. Or rather, inside ourselves *it*, id knows it. We deny it, from time to time, although increasingly half-heartedly as time goes on (or as the text goes on; wears on; wears you down; an illogic of hand-me-downs).

The blood drains away from our optimistic protests. Just so the blood drains away from the writing itself. We see the bones instead, the forms rather than the fleshy content: we move, it would now seem (as if by an inexorable logic, for indeed we have been in this world before, there is little new in the writer springing from the pages of the text, these are old illusions and the top hat is rather threadbare) into a postmodernist world where the need to put flesh on the bone has been succeeded by a type of (again) anorexia, a need to see the skeleton before we can really be sure that the work exists. We want to see *how it works*, and only then can we be satisfied, in an oddly self-defeating version of satisfaction which ensures that no suspension of disbelief can be believed.

## Thinners

The mention of anorexia is perhaps too frightening, too final a stage of addiction to be borne. But it cannot be denied that anorexia is the addicted form of the postmodern. The wish is to be thin, of course: but it is more than that, it is different from that, it is the wish to display *how things work*, how the body works, it is the 'architectonic' wish to display the plumbing, the pipes, the cables on the outside of the body/building rather than inside.[9] It is an aesthetic of display; what it does is to lethally confound secret with secret, so that this display, this pushing the exigencies, the desperation of the body in our faces (in the faces of the readers, the members of the spectral audience, even though by now they have all, I suspect, left the theatre) can at the same time only be held in secret, in for example the festering swamp of the adolescent bedroom where mutating hormones drip from the ceiling and only by curling up, by making ourselves very, very small and thin, can we avoid infection, contamination. Needle replaced by needle; sharp blade by sharp blade; on the edge, always on the edge. The syringe beckons again.

And so (to return from this terror to the supposed replenishments of birth, attachment, dependency) we send these rush cradles off down the river; but every one of them is empty. For every one of them has had to pass over a threshold, the threshold between the inner and the outer; and as we should have foretold, that passing over the threshold has changed everything, always, for ever. All there are now are empty cradles, rocking on the stream. Plenty of rich clothes, if a little shop-soiled; no baby. The passions, the rapture, are no longer there; but where are they? They are lost.

Perhaps you have lost the thread. Perhaps I have lost the thread. Have no fear: the Minotaur sleeps; or he wakes; or he dreams that he is a figure of fun. However: we have moved from the notion of writing as excretion (not a trope which anybody would like to deal with in detail) to a more pleasant image of sending off our words downstream, where they may like the fisher king fertilise the land, may enjoy the delights of the delta, may be washed up and (mis)taken for signs and portents. But regrettably it is not as though the contents of these little boats were simply left at the doorstep, not as though we can see them still lying there, shake our heads over them and hope that next time they might make the transition. No, it would seem as though they have disappeared into thin air; or rather they have been locked away in the liminal land, that land in which we have now found ourselves so often, the land of echoes, repetitions, half-heard sounds, the perfection of the Sirens' island, the rapturous memories of lotos-eaters, of the inhalers of curious plants, the land where we lie half-addicted, still wanting the pleasure of the repetition, still unaware of the skeleton dancing beneath the skin.[10] They are no longer either in the inner or in the outer. They are lost. So are we. From addiction, there is no return; for what comes back will always be different, will be a particular kind of cyborg.[11] Self-plus-drug. Self-plus-absence-of-drug. To try to 'treat' the 'self' alone within this system is folly, the false operation of a defunct moral law. There is no longer any self.[13]

Perhaps this seems a little scary, and it is therefore apposite to turn back to Gothic fiction; and alongside postmodernism, and intersecting with it as it does at all points, it is perhaps unsurprising that Gothic fiction, and the developing critique of Gothic fiction, are crucial loci at the moment, for the re-experience of certain kinds of rapture, and especially the more deathly kind (if we were to grant for one moment that there were others) enshrined in Gothic has a crucial relation to the gradual revelation of this 'emptiness' of which we are speaking (emptily, to or in an empty house; the party appears to be over, but that is only because the meditation is going on, the thinking, the really hard thinking, about where to get the next fix); in other words, it is primarily in and through Gothic that we can dare, if only ironically, to sense that the words in which we deal are actually empty husks, tombs already robbed, meanings already dispersed and held in quite another place.[13] And thus we could loop Gothic back to the crucial issue of somnambulism: the body of Gothic text, of Gothic writing, is precisely an enactment of 'that which goes through the motions', of that which is both condemned to the repetition and yet simultaneously absolved of all responsibility for the consequences of action, the very figure of exemption from the moral law; it is not just that Gothic describes zombies, it is that Gothic *is* the zombie, and always (whatever 'always' might mean) has been in the sense that it proposes the body as the substitute for soul; and its ambiguities of comfort and disturbance stem at least in part from that.[14]

Our pursuit of rapture is inseparable from a need to explore loss further. We shall have to explore, to put contours onto, this 'land in between', this world of the threshold, of which psychoanalysis, it would strangely appear, knows nothing, of which interpretation, certainly and by definition, knows nothing, which even in myth is but hinted at through figures which are half-formed, half-glimpsed, quite improper, the very stuff of *impropriety*, in many senses of that word: this land knows no owner; even the laws of ownership are foreign to it; but so, to take it even further, are the rights of the nomad. More important, however, is the fact that this land we are trying to interrogate is *neither inner nor outer*; it is comprised of things which have been lost, which have been mis-placed, and they lie *between*. Here, perhaps (if anywhere) we may be able to locate rapture; here we can certainly find the 'land of the secret'; here, for all we know (and probably we can, of this, know nothing) we may be able to discover (reveal, dis-conceal, remove from hiding – do we really want to do that?) the abode of the addict, the place to which s/he is 'carried away'.

We can find some glimpses of this land in fairy stories: in the Never Never Land (or in Michael Jackson's reconstructive Neverland), or in all those countries which we visit 'in a flash', from which we return to discover that no time has elapsed, that we are still where we were, that all we have experienced has been a 'glancing blow', an intimation of rapture withheld.[15] But normally we awake from this instantaneous reverie with a pang of the utmost sharpness: for we have seen in that liminal land all the things we have lost, we have seen them transformed, we have seen them 'held' as we ourselves could not hold them. We could not hold them because we could not still time; but there, *in the land of still time* (and, by a bizarre twist, in perhaps the only land where there is indeed 'still time'), there is nothing to erode them, and they can exist there *in the very plenitude of their exemplification of loss* (for if there is nothing which can erode, then neither is there any air to breathe). They live, as it were, within their own halo, their own rapture: their stillness is atremble, afire[16], they live amid the very quintessence of magic; yet all goes on in the one place, in the space between the surface of the mirror and the mercury which backs it, which forms a firm backdrop but which, we know, if the glass, the illusion were shattered would seep away, run off into a little meaningless puddle on the floor; the end of the mirror phase – the cynical revelation, we might alternatively say, of Hermes.

All that effort, all that supernatural strength to keep this 'middle realm' in being: whose strength, where does this force come from in the general economy of inner and outer? What is sapped by its presence? It takes its force, I think, equally from both sides. As it grows in strength, so we experience inner weakness: when we are most sure that all we should hold is in fact held away from us in the world of the threshold, then are we weakened in our resolve to continue, for the air becomes very thin indeed when we have nothing to hold to ourselves, nothing with which to clothe ourselves; except perhaps for textuality, except for the very clothing of lamentation, the garment woven from tears, the cry of loss and even the brave face we put upon loss as we weave poems, novels, plays from a substance which is always already falling apart in our hands and which is in no condition to embark upon a journey. But so also does the outer world grow weak and the pull and strain of its conventions and objective needs get wasted, for the thinness of the air can destroy objects too, as we all know from the museums, and so we experience this gradual double wilting as the demon of the threshold brings more and more things under its command. What would it be like to spend one's life there, in a realm where everything is remembered and everything is forgotten, where, like the alcoholic and the anorexic, we live on air, we know that something is in the air and that it is simultaneously the breath, the substance of life and the source of poison in the bloodstream, life as a wasting, a wasted disease?[17]

## Bad Manners

If it is incorrect to say that hypostasisation provides the structure for this liminal realm, then we might more usefully reverse the thought and suggest that it is the existence of the liminal realm which fuels our need to hypostasise. I refer here not merely to a figure of speech, but to everything which can be considered to fall under the heading of 'the mannered': in other words, the whole realm of institutions, coded behaviour, ritual, role and function. All of this can be seen as a massive response to the loss of rapture, to the ways in which 'nature', whatever that might be, hides itself from us[18]: as a sequence of attempts to seal the boundary, to retain at least *something* inside the household and thus to deny the imaginal power of that impossible gallery in which all our cloudy trophies are hung (and where too we shall no doubt be hung some day). The liminal world thus provides both the *model* for our hypostasisations and also the *reason* for them as we attempt to escape the promise and threat of timelessness, of being 'in between'.

What is this 'in between', we might again ask – for there are evidently two very different possible answers. One would be that we are seeing here some kind of inverted image, some residual memory, of a perspective upon life itself as a time between birth and death. The other would be the reverse of this again, that the after-image, if it is such, is of the time between death and birth, the time spent on the Bardo plane, which has also been known by a variety of names to the ancient Egyptians and others.[19] Is there any real difference? Are these two between-nesses not themselves mirrors of one another, and is not the liminal realm precisely that realm within which the distinction ceases to operate, so that it is a realm neither of life nor of death – a limbo certainly, but imaged differently and without the intensity of population which makes even limbo a more comforting image?[20] For in the threshold world we are describing we cannot find any people. Rather, we can sense their traces all the time, smell their perfume, hear faintly their voices and their music, but they have always departed for another room.[21] Are they more lost than we? Again, is there any difference, for these lost things we are always trying to trace, to follow, are they not the already colonised parts of ourselves, the personalities inside us which have 'gone other', and which therefore exist in an undeniable and unfulfillable relationship to the ego-figured-as-hopeless-pursuer? We are back here crucially on the terrain of the body, for we are in a realm of soul and not of pure psyche, and we are reminded of how the body's own senses perceive the world; and we are reminded also of how for both psyche and body there is a sense of loss which accompanies these perceptions, these perspectives, loss of an interrelation which has never been, loss of a sense of where the past might have come from.

These are some of the things we clothe in words; some of the ways in which we try to uncover the secret, rediscover the rapture.

Erythron turns a corner (he is relieved that he still knows how to do so) into Cricklewood Lane, stumbles, and finds himself on hands and knees, staring into a puddle. Dark night, a bad taste in his mouth, bad wine or corroded metal, cheap perfume across his upper lip. There is a rip in the corner of his tabard, through which the night air passes. Eyes are looking up at him; the brows are knitted.

He looks up at the patch spreading on the lid. The treasure chest is huge, perfectly empty, except for the scroll lying in the corner, as if tossed there carelessly. He knows he must not touch it, lies back exhausted with his efforts to escape. In the patch, there are shapes. Like two eyes; although as he stares they fuse into each other.

He tried to peer closer. One embroidered cuff catches the surface of the water, and the image is shattered; but it reforms surprisingly quickly. The colours do not seem to reflect the obscured sky above him. Are the eyes his own? One seems to have acquired a slight nervous tremor.

As he stares up, the patch seems to change shape abruptly. As it does so, a pain such as he has never known twists instantaneously through his body. He senses his mouth opening in a scream which does not come. It feels as though a ripple has gone through his frame, casting all the organs subtly adrift. One eye contracts, winks.

In a corner of the puddle (do puddles have corners?), he senses rather than sees lettering. His eyes widen; he diverts the gaze, tried to glance sideways (you know he's trying to find the mainline; you know he couldn't hit it sideways). He reads despite himself – what other way is there? 'This is . . . '. Rapidly he turns and stares over his shoulder, upwards at the advertisements, the neon signs. 'Optika', 'McDonalds', a traffic light stuck permanently at red; permanently read.

It all goes black. Crazily, he wonders how come it was not black before. There is, however, a thin light which he can see only out of the corner of his eye. It comes from that other parallel corner where the unwanted scroll lies. It is a curious colour. As he tries to avoid watching it, he cannot help but be aware that it has changed to green.

Erythron remembers the evening, but if feels more as though it is the evening which is remembering him, as though the dance floor is having its own dream in which he is moved like a marionette, like an automaton, as though he is not in control of his own actions. Below the floor, he suspects, there is something further, some other cavern, perhaps some kind of place of profane burial; where the bodies are, where the body might be.

The memories which wing through him like black bats are not his own. He sees a hugely lighted, obscenely overloaded chandelier. His vision is swinging below it, as though he is in constant movement. Absurd words float through his mind. 'This is heaven; heaven is up here. This way. Yield at the Stop sign'.

He has to break away before he falls into this other place, which is, he seems to be saying to himself, the place where the words are, where they have been buried like scripts for an unknown burial service; or for a play with no audience, no actors, the monstrous empty triumph of the ego. He lifts himself onto his knees and, absurdly, falls forward.

One foot kicks the scroll. He cannot help it – it is a big chest, but still none too large for a fully grown minor god. As he does so the texture of the sides of the chest alters completely. They become suddenly transparent, and through them he sees a world of oily slidings and colourings. There is a sound of glass breaking. Inrush.

As Erythron lifts himself, he hears a thin cry, and whips round. It has come from inside himself, from some ventriloqual point from which sound should not come. It is a cry of abandonment. The traffic light has changed. The signs have been replaced by ones in a different language. He seems to walk off down the street as the puddle seeps away into the tarmac.

And as he drowns, he sees the lettering coming at him and wash-

**ing him from all sides. 'This is the secret at the bottom of the . . . '. Everything stops. For the moment. In the moment. He is caught, halfway. The sentence remains incomplete. The cry is unutterable.**

In rapture we lose ourselves; when in the throes of rapture we lose control. Rapture is projected on the fear of the loss of the object, on a sudden awareness of the gap into which things fall.[22] It is a projection of impotence, it convinces us of our strength. All this, of course, must be subjected to further interrogation in the mills of history and of cultural difference.

## It will Kill You, You Know

But of one more thing we can be clear: which is that the terms 'loss' and 'attachment' are very close, so close that we have taken them for psychological and theological opposites. And this is only correct: but we need also to realise that these are opposites which hold each other in thrall, that they are inseparable, that they are the very essence of each other, the hopeless attachment which is the very *manifestation* of loss, the will towards loss which is born of the terror of attachment, which can only be attachment to death, for there is nothing else to which to be attached, nothing else which we can comprehend with our own deathbound senses. We need also to contemplate in this archetypal scenario the binding by way of mutual projections which holds the world's hemispheres together, and our own binding by this difficult binary.[23]

All this is not to deny the exhilaration of loss, the sense of death, as Virginia Woolf put it, as also active, positive, exciting, the sailing close to the wind which is the substance of our explorations against the dark background and which is also the source of that other kind of 'projection' which we know mainly in the course of the psychoanalytic transference.

Transference, translation, the making over through the threshold. The liminal world. What textual moments hold us in this impasse, this terror? I think of Jean Rhys' *Good Morning, Midnight* (1939), and indeed the title summarises the plight, the beckoning, the welcoming, the promise of a new dawn which is simultaneously a move into the darkness.[24]

**In a room somewhere a girl sits, with a man, a man in a position of power over her. They talk; they have a great deal in common; they are getting along very well. Her hand strays to a button near the top of her blouse; she is going through the**

**motions of re-fastening it, although it is not unfastened; her fingers move higher, twitch the collar of her blouse closer together. They continue to talk. Erythron is amused.**

Two stories here, inseparable from one another. According to one story it is, perhaps, the beginning of a friendship, at least of a harmless acquaintance with some potential. *Also*: it is the story of a fear, of an unconscious which reaches out to another, which offers the other violence and destruction, invasion; and which inflects the other with a further fear which it barely knows in itself. The girl's unconscious gesture, the need for protection, the resistance to rape, the simultaneous attraction to display and secrecy, is no whit less powerful than her conscious appreciation of the conversation. Good morning. But at the same time: midnight. Twin apostrophes then, if you like: side by side, the light side by the dark side.

And so, still in a kind of parenthesis, to the ever-unavoidable *Heart of Darkness*, and to the appalling central fact of Marlow's envy; a fact which has been really little remarked upon under the regime of liberal/imperial criticism and is still less acceptable as we seek to shed our historico-centricities, but nevertheless the key to one of the discourses which the text speaks; and it speaks it, to my mind, independently of its many other voices. What it says is: Marlow envies Kurtz. I do not mean simply that he sees him as a great white powerful leader; indeed, I mean the opposite. Marlow knows from the beginning (must do, in the sense that he is retelling an already experienced tale) what Kurtz is; and *that* is what he envies, not his already destroyed myth; envies so much that he seeks to dismiss the power of the unconscious under some strange guise of spiritual non-fulfilment, tries to claim that it is Kurtz who signifies loss of being. One sort of midnight is certainly Kurtz's, and this does not need to be spelled out; but another sort belongs to Marlow, who wishes to stop time, to halt the world in its revolutions, to find some mythical idealised alternative to the cycles of vaunting and dissolution with which only we can be concerned while we are in mortality. No metaphysics for Marlow, as we know; no horror, but only naming; no deep muddy holes, only the matching up to the demands of the Intended, the intention.[25] Where lies Thanatos? Where lies (and who lies about) the filthy possibility of absorption to the point of rapture?

Marlow is the man to whom disclosure is all-important: not to excess, of course, for he is carrying with him on the river-steamer the whole freight of Western moderation and restraint, testing out, if you like, whether it would even be acceptable on a ferry to hell, but as basic truth, as therefore an assertion of the shallowness of psyche and the non-transformative power of thresholds, thresholds which Marlow will not really cross as he glides down his predestined route of stations, clinging on to his suitably reflective self for comfort. But Kurtz holds the secret of the crypt, which is the secret of rapture, the rapture of being the one and only bearer of the secret (unto death), the unbearable secret:[26] for that secret is that the secret will always remain secret, that it is not to be unbound, or fished up from the bottom of the river, or wrested from the grinning skull (Kurtz's skulls, which are a living-dead mockery of Marlow's stations of the cross, skull or crossbones would seem to be the choice), or brought back entire and whole from the liminal land: if you try to do that, it will of course provide you with an answer, for even an oracle has a reputation to keep up, but the answer will be precisely the same as the question, for it will be a *form of words*, and it will thus repeat, echo our own evasion of the fact that the secret lies elsewhere.[27] In bodily tissue, perhaps? The secret is that the secret is not for saying, except in the cults which practise death-names: Marlow knows this, knows that he has to – has to in order to preserve his own 'skin' – move the notion of the secret (which is also the heart) from inside to outside, from kernel to halo, but he can *understand* all this only as in a dream, only in the long shadows of recollection, only as a servitor of the dead Kurtz. The true enslavement is his, and it is an enslavement *gained*, fought for as a means of assuaging envy.

However: to return to Rhys and therefore necessarily to the perils of the demon drink, while continuing to be aware that we are still on the great river, still keeping in contact with the long polluted curve of colonisation. We can state the encapsulation, the pain (for they are the same thing) of *Good Morning, Midnight* very simply: what happens here is that a figure moves closer and closer to a pool (a well, a lip) and ends by disturbing its surface (we might say that the pail of self is spilt); when she thus passes to the other side she finds there waiting for her what she has feared, what has terrorised her for so long. We have to add, banal though it is, that the figure of the waiter (the haunter, the servitor) is herself, but what is truly awesome is Rhys' abrupt portrayal of the difference between these two selves, a portrayal which is *nowhere* spelled out; for it is the quintessence of all difference and yet it is, in one sense, totally imperceptible: it is the difference between self-as-subject and self-as-object, between a self which puts forward its own projects into the future and thus saves itself, always at great risk and with the utmost difficulty, from the passages of sickness and death, sickness unto death, which haunt it;[28] and a self which has ceased upon the midnight; in pain; but now finds this pain bleached as white as snow for all its differentiating projects – which are the spars on which we project ahead of ourselves notification of our internal multiplicity – have failed, fallen forward, lie upon the floor of shadows. The automaton, the addict, the alcoholic, the opium-eater has come into being, and is perceived instantly as on the one hand carrion, prey, as on the other the masculine molester of all our nightmares, the interfering animus which will always cut our projects down to size, will always be already there in the bedroom, the 'nasty man in the bathroom cupboard' who is death's joker, the carrier of his calling card which will brook no delay, the one who comes to say: 'Is it this trivial? Is this all you have ever managed to wish for?'

## Non-Addicts Anonymous

When we batter the dream into submission, as we feel we have to try to do, and enter into our armoured continuing quotidian self, we frequently get things in the wrong order; it is our purpose to commit such reordering, it is our purpose to lie. We who have anything to do with fiction, we fastidious and sepulchral readers, should know that. We suppose, with faint and false regret, that it is the construction of the self which entails the suppression of the dream; but really it is the necessity to suppress the dream, the need to relegate the hallucination, even when we know that it is precisely hallucination which is the mark of the human in the very depth of humanity's non-humanity,[29] which produces the self-as-armature, as-musculature; we might add, whatever our gender, as male. Here we are on the terrain of what we may describe as the godly hermaphrodites (and there will be more said about this in a later chapter), and they are, as always, playing with us: they have us at our mercy not only nightly, but also in the 'good morning'. We might, had we time, look at how hermaphrodites are treated in hospitals; but we are being rushed on by a wind from nowhere, by a set of unfounded recollections, by the need to remember a time when we were ourselves, which we of course have been, in no time at all.

But also, at an inevitably more trivial level, we might at least begin again to look afresh (it is never, always too late to begin again) at our dealings with text; and particularly at what might now emerge (from the shadows) as our hatred of textuality, of the ways in which it constantly reminds us of our most unreal, most unsatisfactorily hallucinated moments. We are filled full of the rhetoric of imaginative riches, and at one level we have to take these seriously because we are thus commanded by Hades, and he brooks no disobedience;[30] but at another, still deeper level we are filled with contempt, with private despisal for this residing in moments of leisure on the long uphill climb; we are all dead mountaineers. We do not say, yes, this text offers us a house in which we might reside (and I now speak of the 'we' of the West; in Chinese culture, at least, it seems to me that things are arranged differently because the curse of a supernatural bringing-to-consciousness of the things of the unconscious has not been laid so heavily[31]); we say instead that the text must always be an adjunct, an adjuvant, a way to learn, an unwilling servant of the moral law. To transpose this back into the discourse of the two crucial realms of experience: why should it not be the case that it is daily events themselves which are 'merely' a way to help us to learn how to really live, to live in our dreams, our hallucinations, our narcotised trances?

One answer is obvious; because, we say, to live in our dreams is to live to ourselves as individuals alone. But once again we are here the victims of a self-imposed inversion; for it is not that our *dreams* are individual but that what we most passionately want to do to them is to *make* them individual, to sever them from the deeper life, to hold our rapture to ourselves, whereas in fact they and they alone promise us a sense of community, of communion. All this, we might say, not without a certain sense of relief, we have lost; all this we have succeeded, at great cost but with tremendous determination, in losing. If we could remember that life is there to help us with our dreams, then we might not become so frenetic, so over-determining; but there is no way out that way (because that is the western way, the way of achievement, we might say, but then other ways might indeed be unrecountable – unless we are simply to say, and leave it at that: I am Dao – the way).

I have said various things so far in this book about the differences between East and West, and I am aware of their inadequacy. Yet they have a symbolic value, and I now want to put it like this. There is a world in which some statements make sense, and a world in which they do not. Let me put forward one such statement. It is this: the greatest value a person can achieve will be felt when, in the course of a travelling life, s/he dwells for many days in a city and then leaves; and it is as though s/he has not been there.[32]

What price such a 'value' in the West; or under any monotheistic system? What price such a thought to a psyche under the dominance of a notion of proselytisation? What would be the price that would be placed on a rapture which consists entirely in ignorance, in mutual forgetting? The gearing of the 'earthbound' life, the life of the strangely non-addicted, is to achievement, to *making a difference*; and this is where we can sense the circling back to a general critique (trivial it may seem, and be) of Western schools of literary criticism, and especially the infatuation with interpretation. For below all the bluff and bluster, all the rhetoric and wind, there is a commitment, almost a sacred devotion to making a difference, in so many, and such obvious, ways that I need not state them. Yet this is perhaps not the only path.

Deleuze and Guattari, it is true, do approach, if rather full of rhetoric and wind, another path when they talk about planes of consistency; yet even this takes thousands of plateaus of effort. When shall we be able to say that peace is a desirable end, and better still, a desirable and workable procedure? We might alternatively call it equanimity; either way, to contemplate such a goal would be to begin to offer a seal on the distances between the intellectual pride and self-distancing at the moment carried to its farthest extreme in criticism and philosophy and the sense of urgency which is perhaps all that currently remains of the residual humane (but also inseparably abhuman) impulse. All of this we blame on politicians; we do not reflect often on the poverty of their education. But this is perhaps (like everything else) a trivial aside; the question remains: how can we address, or be addressed by, rapture?

# 10

# Constructing a White Space

Here is one way, and I want in this chapter to focus largely on the Scottish/Cornish poet W. S. Graham, in respect of whom a tradition has interestingly emerged: he is seen as a poet dogged by bad luck. It was bad luck that his early work fell so heavily under the influence of Dylan Thomas; bad luck that his most considerable volume of poems was overshadowed in its year of publication by Philip Larkin; altogether bad luck that he should choose to write in a vein deeply counter to Movement norms. But there is – and here we already touch on Graham's own themes, which include rapture – a limit to the accidental; we cannot best get at the importance of this highly individual body of poetry by claiming to pare off its excesses, by treating the early volumes as mere training, or by – and this is where the conventional approach appears to have ended up – simply regarding Graham as better the less he writes.[1] Critically, he has been turned into a monument to linguistic suffering who, by his silent contortions, provides us with a signal reminder of the fate of the consciousness freed into a 'different' realm by his resistance to attachment. But Graham's poetry describes a specific trajectory. Over the course of seven slim volumes, we can see his writing moving, sometimes hesitantly and sometimes with exultation, in a state we might fairly, if over-resonantly, describe as ecstasy, from the full to the empty sign; from the plenitude of connotation to a more bounded space of denotation; from white heat over the 'white threshold', through the liminal space to the white degree zero.[2] From an inclusive consciousness which 'seems to have no circumference, and to merge with whatever he writes about',[3] Graham moves, and in moving moves *us*, towards the deconstruction of the subject, a measured and ironic dissection of himself and his reader; like the magician in Robert Coover's story, 'The Hat Act' (1969), he enrols his reader (our reader, dear reader, the constant reader) as his professional assistant and then proceeds to dismember him, although unlike the magician, the conjuror, the dealer in overt hallucination, he does so not in front of a large paying audience but in the pursuit of more private and, perhaps, vengeful satisfactions.[4] For Graham is not a comforting poet: over the years he demonstrated in his poetry an increasingly anxious pallor before the unlocked might of language, the inescapability of the danger of a rapturous engagement, and there can be little doubt that he meant to allay some of his unease by passing it on.

## Of Liquid Grandiosity

With hindsight, then, we can see the first four volumes – *Cage Without Grievance* (1942), *The Seven Journeys* (1944), *2ND Poems* (1945) and *The White Threshold* (1949) – as an initially rather cheerful encounter with the contents of Pandora's box, with the inner mysteries of the labyrinth. Graham here revels in poetry as if in a child's playroom: adjectives and propositions are profuse, words change their syntactic functions with deliberate sleight of hand, complex and repetitive forms are whirled before our eyes.

> I worship a skylift of Narnain blaeberry globed
> Priestlike sealed in a tensile sac in a nerve
> In the vein-geared bubble of vision.[5]

Meaning, for the early Graham, is liquid: sweet and dangerous, it is to be contained in poems as in a grapeskin, available to the 'tongue like a stamen' which can blindly share the verbal euphoria. Thus although many of the poems in *Cage Without Grievance* are syntactically strange, they are not loose but taut, crammed with too many connections, too many separate relations between words, complex, showy and pointless like, for example, the Brussels Atomium. And, clearly, Graham is aware of this: the imagery of poems like 'Over the Apparatus of the Spring is Drawn', 'As if in an Instant Parapets of Plants', 'There was when Morning Fell' is unified around a single concern, the relation between exuberance and architectonic structure. 'Over the apparatus of the Spring is drawn/A constructed festival of pulleys from sky': the world of these poems is riotous with foliage, but it is curiously stagey, full of arbours from *A Midsummer Night's Dream* in which at any moment part of the scenery might fall away to reveal a world of rather primitive machines, the machines which keep up the simulacrum of rapture. And this sense of the interpenetration of the free-flowing and the prearranged or determined is, in a shadowy way, related also to the poet's own identity, even at this early stage:

> After, when who I was
> Stands rarer and as fair as natural hawk
> My death will need no roof
> To trellis Spring's horizon from my head.

Laid out with bloodshot pennies on my mind
My dead discovery in evening corridors
Shall bring this crossbeamed sycamore of steel
To brace my crowded heart.[6]

Almost hidden within the contorted syntax, as within an over-lush forest, there lurks a fragile ego, incapable on its own of withstanding the sheer press of the outside, looking toward death, or at least the certainty sanctioned by the approach of death, as a crutch or breakwater. There is irony in the insertion of the word 'natural': where for Ted Hughes the association of the hawk with freedom, blood and cycle might be assumed, for Graham the very category of the natural is dubious:

I, no more real than evil in my roof
Speak at the bliss I pass I can endure
Crowding the glen my lintel marks,
Speak in this room this traffic builds
About my chair and table for my nature.
I feel the glass collide with light and day.[7]

Again, some of the difficulty is wilful, and the insistence on subjective relativism callow: what is interesting, however, and again it is a keynote of many of the early poems, is the 'collision'. For the world of these poems is not static and unified; it is one in which the ego has to try to shoulder itself a space, try to find standing-room in a world already crowded; but to 'build' (as we have seen before), to try to find coherent identity and personal location, is simultaneously to enter into conflict of kinds that one could not foretell in advance. The poetic implications are obvious: Graham is not a believer in the pure word, language is already unspeakably profuse, the stage (with its attendant though already vanished audience of the dead) is already set for an as yet undreamed-of play. The poet can only try to move the scenery about, as 'through all the suburbs children trundle cries'[8]; neither the woods of Arden nor the cries of poverty or boredom reveal anything of the underlying reality of the world.

This set of half-completed metaphors about the secret springs of action and control is strongly present in *2ND Poems*: 'Explanation of a Map' deals in the contrast between surface and deep structure, and 'His Companions Buried Him' offers us two neatly encapsulated images:

Always by beams of stars (and they disclose
India Africa China Asia then that furry queen)

I see Earth's operator within his glade
Gloved in the fox of his gigantic hour.
. . .
Always by beams of stars (and they disclose
That furry queen who saunters on night's boards)
I see Earth swing within its own explorer
Who dangles each star lighting up his map.[9]

In the first stanza, the secret knowledge is of the illusory quality of freedom: the dramas of history, even those which 'carry us away' with the greatest efficiency and joy, are staged for us by technicians, pilots, telephone operators, intelligence men (whatever they might be) crouched in the thickets. It is they who can fairly claim 'gigantic' purposes, destinies, not the rest of us for whom the 'furry queen', the residue of an unrecountable hallucination, is all we need to know. The last stanza narrows the focus still further: the planet itself is reduced to a plaything, the stars to coloured lights, and we, presumably, to the unnamed dying alluded to in the poem's title.

The lushness offered by the visible world and by language is thus illusory: and in this context it is hardly surprising that Graham should next choose, in *The White Threshold*, to try to renounce these overpowering illusions in favour of a grittier, harsher attempt to break through to bedrock. Calvin Bedient says of the early volumes that the poet 'has backed so far from common discourse that he makes us conscious less of what he sees than of his effort to escape convention'[10], but the poems *feel* more the products of a writer in a cave, looking out across an unnameable threshold. In (indeed) *The White Threshold*, Graham turns his back determinedly on his absorbing but cloudy trophies from the underworld, and moves out to the mountains and the sea. And this is accompanied by another change: for the explosive fullness of massive instantaneous signification he substitutes the more continuous pressure of time: short, effusive lyrics are replaced by lengthy, slender ballads and the terrifying choric structure exemplified in 'The White Threshold' itself:

Let me all ways from the deep heart
Drowned under behind my brow so ever
Stormed with other wandering, speak
Up famous fathoms well over strongly
The pacing whitehaired kingdoms of the sea.

I walk towards you and you may not walk away.

Always the welcome-roaring threshold
So ever bell worth my exile to
Speaks up to greet me into the hailing
Seabraes seabent with swimming crowds
All cast all mighty water dead away.

I rise up loving and you may not move away.[11]

## Great Crack

The ballads, 'The Children of Greenock', 'The Children of Lanarkshire', 'The Lost Other' spin out like fishing-lines; we become already aware that this rapture is of the sea, is signed by the sea, is lost in the sea.[12] In 'The Children of Lanarkshire' in particular it looks at times as though Graham is deliberately replacing linguistic density with an absent-minded casualness, as though he wishes to postpone climax as a way of avoiding the overriding problem of bringing together the scattered and dislocated self:

And under waters of a monstrous language
Its glow and game writes on the age
Here loud with beast and flying offices.
And April rising from the laws

Finds in my nosed and fostering pocket
Kingcup myrtle lintroot for my foot.
And a good black thorn for my head.
And a linty to sing at my deathbed.[13]

The last two lines are fragments of the past, repetitions in the echo chamber, not writable by the individual poet, and this is surely the point: Graham has now identified that hidden force which surreptitiously makes and remakes the world behind our backs (or when we leave the theatre after each night's tragedy) as language; he has realised that the discourse in terms of which he is trying to write has itself a 'monstrous' and material presence which presses heavily upon the poet, but which is itself only a petty survivor from the sea-wreckage which is all we shall bring back from the sunken trawler of our dreams.[14]

The movement into the open air, some would say, is not altogether successful: his rhythms, certainly, are liberated by this unclogging of the arteries, but a poem like 'The Search by a Town', which promisingly begins

'This step sails who an ocean crossed/and mountain climbed', nonetheless becomes redolent of Blake's doomed and circular 'Mental Traveller':

For ever as the seeker turns
His worshipping eyes on prophetic patterns
Of shape arising from all men
He changes through, he shall remain

Continually stripped and clothed again.
The morning loses sound and man.
The glow invents the worm. His saint
Invents his food and feeds his want.[15]

The self here moves together and apart in purposeless gyration, solving problems in the external world which have in fact arisen purely through its own structure. The sea, as we might expect, proves even more problematic: it allows Graham the minor triumphs of 'Shian Bay' and 'Gigha', but it also prompts the reflections at the end of the third of the 'Three Poems of Drowning':

Now in these seas, my task of the foam-holy voyages
Charted in a bead of blood, I work. I answer
Across the dark sea's raging bridges of exchange
Proclaiming my own fought drowning, as loud laid under.
All arriving seas drift me, at each heartbreak, home.[16]

From Pandora's box we move, it would seem inevitably, back to Chinese boxes (although not, at least visibly, to English hedges): the complex poise of the ending, whereby we are not certain whether homeward drift connotes safety or failure of communication, or whether we are intended to see the two as necessarily interwoven, is precisely the poem's problem: whether the very *achievement* of that 'complex poise' is not itself a betrayal, a refusal of communicative direction and a consequent submergence in the endless, pointless, rapturous flow of the sea. Might it be the case, Graham appears to be asking, that the density of language ends by stripping *us*, as subjects, of meaning?

Because *The White Threshold* marks out the beginnings of new formal directions for Graham, what tends to have been underestimated in it is its often successful deployment of the older mode of plenitude, notably in the 'Two Love Poems' and 'The Bright Midnight', in which the resonances from Dylan Thomas remain but are set against a different kind of voice, derived from Gerard Manley Hopkins and from the seventeenth century, almost as though, despairing at this time of finding his own voice amid the newly revealed labyrinth of language, Graham at least determined that he would test the Thomas fluidity against a poetry of sinew:

> Since there (spun into a sudden place to discover)
> We first lay down in the nightly body of the year,
> Fast wakened up new midnights from our bed,
> Moved off to other sweet opposites, I've bled
> My look along your heart, my thorns about your head.[17]

The voice is not in itself original, but hearing a dialogue between Donne and Thomas is nonetheless an adventure of language, another step out of the forest; but it is also, of course, a revelation of further depth within the sign, depth which can be interpreted as resonance or duplicity.

Graham's early works we might then see less as variously successful or unsuccessful isolated attempts than as the complicated and hesitant beginnings of a narrative which can be seen running through his texts. I am therefore less concerned with the quality of individual poems than with the directions of a large poetic enterprise, and with getting our bearings in Graham's world before coming to firm decisions on the identity of the objects within it. We can follow this hazy, winding, hallucinatory narrative through his three later books, *The Nightfishing* (1955), *Malcolm Mooney's Land* (1970) and *Implements in Their Places* (1977).

The structure of *The Nightfishing* is complex, and important because the volume as a whole represents an attempt to bring the overflowing world of experience into relation with meditation on the draining away of the ego: the sea gives, but the sea takes away. The central long poem, 'The Nightfishing' itself, contains a central section in which we are immersed in immediate experience, but this is framed between sections designed to cast doubt on the sufficiency of the unreflective empiricism which such description entails:

> The rigged ship in its walls of glass
> Still further forms its perfect seas
> Locked in its past transparencies.[18]

When Bedient says that 'few poems in the language resonate with so full and immediate a response to life',[19] this is certainly true of the central section: but that section is presented less for absorption than for criticism. Graham seems to see it as representing one, wished-for, way of achieving wholeness, of returning to the occluded possibility of the rapture; yet also as a way impossible or illicit in the real world, achievable only within the framing confines of text. Thus the relation between the fully described experience and the half-hearted and half-glimpsed relations to the outer which are permitted to us in everyday life remains an ironised one, and this is pointed up by the other poems in the volume, which by no means share the easy, complicit tone of the fishing description.

## The Ghost is Behind You

In the first section of 'The Nightfishing', the poet is 'called' by 'the quay night bell', but his response is ambiguous:

> I bent to the lamp. I cupped
> My hand to the glass chimney.
> Yet it was a stranger's breath
> From out of my mouth that
> Shed the light. I turned out
> Into the salt dark
> And turned my collar up.[20]

Ostensibly the narrator makes his way down to the herring-boat; but at the same time the poet embarks on his own descriptive voyage, thus assuring us that the poetic mode he is about to use is in no way to be seen as 'natural', but instead as an artificially constructed work which may gain the weight to stand firm against the erosions of memory and the intrinsically fragmentary nature of perception and reflection. And indeed there is a further more troubling level at which we are brought to doubt whether either of these journeys is happening in any realm other than that of dream, rapture, indeed addiction in, here, the sense of irrevocably repeated images:

> Far out faintly calls
> The continual sea.
> Now within the dead
> Of night and the dead
> Of all my life I go.
> I'm one ahead of them
> Turned in below.
>
> I'm borne, in their eyes,

Through the staring world.
The present opens its arms.[21]

Graham manages to find (and perhaps he also suggests that there is no alternative trajectory) new uses for ancient imagery: if the sea is dream, how can we find in it any source of purchase? Yet this is the point: for only at sea are we freed from the 'arrangements' that take place in secret, hidden, unseen glades, only by plunging into flux can we escape the crushing massiveness of linguistic preformation. And so, says Graham, 'we'll move off in this changing grace./The moon keels and the harbour oil/Looks at the sky through seven colours'.[22] What the last phrase establishes is that the escape which the sea represents is an escape from a particular kind of perceptual separateness which we have tried to address before (or at least I have): the central description is based, not on the poet looking at the sea, but on a dialectical relationship including an attempt, reminiscent of Hopkins or of John Keats' 'in-feel',[23] though also perhaps of a certain kind of 'pre-cyborg', to see and feel through the sea's blue senses: 'our bow heads home',

Into the running blackbacks soaring us loud
High up in open arms of the towering sea.
The steep bow heaves, hung on these words, towards
What words your lonely breath blows out to meet it.
It is the skilled keel itself knowing its own
Fathoms it further moves through, with us there
Kept in its common timbers, yet each of us
Unwound upon

By a lonely behaviour of the all common ocean.
I cried headlong from my dead.[24]

In *The White Threshold*, Graham perhaps approached an impasse: on the one hand he sensed the power of language, the sinewy yet frail strength of text to resist purposive shaping, while on the other he took on a certain responsibility for agency which writing entails, thus sharing language's historical guilt. Here we see him trying to shed that guilt, trying to enable the sea to write itself, humbling himself before the power of the word and allowing the waves of description to wash over him and submerge the resistant subject, resistant at all times to the overwhelming possibility of transport, as if hoping that he could by those means exhaust the enemy.

What is produced, however, is change in the poet, and particularly in his sense of (liminal) place:

> So this is the place. This
> Is the place fastened still with movement,
> Movement as calligraphic and formal as
> A music burned on copper.
>
> At this place
> The eye reads forward as the memory reads back.
> At this last word all words change.
> All words change in acknowledgement of the last.
> . . .
> Here is this place no more
> Certain through the steep streets
> And High Street form again and the sea
> Swing shut on hinges and the doors all open wide.[25]

But whether this change solves any problems remains ambiguous: in one way the poet's immersion has devalued other experience, enabled a meta-language but at the expense of the sense of home. Immersion in the Other has produced not reconciliation but exile; the haunted stillness of the port enshrines traces of the poet as he was before, progress is subverted into that very doomed attempt at recapture which we seem to encounter whenever we are in the presence of an attempt at the 'recount'.

> Home becomes this place,
> A bitter night, ill
> To labour at dead of.
> Within all the dead of
> All my life I hear
> My name spoken out
> On the break of the surf.
> I, in Time's grace,
> The grace of change, am
> Cast into memory.
> What a restless grace
> To trace stillness on.[26]

The attempt to use the sea as image and touchstone, to generate energy from its stored metaphoric power, has partly backfired: the sea now has added to its blind enraptured power a voice, whereas the fecundity suggested during the actual voyage dries up on the poet's tongue when he returns to land. The sea has caught the poet as the poet has caught herring; as he hauled them up to the surface in nets of words, attempted to impose precision and order, the sea fought back. 'Far out faintly calls/The mingling sea'[27], mingling in defiance of order and integration, calling out with the paradoxically chaotic voice of language itself, imprinted with the thousand other voices, those glancing blows which impede our direct vision of the world. Under these circumstances, the poet's fragile ego cannot survive; change, after all, is the sea's realm, and the human being cannot bear this much of it:

So I spoke and died.
So within the dead
Of night and the dead
Of all my life those
Words died and awoke.[28]

But the death of the ego is simultaneously a kind of non-human liberation, for the poet dies so that the word may have its own life. The thought is an alarming one: Graham implies that language feeds, vampire-like, on death, on what is irrevocably past, on the residue of the echo. Catching the herring (hearing) was, perhaps, a present act: but no matter how immanent, to write experience, to provide an account of the rapture of the immediate, however violent in itself, remains a distortion, a further savagery, and one within which the poet finally consumes his own substance, leaving phantom words hovering over the resultant double absence.

The 'Letters' and 'Ballads' meditate variously on this collection of themes, some less pessimistically than others. 'I am/Trusted on the language', begins 'Letter II', but this hope turns into an agonised pleading with the bonds of the past:

Take heed. Reply. Here
I am driven burning on
This loneliest element. Break
Break me out of this night,
This silence where you are not,
Nor any within earshot.
Break break me from this high
Helmet of idiocy.[29]

## Losing It

Implicit in many of the poems is, as we might by now expect, an inverted model of communication: when Graham utters words it is precisely the case that he *loses* them, they are carried away, and utterance thus demonstrates not communication but separation. Language has power, mostly for destruction, always for obfuscation; far from freeing us to make contact with others, it effectively bounds us, reminding us whenever we choose to collaborate with it that only by its permission can we prepare a meaning.

Cast in this gold
Wicklight this night within
This poem, we two go down
Roaring between the lines
To drown. Who hears? Who listens?[30]

The obverse side of the close involvement of the herring fishing scene is withdrawal and violence, reflected in the crudity of 'Baldy Bane':

Through the word and through the word,
And all is sad and done,
Who are you that these words
Make this fall upon?
Fair's fair, upon my word,
And that you shall admit,
Or I will blow your face in glass
And then I'll shatter it.
Lie over to me from the wall or else
Get up and clean the grate.[31]

If words cannot be used for communication, perhaps they can at least be effective weapons; but the impotently threatening figure of Baldy Bane, drunk and powerless, lost within an addiction which renders him a figure of ridicule and humiliation, the 'bane' of good sense and moderation, undercuts even this possibility and gestures towards the frozen wastes which we shall encounter in *Malcolm Mooney's Land*.

*Malcolm Mooney's Land* contains several significant minor successes: the elegy for Peter Lanyon, 'The Thermal Stair'; the love poem, 'I Leave This at Your Ear'; even the splendidly kinetic and colourful portrayal of a fruit machine in 'Press Button to Hold Desired Symbol', despite the dubious nature of the underlying set of puns. But these are suspended, as in aspic, in a world which has recognised the stasis of rapture and which is thus largely without outward-going vitality, a world which recognises only immobility as a possible posture of defiance. The coordinates for Graham's vision here are, on the one hand, the Antarctic scenery of the title poem and, on the other, the long series of circular or regressive linguistic (textual) meditations which run from 'The Beast in the Space', through 'The Dark Dialogues', to 'Approaches to How They Behave' and 'Clusters Travelling Out'. Those poems which escape the command of the debilitating inner are the rarities, sparks cast off by the hammer with which Graham seeks to pound a glimmer of truth out of the distortions of the world (Los's hammer, for Blake, the hammer which seeks to reconvert us to the real – by which Blake means imaginary – world even while he senses that in fact things are flying off – like sparks – in every uncontrollable direction); yet the paradoxical strength of these poems is that the poet is fully aware of the debility, is able to take the tonal thinness and, largely by use of his twisting, squirming short lines, stretch it beyond expectation. The effect is of a discourse virtually shorn of predictable sources of interest – compelling imagery, character formation, narrative – which nonetheless succeeds in exciting us by its absolute determination to attend to words in a self-reflexive way, no matter what the danger and no matter how attenuated the rapture invoked.

And there is danger in 'Malcolm Mooney's Land'; the landscape reminds us of those frozen wastes through which Frankenstein and his monster presumably still endlessly pursue each other, hoping against hope for an answer to Oedipus' little difficulty. The explorer who is the supposed author of the poem seems deeply uncertain of the line between the human and the 'monstrous' Other: 'Elizabeth/Was in my thoughts all morning and the boy', but later Elizabeth becomes the 'furry/Pelted queen' whom we have met before in the glades of illusion.[32] Out here in this uncertain land she is joined by a cast of other familiars, witches, animals, hallucinophagic spirits: the invisible fox who leaves 'prints/All round the tent and not a sound', the landlice, 'always my good bedfellows', the 'old sulphur bear/Sawing his log of sleep/Loud beneath the snow', the 'benign creature with the small ear-hole,/Submerger under silence'.[33] They and the explorer share, it is interesting to notice given our ongoing difficulties with hearing the case or the text, a world of minimal sound: the purpose of the journey (although whether journeys have purposes is a thought always under siege here, wherever here [or indeed 'hear'] might be) may be to isolate the smallest of all possible sonic units, freeze them, and see whether by these means some sense may be distilled and the endless echo of addiction finally (or at least temporarily) stilled.

Enough

Voices are with me here and more
The further I go. Yesterday
I heard the telephone ringing deep
Down in a blue crevasse.
I did not answer it and could
Hardly bear to pass.[34]

Or could it be that sound and illusion of meaning simply expand to fill up available space, that to cheat ourselves of normal human converse, however inadequate, is simply to allow the sounds of night and ice, the unending buzzing, to take over?

Out at the far-off edge I hear
Colliding voices, drifted, yes
To find me through the slowly opening leads.

Tomorrow I'll try the rafted ice.
Have I not been trying to use the obstacle
Of language well? It freezes round us all.[35]

At this point, language itself has become the tenor for a complex set of interlocked metaphors: language is the great obstacle to knowledge of reality, whether of the world or of others, yet it is also the only available site for activity, and as such it turns into a deadly trap, or rather, perhaps, it harbours within its own striations and folds a host of partially seen dangers. These dangers become brutally realised in 'The Beast in the Space', which is in some ways a more important key to the volume than 'Malcolm Mooney's Land' itself, in that it pares down the poem to an attempted description of its own creative process:

Shut up. Shut up. There's nobody here.
If you think you hear somebody knocking
On the other side of the words, pay
No attention. It will be only
The great creature that thumps its tail
On silence on the other side.[36]

The technical manipulators and string-pullers of *2ND Poems* represented an image of language as determined by rigid, para-human rules; the 'Great Beast' of *Malcolm Mooney's Land* shows us instead language, as we have seen it before, at the apparently willing service of the maliciously inarticulate and inexplicable.

The beast that lives on silence takes
Its bite out of either side.
It pads and sniffs between us. Now
It comes and laps my meaning up.
Call it over. Call it across
This curious necessary space.
Get off, you terrible inhabiter
Of silence. I'll not have it. Get
Away to whoever it is will have you.[37]

That which lies between the writer and his implicit audience, which we have thought for several chapters might be dead, or at least on the point of giving up the ghost, has come alive: stirred up finally by continual prodding, it has woken to guard that mysterious liminal area which we have explored but through which, nonetheless and despite our doubts, dear reader, communication has to flow. It can be, temporarily, tamed, but remains unreliable, random; because it is the spirit of language, it is a human creation, but because we have lost our grip on our own construction it is out of our control, the impossible soul of the abhuman. Our alienation, not only from words but from most aspects of our lives, emerges symbolically in 'The Lying Dear', where a poem which starts off by being about sex falls foul of the beast, and ends up catapulted back into no-man's land in an addictive dialectic:

Her breath
Flew out like smoke. Her beauty
Twisted into another
Beauty and we went down
Into the little village
Of a new language.[38]

Words act as an inverted Aladdin's Lamp, sucking in energy and meaning.

In 'Dear Who I Mean' (and this will not be the only time that this has been the only 'recourse' open to the attempt to recount the moment of hallucination, ecstasy) the only solution offered is silence:

When the word or the word's name
Flies out before us in winter

Beware of the cunning god
Slinking across the tense
Fields ready to pretend
To carry in spittled jaws
The crashed message, this letter
Between us. With two fingers
I give one whistle along
The frozen black sticks
To bring him to heel.[39]

The most primeval power of the gods is to name, and to confer life by naming; in Malcolm Mooney's land, symbolised by telegraph poles, symbols of distance isolated in the waste, the gods are always ready to take our proper names away.

 the quick brown pouncing god
Magnifies towards us.
He crunches it up like a bird.
And does not leave one word.[40]

If in the early poems Graham practised an excessive expansion of consciousness, dispersed his location and perspective, here he has come full circle: he is a tiny black dot in a white landscape, unable to move and all but robbed of speech. The sparse words come through gritted teeth; far from being 'trusted on the language', he appears to have scant hope that any of his words will still mean by the end of their impossibly difficult journey through the space occupied by the beast.

## Caught; Not Out

In 'The Constructed Space', there is a certain amount of fighting back, even if obviously doomed. If the boundary between sender and receiver is not rigid and immutable, if it contains pockets wherein words can be swallowed, might it not be possible to find our own space somewhere within that masterless realm? Such a space is suggested, not very hopefully, 'a public place/Achieved against subjective odds and then/Mainly an obstacle to what I mean', yet the brilliantly and intricately worked final stanza does after all allow some possibility, sanctioned perhaps by love, or perhaps by sheer shared effort:

I say this silence or, better, construct this space

So that somehow something may move across
The caught habits of language to you and me.
From where we are it is not us we see
And times are hastening yet, disguise is mortal.
The times continually disclose our home.
Here in the present tense disguise is mortal.
The trying times are hastening. Yet here I am
More truly now this abstract act become.[41]

The 'caught' habits of language are finely ambiguous: infected, but also trapped, language itself trapped by the beast but we as speakers trapped within it. Thus a complicated paradox: the ego needs first to shape a space for itself, in which something can be abstracted from the literal meaninglessness of the continuous present – a task which art has habitually set itself – yet this very space can become an inescapable enclosure. The phrase 'disguise is mortal' signifies the problem: it is a mysterious shape, emerging from the snowy mist, both ends lost in ambiguity, simultaneously affirming hope for demystification and the endlessness of illusion.

'The Constructed Space' remains the highpoint of hope in *Malcolm Mooney's Land*, the point at which Graham comes closest to emerging from 'white-out in this tent of a place'[42] and building (building, endlessly building) some kind of more stable shelter against the cold winds. 'The Dark Dialogues', 'Approaches to How They Behave', 'Clusters Travelling Out' represent a series of attempts to reach out and touch words, but they become increasingly tentative: the clusters end up travelling beyond reach, the attempt to give an account of how words behave remains an anthropological ruin. 'I always meant to only/Language swings away/Further before me'.[43] What is most painful in these meditations is the increasing weight of guilt; Graham becomes almost childishly tearful (like a drunk) before the accumulating evidence of his inadequacy, the failure of his attachment, and that guilt which he has previously tried to account for in terms of the pre-empting of language by history now starts to fall back onto his own shoulders.

Before I know it they are out
Afloat in the head which freezes them.
There I suppose I take the best
Away and leave the others arranged
Like floating bergs to sink a convoy.[44]

There are other brief moments of strenuous hope, and more of a wry humour, especially in epigrammatic form, presumably because a brief sally into monster country scars less badly than a lengthier engagement; but perhaps the overall tone is best summarised in an extract from 'Clusters Travelling Out':

> I am learning to speak here in a way
> Which may be useful afterwards.
> Slops in hand we shuffle together,
> Something to look forward to
> Behind the spyhole. Here in our concrete
> Soundbox we slide the jargon across
> The watching air, a lipless language
> Necessarily squashed from the side
> To make its point against the rules.
> It is our poetry such as it is.
>
> Are you receiving those clusters
> I send out travelling? Alas
> I have no way of knowing or
> If I am overheard here.
> Is that (It is.) not what I want?
>
> The slaughterhouse is next door.
> Destroy this. They are very strict.[45]

Graham has arrived in the 'prison-house of language', poetry is reduced to ephemeral communication in a concrete environment, as the slops are emptied (we have come across these dealings with the detritus of the cooking of soulstuff before); thus also language, in the service of Graham's still continuing and appallingly thorough attempt to find the one true, unpolluted, self-referential word which will destroy the beast and magically open the door it guards.[46]

It seems doubtful whether Graham would attribute the difficulty of communication to a historically specific cultural condition, the sparseness of his own words to the draining of meaning effected by, for instance, commercial debasements of language, but of course we remain permitted to investigate such attributions. On the whole, rather surprisingly, critics have not done so; they have preferred to see the changes in Graham's work as indications of a purely private syndrome, and the reviews which greeted *Implements in Their Places* when it appeared suggest a kind of almost morally blameworthy atrophy. 'In what . . . looks like a carefully anxious career, Mr Graham has slowly ground down his work until it is by now concentrated on a small handful of subjects essential to himself', wrote Douglas Dunn, and '*Implements in Their Places* is very much a book for private meditation, no matter how public the theme of communication might seem to be'[47]; but both claims undermine the 'careful' dialectic which Graham has built up. The grinding down is performed, not purely by the poet, but in the course of the continuous confrontation between the force of subjectivity and the weight of language, between rapture's intensities and the 'strata' through which they have to be inadequately transmitted; the 'private meditation' may itself be a forced mode, may be the only pocket of resistance left for the poet in a time when the telephone lines are down. The very first poem in the collection is called 'What is the Language Using Us for?', and is a defiant restatement of the earlier pressing themes, an indication that this volume is going to provide no easy escape from an encounter which is now taking on the dimensions of an epic wrestling match, a fight between the moral self and the heavyweight produced by all that circumvents the victory of what George W. Bush so disarmingly (yet, of course, fully armed) refers to as the 'good guys':

> What is the language using us for?
> I don't know. Have the words ever
> Made anything of you, near a kind
> Of truth you thought you were? Me
> Neither. The words like albatrosses
> Are only a doubtful touch towards
> My going and you lifting your hand
>
> To speak to illustrate an observed
> Catastrophe. What is the weather
> Using us for where we are ready
> With all our language lines aboard?
> The beginning wind slaps the canvas.
> Are you ready? Are you ready?[48]

The resources of Graham's imagery of rapture – the sea, the wind, the wastes – are reinvoked in the service of an introductory poem which introduces only its eventually non-existent self; even beginning is replaced by reflection on the possibility of beginning, bracketed and abstracted in an extreme phenomenological parenthesis according to which the 'thing-in-itself' left for pure apprehension is the pattering of life in language's wainscot, *before* the writer or user himself starts to interfere.

## Tooled Up

*Implements in Their Places* is a volume which broadens the site of poetry. Graham's perception of the materiality of language forces him to bring the whole question of the social relation between poet and reader into the arena, and in many of the poems this actually becomes the content. The subject matter of 'Untidy Dreadful Table' is the poet himself in the act of writing; the subject matter of 'Imagine a Forest', a poem written in the second person – singular – is the reader entrapped by the poem's coordinates and by his own prior experience of poetry – 'you go in a deep/Ballad on the border of a time/You have seemed to walk in before'.[49] It is not at all that Graham has found a way through the obstacles; it is more that, having observed the monsters which impede communication, he is now concerned to bring up more lights on the stage (you no doubt remember the stage, dear reader? do you remember the play?), to bring us and himself into greater proximity with the beast. But what happens is therefore a set of preparations: the meanings of the title of the volume are multiple, but one important one shows Graham arranging his tools for a further round in the struggle – whether or not that round will come.

> This morning I am ready if you are
> To speak. The early quick rains
> Of Spring are drenching the window-glass.
> Here in my words looking out
> I see your face speaking flying
> In a cloud wanting to say something.[50]

What Graham seems to have done with this singular discourse is to press through an almost adolescent subjectivism and come out on the other side; in order to squeeze through, he has had to – or perhaps more to the point, has determined to – jettison some of the paradigmatic resonance which poetry enables to flourish, as if that were baggage too heavy for the journey (through the Antarctic) and is left with the thinnest and most sinewy of syntagmatic chains, pared to the bone but as powerfully linked as steel hawser.

On the whole, the concentration on the poet's activity is less satisfying, perhaps because Graham has already tapped the vein, than the new attention to the implied reader. 'Language Ah Now You Have Me' makes us begin all over again (yet again) when we no longer feel we need to:

> Language ah now you have me. Night-time tongue,

Please speak for me between the social beasts
Which quick assail me. Here I am hiding in
The jungle of mistakes of communication.[51]

But 'Ten Shots of Mister Simpson', one of the most important poems in the volume, has power and grace in sinister combination. It seems initially a direct address to the reader:

Ah Mister Simpson shy spectator
This morning in our November,
Don't run away with the idea
You are you spectating me.

On the contrary from this hide
Under my black cloth I see
You through the lens close enough
For comfort.[52]

Graham's attitude has changed: from a worthy, but increasingly self-pitying, fear and guilt before language, he has moved into a posture of greater aggression – why should we be scared or humiliated by our own inability to recount? Here we are directly threatened by the awful complicity of 'our' November, 'close enough/For comfort'. Why, the poem appears to ask, should the poet be the only one terrorised by the beast? Or, to put it another way, why should we as readers not also be made to feel the threat of unnaming and the meaningless, the terror of loss which has, after all, been on the horizon from the very beginning? Graham then swings between Mister Simpson and a further reader:

Look at him standing sillily
For our sake and for the sake
Of preservation.[53]

'Preservation' sounds very like a jibe at Larkin's insistence on the possibility of a poetic conservation of real experience: the alternation between Simpson and a further Other ensures our discomfort, demonstrates that even the elitist complicity offered is itself fake, that language's duplicity does not always merely confound the poet, it can also provide the poet (the text, the withheld secret of the text, the lost rapture) with the means to confound us.

The growing irony in Graham's stance moves at times (as we might hope, and, under addictive circumstances, fairly anticipate) over the boundaries of literary gentility into sarcasm: at the end of 'Enter a Cloud' Graham, still the stage magician, emerges from behind the curtain to provide a fitting conclusion to his act:

> Thank you. And for your applause.
> It has been a pleasure. I
> Have never enjoyed speaking more.
> May I also thank the real ones
> Who have made this possible.
> First, the cloud itself. And now
> Gurnard's Head and Zennor
> Head. Also recognise
> How I have been helped
> By Jean and Madron's Albert
> Strick (He is a real man.)
> And good words like brambles,
> Bower, spiked, fox, anvil, teeling.[54]

At a stroke Graham's abrasive wit scythes through sterile problems of metaphysics and defines the text as fiction within self-conscious fiction. Earlier in his career, when asked about his influences, he mentioned only modernist writers, leaving out, to the consternation of some critics, more overt influences like Thomas and Hopkins[55]; whether or not this was a fair account of the poems to that date, his later work has certainly vindicated a similarity of attention to, say, Beckett, and *Implements in Their Places* demonstrates a constant dislocation of form and role which reminds us at several points of Beckett's 'prose'. In 'Johann Joachim Quantz's Five Lessons', a different but related comparison springs to mind: the frozen postures, the stylised speech, the chill intensity of estrangement are the devices of the 'new German cinema' of Rainer Werner Fassbinder and Werner Herzog:

> Karl, you are late. The traverse flute is not
> A study to take lightly. I am cold waiting.
> Put one piece of coal in the stove. This lesson
> Shall not be prolonged. Right. Stand in your place.
>
> Ready? Blow me a little ladder of sound
> From a good stance so that you feel the heavy
> Press of the floor coming up through you and
> Keeping your pitch and tone in character.[56]

Beckettian fragmentation and neo-Brechtian stylisation are, despite everything, not improbable refuges for the consciousness harried by a promise of repetition which will nevertheless not repeat, the potential for an eternity of dropped calls.

## We Move in Delusion as the Night . . .

Strangest among the poems are the three little horror stories, 'The Gobbled Child', 'The Lost Miss Conn', 'The Murdered Drinker', in which minor newspaper pieces are turned into Graham's distinctive five-lined non-rhyming ballad stanzas; but more significant is the long title sequence of seventy-four pieces, fragments or epigrams, beginning 'somewhere our belonging particles/Believe in us. If we could only find them'.[57] Rather than attempt the de-hallucination which would be involved in marshalling these pieces, Graham has preferred to leave them to stand on their shelves, racked like tools, implements or items in the *pharmakon* of delusion, available for use but not foregrounding their participation in the textual act. It is as though we have come (yet again, some readers would say; but then again, how many authors would freely declare that their narrative has ceased, or worse, has never reached the point at which it might begin?) to a place where movement has ended: since such movement might disturb the sulphur bear, release danger and destruction, Graham has become, temporarily, an armourer rather than a fighter: here, he says, are some weapons, some things or words (hanging on the wall of words) which you might find protective or preventative, but I am not about to dictate their use. And this confronts us with a choice: whether to believe, with Mister Simpson, that we can take up a passive stance to the problems outlined, or whether we are fatally embroiled in an active situation. Graham is ironic about our options, and also about our potential: in one poem he leaves us space to write in our own implement, adding after the empty lines:

> Do it with your pen.
> I will return in a moment
> To see what you have done.
> Try. Try. No offence meant.[58]

It is as though, having tried in poems like 'The Constructed Space' to persuade us of the possibility of activity by relatively non-directive means, he is now reverting to more old-fashioned pedagogy. His patience with his audience (does this remind us of something?) is fast running out, and we feel increasingly doubtful about the intention of his embraces:

> You will observe that not one
> Of those tree-trunks has our initials
> Carved on it or heart or arrow
> We could call ours. My dear, I think
> We have come in to the wrong wood.[59]

Further reflections are prompted: whose fault, for instance, is the mistake? And what might proceed to happen if this wood is, after all, not the nice safe one which we habitually think of as (woven) text, but a wood, a forest which is altogether more wild and deep?

In *Malcolm Mooney's Land*, Graham's emptying of the over-determined and overladen sign was almost completed; greater perfection might only have been possible, we might surmise (and schizos all over the world might agree if they were allowed to) at the level of white noise. *Implements in Their Places*, courageously assuming that at least *that* minimal communication reached its audience, proceeds to supplement it with a question: what are we going to do about the increasingly rapid evaporation of meaning? It is as if the magician has turned into the animal-trainer, in several different senses: he wishes to train us in the use of his implements, but at the same time he wants to show us the limits of our own freedom, the extent to which we rely on the writer, depend on strength to control language. Graham feels he has become the victim of the transference, that his strenuous negations have somehow made the reader dependent on him, and *Implements in Their Places* is a defining, and a partial (and impossible) shedding, of responsibility. There is no point, the book claims, in moving through the mazy thickets, the labyrinths of language unless we become able to do it by ourselves, without a helpful guide at our elbow. Thus the emptying of the sign turns into an emptying of role: where the romantic conception of the poet ends in apotheosis, Graham's conception of the writer (the beckoner) ends in absence and silence; 'rapt'.

# 11

# Towards a Homeopathic Erotics

And so to another question about rapture, secrecy and addiction. What is it that, as constant readers, we want Sylvia Plath to be? A virgin goddess, perhaps; a woman who has not had to do with men, and beside whom all men can appear only as brutes and liars. A blazer of trails, also, someone who has had a close encounter, and whose lamp might still light our way to particular shores, even if this seems counter-intuitive in view of the motif of suicide, the rapture of finality, the finality of rapture.

For on these shores, she still lingers; behind these wishes lies a further one, which is to keep Plath alive, to continue to treat her as our contemporary. So it is, of course, with those who die young, stay pretty; in a different rhetoric which is nonetheless applicable to the addict, 'age shall not wither them . . . '. It is as though also through Plath we seek a kind of inoculation: as though contact with this peculiarly sacred body, sacred in its taboo status, in its hiddenness, its secrecy and in its exposure, will grant us some boon which will go beyond the trammels of materiality and give us a glimpse, a *soupçon*, some tiny but infinitely precious amount of a substance which is, as it were, homeopathically related to death, and just this tincture will enable us to rest easier, to preach our gained wisdom and experience without having to be present ourselves on the fatal bank where alone that wisdom and experience can be validated.

Homeopathy, of course – the passion of similarity, if you like, although other readings are possible – is one of the great secrets of text. Administered in the right dosage, literature can cure us of most of our ailments, so the myth runs (and Deleuze's rhetoric of 'therapy' is emblematic here[1]), and so the poet/healers, emblematised for example in Keats and his curious relation to disease and pharmacology[2], have been pressed into service along this line of argument: the wound, the gap from which creativity flows or pours, the loss which we then seek to assuage, all these manifestations can be dealt with by the patient application of surrogate quasi-medical equivalents. This myth itself is soaked and steeped in rapture, in the notion of the suffering artist, of Dylan Thomas, Brendan Behan, Francis Bacon; a romantic myth, of course, but one with a longer mythic backdrop, at least as far back as Epicurus and his garden of pain – philosophy as a drug, thought as a staving off of death.

## Methadone; the Future Perfect

The inoculation with which we come face to face in our dealings with Plath is, however, more complicated, more many-sided, more undecidable: because of the nature of suicide. Suicide – of which many things may of course be said – has nonetheless intrinsically to do with excess and the imagination but in a doubled and undecidable way: it has to do with excess *of* imagination, with a flood of impressions of what the future might bring if time is indefinitely prolonged along a 'normal' axis; or at what distance the present might be standing from a sanely, drily apprehensible and rationally manageable life; or the ways in which the past might not desist from rising up against us; or a combination of these three temporally-located terrors. It has also to do, however, with an excess of the will to defeat imagination – for these very reasons, but also because of a lack of faith in imagination itself, and thus at least one route towards suicide lies through a denigration of creativity, through a willed destruction, such as the addict enacts, of the capacity to change. Suicide is the last and most extreme of uncreative acts, or perhaps we should say it is simply the most desperate, it is the end – the goal, the perfection and the closure – of alchemy, the final and fatal attempt to convert the dross and base metal of quotidian life into the blushing silver of rapture, memory and reputation: it is an attempt to strike out beyond the world through a movement within and a movement without time: 'without' in the sense of the purported possibility of removal to a higher sphere, 'within' in the sense of history, an attempt to move beyond the petty disregardings and slights of the present and find an ecstatic salvation beyond the grave. It can therefore also be seen as an attempt at a premature opening of the crypt, or the psychic reverse of premature burial; it is premature awakening, it is saying that the time spent underground is not too long but too short, it looks forward with an uncanny expectancy to a time when the record will be set straight, when the crypt will yield its secrets and one will be proved to have been what one had claimed to be all along . . . an attempt to bring the posthumous within the boundaries of life, to assert necrophilia among the perversions and thus among the sources of joy.[3]

My tenses, perhaps, are getting confused here,[4] and that is as it should be for suicide is an act which presupposes its own special tense, the *future perfect*, in all the senses of that phrase. In order to hypothesise the future perfect, it is necessary to call into being another, stranger tense, perhaps not fully representable micro-linguistically, which we may call the 'present absent'. It is this symbolic tense, this sign, this absenting of the accountable self, under which we are fated to read Sylvia Plath: she has indeed set up a 'cemetery guard', as Derrida puts it, she has encapsulated an

Althusserian 'life in mourning',[5] yet what she has also done is to conjoin this with a zest and an energy in her writing which continually involves us in further, unwelcome dialectics: the *jouissance*, the rapture is still there, it pokes out at us, vulgar and agog, between almost every line: it embarrasses us, like the presence of those who are committed to a trajectory of 'difference', and we do not know what to do with it.

But something must be done with it. One thing we can do with it is to refer it to a kind of childlikeness, a version of dependency, and in doing this we further reinforce the myth, for this virgin child that we now invent is precisely she-who-is-to-be-reborn, and is precisely also further valorised by the sense of life-promise with which she is now invested. Plath has not invented, or left us, a crypt: she has invented and left us a machine for the rapturous reproduction of death, one which continually implicates us regardless of the careful dealings we try to have with it. We try to choose our stance towards it carefully – biographical, diagnostic, mythic, aloof. It makes no difference, for the present absent is always already there, guarding the remains: we cannot approach without paying our dues, and once we have paid we are automatically sucked into the *topos* of the poetry, the paying customers who want only to see a head of flame-coloured hair rise from the dead, the 'peanut-crunching crowd' who have nowhere to go unless we confirm our role as the customers of death's brothel, clients of the spectacle which devalues the body beyond recall.[6] For one thing that lies behind this is a conniving, ironic hatred of the body (familiar by now in a general sense, but here specifically the female body, and thus the hatred passes down through the generations, especially in terms of the motif of the virgin birth: one thinks of the disastrous hymn line, 'Lo! He abhors not the Virgin's womb[7]): in these poems and in these our readings the body is martyred again and again while psyche winks and encourages us in our mock transcendences, which are the very image of the 'dry salvages', couplings without the pull and tremor of flesh on the bone, geometric consummations as the desire of the heroin addict dissolves, falls back on itself, loses sight of the other and loses also the power of action, sexual or otherwise.[8]

The body, we might say, is thus martyred – as it so frequently is in nursery rhymes, fairy stories, with their continually coded messages about the gap between the latent and the manifest; for whereas all narrative may be forced to exist on both of those levels, only in the materials specifically 'cooked up' for those between the ages of, say, six and twelve will the notion of latency itself become the topic and substance of narrative, the ramifications of hiding and hiddenness the very stuff from which the discourse is woven; and this combined with a *purpose* so shrill as almost to rise above the levels of normal hearing, which is that the body must be disavowed, its promptings stilled, and that in the name of this stilling, this calming of the prohibited possibilities of rapture during the period of psychological and biological latency, even the sacrifice of Struwwelpeter's fingers, an emblematic mutilation which is also the sign of the punishment to be meted out on those (like little Hans) who seek self-pleasure, the condemnation of the autoerotic for its evasion of the order of reproduction, is to be seen as but a minor part of an essential national curriculum.[9]

## Cauterise

I want to dwell at some length on – or perhaps within – a specific poem of Plath's, 'Nick and the Candlestick' (1962). 'Jack be nimble, Jack be quick/Jack jump over the candlestick', goes the originating text; but *not* Jack, Nick: Plath's son Nicholas, of course, but what other Nicks or nicks, namings or markings, are implied here? The jumping demon, the creature of fire who may nevertheless be terrified by fire: this might be an equal game, for there are many creatures of the night which can be scared away by the candlestick, yet there are others who seem to come specifically to crouch in the shadows that candles cast, who can never be made out with complete clarity but whose eyes, scarlet and green, flicker and blink in the light reflected precisely from this 'stranger' flame by whose means we seek to banish them. The candlestick is capable of conjuring its own 'Old Nick'.[10]

We can perhaps, or so we might hope, surmount some of these problems by a sense of measure. For the candle in its slow burnings has also historically been an instrument of measurement, it is said to bear a precise correlation to the passing of time, one which can be measured in a series of nicks down its side, mock attempts to halt the flow and seepage, but ones which also remind us that psyche can at least do something to measure if not to retard the passing unto death, unto the guttering of the candle, the moment when night irredeemably comes. Yet does rhyme, the transition from 'nick' to 'stick', really mark mastery or instead a submission to blind forces, forces beyond meaningful control? Do we pass on from this rhyming title with a sense of something clever having been achieved, or with a sense of the failure of cleverness before more massive pressures – the conundrum, again, of a life which ends in suicide, the act of supreme self-control which signifies its equivocal other, submission before the uncontrollable, an over-hasty lowering of the (cemetery) guard leaving us with a flood of unrealised intentions which are the very substance of hauntings, of the attempt to pretend that the dead continue to live at the centre of the household, that

Plath still cares about her reputation, that her divinity is not to be assailed and that a certain secrecy might be the guarantee that the 'public' will be kept out, that only we – or I, the singular reader – can achieve the necessary communion, can penetrate the secrets of the grave or of the life lived on a plane segregated from the normalcies of time and the moral law?

'The butcher, the baker, the candlestick-maker/Cast them out, knaves all three'; so goes the nursery rhyme. Knaves, presumably, because of their power: the bringers of sustenance and light, or rather, because the rhyme deals with a maker of candle-*sticks* and not of candles, those who handle these sources and bring them to us safely, free from the possibility of being burned by the nightly fires or contaminated by bad blood, seared by the rapture. This power can be readily feared and reviled, these were the *men*, we might say, who had society by the throat, their wares were non-negotiable. Simple Simon, to continue with the nursery rhymes, got nowhere with the pieman; nor could Old Mother Hubbard find any way of pleasing her all-consuming dog, or even of interpreting or foreseeing his wayward and (structurally) endless desires, the dog which so frequently represents that which pursues us, that which cannot be slaked, the dog as endless, the black dog, terminally 'dogged', whether the imagery attaches itself to addiction or to the depression which is, one can only presume in the absence of 'terminal evidence', the constant accompaniment to the presentiment of suicide.

I am a miner. The light burns blue.
Waxy stalactites
Drip and thicken, tears

The earthen womb
Exudes from its dead boredom.
Black bat airs

Wrap me, raggy shawls,
Cold homicides.
They weld to me like plums.[11]

And so the poem begins, although its roots, its origins, are lost in a history of childhood, in a re-enacted scenario of dependency. And so we are also called upon, again, to begin: by, for example, bifurcating this 'I', creating – as is the business of the poem – a forked animal. On one side, the 'I' is the unborn baby – 'the' and not 'an' unborn baby because of the directness of the address, the non-necessity of explanations, the consequent absolute assurance that this is the harbour of centrality, the giver of meaning, not one among many but the signifier, the exemplum of life. On the other, because it is a 'miner' and thus purposive, seeking to penetrate the secret (and thus to recover riches, precious metals, a substance at the bottom of the treasure chest with an overarching value and beauty), looking inwards for clues, endowed consequently with consciousness which is here being transferred from outside to inside; it is the maternal psyche, inhabiting in the realm of the imagination the insides of its own body, a messenger from higher levels which has moved down from its lofty station to explore those deeper, darker regions 'where the body will blacken and turn into coal'.[12] Thus the two halves of this forked beast are searching for each other (perhaps it is no accident that this is a major trope of Hughes's *Crow* sequence [1970][13]) but in doing so they adopt the imagery of the third, the real Other, bifurcation becomes triangulation, for miners are not babies, they are not for the most part mothers, they are adult males, the arbitrators and dominators of language, and thus paradoxically the only meeting point; the only meeting point especially if the other participants in this monodrama are in a state of ironic alienation, are in any case discoursing precisely about the separations within the supposedly integral organic body.

And thus in this potential meeting there is danger, poison in the air, although the blue of poison takes up its station also as the blue of the candle's heart; and thus the very centre of this projected meeting, of this coming together which already reverses the notion of birth as an outgoing, is poisoned, dangerous, freighted with death. We are in the wrong zone, we are the other side of curtain – perhaps watching from the wings as our own drama unfolds. Where the fertility of the underground ought to be, we come across only the chthonic depths, the stilled underworld.[14] The heart has been infected, perhaps cut out: rapture – passion and anima – remain forever elusive through these whispering halls, in this long-closed mine; *she* gives off no clues to her whereabouts, and has in any case been absent for ages – through the ages – as the stalactites 'drip and thicken', slowly flood down like the candle over the candlestick, obliterating all mark of distinction, engulfing whatever directional signs should be here to guide our explorings.

If these are tears (rather than 'tears' in its alternative pronunciation, in the sense of rips or rents in the fabric, which is also part of the discourse) then they are tears of fatigue; they mourn, but what they mourn is the forgetting of the mourning process and of the object of the mourning.[15] This 'earth' is the earth shovelled and shaken over the coffin, the earth which conceals even under the guise of memorialisation, not the earth from which all things spring; the 'dead boredom' promises no cyclical turning, nor renewal, but a ghostly repetition, 'all passion spent', a lack of affect which cannot be bothered even to expunge slangy hints ('dead bored') from a language which, despite its debasement, the debasement of the speaker for whom all things are fatally the same, otherwise seeks to operate in a different dimension. It may be that some of the tunnels of this superannuated mine are still open, but even they are in 'grave' danger of closure: some clotted, swelling substance, which is not grief although it pretends to be a simulacrum of grief, is flowing slowly along the passageways and will in the end block off all avenue of escape. Like a cold lava flow, perhaps; or like the sterility of pointless blood; or like the endlessly repetitive contents of the needle; like candle wax, of course; like all the nameless fluids of the interior of the body, which is resigned to non-acceptance and which cannot therefore be relied upon to put in its share of the effort to achieve a clean or felt birth.

## Poisoned Wombs and Dripping Wax

We are here face to face with a malignant heritage; it is the malice of revenge upon the body, which will respond to being imagined as the cave of death by *becoming* a cave of death filled with self-in(tro)jected venoms under a homeopathic guise, which will react to being referred to as poisoned by becoming poisoned and by poisoning that which falls within its borders. The body will not 'naturally' kill; but if it is to become a killer, then it will be of necessity a *tueur sans gages*, for such reasonings are not its province and in any case perhaps we are overly romantic is assuming the body's wish to survive at all cost, to resist damage.[16] These are also, obviously, the ragged hangings of the insulted womb; but what is withheld in this labyrinth (the labyrinth is with us all the time, on the edge of vision, confusing our sense of what is at the centre and what is at the margin) is the agency, the possibility of hovering between introjection and paranoia: as so frequently, we are here in the realm of the threshold, of the question of what happens, in this case, to the woman-when-she-writes, of the masculisation of the female writer such that this interiority becomes something to be spurned, a sign of inner weakness, an implantation of a demonised Hades at the source of life. These misinterpretations, these negative transformations of psyche as it takes up the pen, as it succumbs to the ubiquitous pressure of textuality and thereby becomes other than itself, it is these which weld to us like plums; not, of course, 'really' like plums, but *like* those things which to a superficial glance are *like* plums, like surely leaches, bloodsuckers, which grow fat like overfilled syringes on the poisoned blood, which mock well-being and good health and which cannot be prised apart from us; and like therefore, of course, the bloodsucking health and vitality of the foetus considered in its negative incarnation in these caves of death.

Old cave of calcium
Icicles, old echoer.
Even the newts are white,

Those holy Joes.
And the fish, the fish –
Christ! they are panes of ice,

A vice of knives,
A piranha
Religion, drinking

Its first communion out of my live toes.

From the blue of the Davey lamp and of the candle's heart, through the red of the appropriated blood of the plums/leaches, and now (with the ghost of Graham) into the white, the calcium/chalk, icicles, newts which have spent too long underground: there is nothing living here and yet this absence can itself be seen under certain circumstances as a monstrously friendly alternative, or at least it is to be hailed in friendly terms – 'old cave', 'old echoer'. If this is indeed alienation, then it also bears within itself the pallid seed of its own replacement; the harbinger of an intimate acquaintance with whatever it is the organic body has become, with the fossilised form which has arrived to replace and succeed the physical, the transmuted body of the addict.[17] The narrator here is one of the undeceived: not taken in by these vestments of purity, she can see the hypocrisy of nothingness yet she can also admire the hypocrites, admire the putting on of the semblance of death as a gesture which outweighs in its commitment the more febrile earthside emotions of the upper world.

Let us pause for a moment (as Graham does for an indefinitely extended moment of white-out) on whiteness. The white coverings of the newts are the white robes of friars, the whited sepulchre, the whiteness of a sexless avocation; their very pretence bears a deeper truth than, presumably, the other pretences which have produced this effect, the passions which have relentlessly produced this coming birth. So this world of the cold, the white and the sharp is violent and threatening, but it is also welcome: in its purity, in its hallucinatory rejection of the colourations of life, it revalidates the repulsiveness of the body, reaffirms the crucial disavowal, provides a vivid imagistic counterblast to a discredited discourse of the organic. The words here overflow in a kind of rapturous panic: 'Christ!' the expletive and Christ as symbol, as it all too frequently is, for torture of the body; 'panes' and 'pains', the coupled imagery of smashed glass and the blood flowing; 'vice' and 'vice', held fast by the double dilemma of sin and sinlessness – we need to ask which here is indeed the 'vice', the succumbing to sexual domination which is here assumed as the blameworthy origin of this inner death, or the religion of purity which forces us continually against the body, which has produced this evacuation of inner space, the endless deferral of this projected 'meeting' which will, perhaps, never now take place.

As the words overflow, so the syntax also breaks and bubbles – like wax. Singulars and plurals mix and confound; qualifiers shift and sway ('A piranha/Religion'); agents and those acted upon change their roles in a parody of the polymorphous, in a simulacrum of (textual) rapture. Perhaps we might see these as the dislocations attendant upon drowning, the fate of swimming about in the insides of oneself and finding the interior waters cold beyond recounting. Perhaps they are also, however, the graph of the sapped body, a revelation of imminent replacement, a myth about the birth of the Other inside the self which does not shirk the moment of *kenosis*, of emptying, the moment when the self becomes only a functional cover, a cover-story, for whatever is new and which will, by its own life, retrospectively invalidate the monologues which one has told – which one is indeed, even now, struggling to continue to tell – oneself in order to maintain balance in this flooding world of old caverns and tunnels; which is surely by now also recognisable as the cold, pathic realm of dream and addiction in which change does not really occur, only a series of incarnations which figure as revelations of that which can never be truly surprising.

> The candle
> Gulps and recovers its small altitude,
>
> Its yellows hearten.
> O love, how did you get here?
> O embryo
>
> Remembering, even in sleep,
> Your crossed position.

Where change does not really occur, perhaps, yet a realm also where further depths will not be consonant one with another, and where there is always the possibility of crossover from one personality to another, from one severed element of psyche to a different one, as happens here at the midpoint of the poem. Let us traverse this midpoint, inspect whatever lies beneath this threshold, by means initially of a recapitulation.

We can see the poem as negotiating a problem of scale, questions about proximity and distance, an opening of the solid shape of the body (a re-forming of the body's own openings) so that light can be seen between the 'shutters', the formation of a latticework which sets one perspective off against another so that a 'third' can appear through the shapings. The intimacy of connection figured by the umbilical cord (although if this has appeared within the imagery, it has been only as a thing of bits and pieces, to be strung, artificially, together from rags, shawls, plums which might be leaches) is drawn out to an impossible length by the fictions of unknowing and non-recognition. This is a struggle to the end, a sickness unto death; and then we change the perspective, we turn the chart, as it were, on its side; we feel the alternative intimacy of the old cave and the old echoer and we are looking at a picture reversed, where light is shadow and shadow springs into focus as the intimate, the proximate, the close, so that the bonding of living bodies recedes to a distance to be transited only by the artificial means of long-distance communications, symbolic communions, the mechanisms of *tele*. What is close now, what is pressing and friendly, what takes us by the arm as we too slap it on the back and hail it in the accents of an old sharing, is death; not the substance which tries to fill the space but the *space itself*, the vast and cheery camaraderie of emptiness.[18]

## Scar Tissue

And, of course, the ramifications are much greater than this. For if this massive shift in perspective (and it is here emblematised in the 'crossed position', the cross over the threshold which has a curious warding function) confronts us with the emotional solidity of emptiness and relegates this physical fullness of pregnancy to the immaterial distances, as the chart, the lattice, the slats of the shutter swing through ninety degrees, then we are left also with questions about the *new form of the 'non-existent material'* which will come to 'fill' the emptinesses which we now celebrate. Whose voice do we hear as we shout through the echoing halls, what replaces the forgotten baby now redistributed in fleshly abandon at the ends of the earth?[19] What, we might alternatively ask, responds as we inspect the secrets of the body seen as damaged beyond recall, sunk in a realm of risk where every gamble might result in death, where we have grown so habituated to death, where we have been living with the imminence of death for so long that only the tiniest of movements, the most minute of changes of dosage in a world where already the dosage of the homeopathic is minute, minutely measured, is possible?

Here it would seem that it is one voice, one voice only: our voice, our one and very own, dependent on our readerly gender *but* automatically and always 'discounted' through the recurrence of Echo, the impossibility of a new narration, of an authentic 'recount'. What is an 'echoer'? Is it a device which mechanically makes echoes; or a being who/which echoes our words; or a stimulus, an activator of echo? There is no set route through this triangular structure which, you will see, sets also in motion the further triangulation of machine, follower and leader; let us cast these second and third positions in terms of the mother and the foetus, and then in first position, as the device which makes echo, we shall find that we return to the problematic masculine we come across in any triangulation – and triangulation, of course, is also etymologically the process we use when we are trying to find out where we stand, whether our feet are on the ground; or alternatively under, we might say, the apparently stable earth. Or we might see in these three terms the endless evasions of the addict: are we speaking here of victimhood or of agency, of the unconquerable supremacy of the machine before we must inevitably succumb, or of a celebration of lack of will which is its own perverse course of power, of triumph, of escape from the most obvious and well-regarded means of social control?

And so: this voice which is the only possible source of stability, reliability, emerges also by this point in the poem as radically under-mined, the monologic myth is overturned and we are back in the labyrinth, in the 'gallery' among the contradictory and self-serving images of the Other, which is also the remains, the residue of our 'self' in 'other' guise.[20] The 'opening' between mother and foetus, the gaps in the ragged curtain or shawl, these are also the gradual forcing apart of that-which-had-been-at-one, the reopening of the birth experience of separation, which in the context of this *pre-birth* poem therefore doubles back on itself, birth as a memory of the birth which is to come, all births superimposed one upon another so that one cannot tell what is memory and what prefiguration, whether every birth is not a rebirth, every high potentially different even when some part of us knows that it will be exactly the same: 'is there only this?', the depressive (repeatedly) asks; is this all, is there nothing *more* with which to colour in our child's painting-book of expectation? Who in these caves could deny that to emerge from them – at all – is to be *reincarnated*, and thus that reincarnation, the well-publicised and well-advertised secret of Lady Lazarus, is a show-woman's trick, but crucially a trick whose final trickiness consists in the fact that it conceals from our startled gaze an eminently non-tricky truth, a truth which is *exactly identical with the trick itself* . . .

And so, to return to the poem at the point of its own reincarnation, its own 'recall', not entirely unreminiscent of the rebirth of Heathcliff which bears a similar relation to a descent to Hades, but differently 'crossed', as we might expect:[21] we return with a 'gulp', a gulp of air with which we try to recover all at once from the dislocations of the nightworld, to suck in something which will act as a homeopathic solution to the engulfment, the relegation to a land of unrecountable secrets. We gulp also with fear, with surprise, with anxiety, we try with a gulp (across the gulf) to get enough substance suddenly inside us to cope with the exigencies of the outer, the gulp is a symbol for reincorporation with all its attendant difficulties and the impossibility of reincorporation's final project, the engulfment of the world, the gulp which reveals only a gulf, the gulp which feeds on and in the gulf, the eminently solid substance of emptiness, and the yawning, the desire . . .

Yet the problem of scale is upon us and will not go away. Are we dealing here with the earth-shattering, the breaking apart of volcanic tunnels under the pressure of this chilly lava which is also the throbbing blood, or just with another birth, another baby, another mine on the brink of closure, another closure which will put an end to all that is . . . 'mine'? In other words, are we dealing here in the pomposities of 'altitude' or in the ironisation produced by 'small', by what 'measure', by what nicks in the candlestick shall we remember or reinvent a sense of (human) proportion when the human itself threatens to overwhelm (or to be overwhelmed by) the small candle of reason by which we have elected to measure its indefinitenesses? Well, by and only by the heart, comes one answer from the regime of hope which stands at the threshold of the poem (which guards against the sinking, against the subjugation which always menaces): by the heartening which stands over against the excavations of the centre, the mining which is also an 'un-*mine*-ing'; through this 'heartening' we may be able to put back something of what we have mined, reinvent some kind of 'infeel' to compensate for the never-ending trope of 'output' (for yes, although this is always discounted this *is* also, inevitably, a poem about that most unlikely of topics for Plath: mining. Quite aside from all the puns. Of course it is. And mining is inseparable from the risk of poison, from the risk of rock-fall or avalanche, from the terror of being buried alive, of finding oneself in a realm where no text can account for the omnipresence of hallucination – even when, as in the rare cases emblematised in Larkin's 'The Explosion' (1970), itself a decisively liminal poem in the poet's *oeuvre*, such hallucination can be represented as humane, benign).[22]

And to the presence of that continuing slight movement of the heart, guttering and potentially poisoned as it might be, there is no clear question to put, and therefore the address to love in the next line slips away necessarily from separation of persons – falling again into a triangular structure, an address to the god, an address to the foetus, an address to some darkened Other, perhaps even masculine, whose presence here can be recognised only as part of the globalisation, the rejection of separatenesses, represented in the heartening; although to allow its presence within this halo, this gentle flame, is not at all the same as to allow its naming: some things are still forbidden, still held in secret, some wounds must be permitted more time to heal, and that itself is a cover-story for the necessity of keeping the wound open, because otherwise . . . well, apart from many other things, Hephaestos, the wounded god, would cease to 'inspire' us, we would find we would have no breath, it would be terminally useless to gulp, the organs which might enable us to effect a return to the outside can no longer operate, we have already placed them at the service of a different goal, placed them at terminal risk.

## Pure White; the Needle

Anyway. In any way. In the next line this undecidable can be left lying around no longer and is fined down to the embryo, but only in order that a parallel set of undecidabilities can be placed within the embryo's purview, a catalogue of difficulties which, unfortunately, there is no space to plumb here, or perhaps anywhere; we all know how difficult it is to call a plumber, but at least we need to make mention again of the 'crossed position', the implication of the foetus through Christian imagery in the world of the 'holy Joes' so that in this newly emerging world where love has a place an expansion occurs which paradoxically but inevitably leads to the potential inclusion of that other side, of, for example, the shadow of the cross, of physical torture and the torture *of* the physical represented (as in addiction, as in the world of the needle, in the world where sharpness of penetration holds an uncanny equivalence to sharpness of perception even while the senses dull, grow disorganised, spread rhizomatically to the 'point' where nothing can be reduced to a singleness of text, where monolithic control is prevented at a certain irredeemable price) in the holy Joes, in the sharp-edged but spreading whiteness, in the removal of colour and vigour (according, at least, to Western imagery of the 'white') as love sows the seeds of its own demise or transformation. And so when we hear that 'The blood blooms clean/In you, ruby', we remember that every statement is itself crossed by an alternative statement which is not the less real because its incarnation is in secret, in the shadows; and therefore the possibility of polluted blood, of an unreflecting crystal, of an impure stone, is something also that is with us in this crossed, tangled, slatted world which is still gaping wide as we seek to bring its contours together into a single withheld and deferred image, deferred as the birth itself, deferred as the potential realignment, recapitulation of humanness might be under these circumstances where birth and death are struggling over their spoils, fighting for a bloody trophy.

And so, perhaps, even more determinately with the next sentence, 'The pain/You wake to is not yours': the negative indicates with precision what is hidden here at the first level, which is that this pain, the pain which is ineluctably linked to the rapture, is *nevertheless* not to be escaped. Yet at the next level down, the 'yours' comes into a different and more complex tension with the evacuated 'mine' (yes, we are here again in an evacuated mine where the canary has ceased to sing, where the 'yellows' have been forever occluded), for when we are dealing in these realms of disavowed jealousy, which is the mood pervading this part of the poem, then we discover to our consternation – or we choose not thus to discover, or on occasion it is discovered *in us* – that it is more than possible to be jealous of another's suffering, pain, and that the need to preserve our individuality, our singularity, might render it on occasion even necessary to deny that dark grace of the Other whereby a character, an undeniable co-inhabitant of the world, can be conjured into ineradicable existence exactly by her/his pain; and what, then, if we feel the beginnings of this pain that will guarantee the existence of the Other and thus produce pressure on our own living space, our own room to be, what if we feel this pain beginning *inside ourself* and yet simultaneously *inside the Other*, who is also inside ourself . . . whose pain is this anyway (and I mean the birth process here as an image for the housing of the multiplicities of psyche; or of anima[23])? By what homeopathic process might we now banish the inquietude, the simmering 'memory' of this 'cross' between the generations which does not, quite, seem to be assuaged by the friendliness of our commerce with old death, the menacing (to others) big brother by whose assistance – or simply by the force of whose silent threat – we had hoped we could bring the rest of the world to heel as easily as, many years ago, we seem to recall that we could in the school playground? Of this pain, and of the desire for pain, there is much more to be said; I shall try to readdress it later, although the approach to pain, the incorporation of pain, is always uncertain, problematic. What if we entertain this hypothesis: that those who most fully deserve our sympathy are precisely those whose desires cannot be achieved except through the infliction of pain, what if the sadist is the person (if that is a proper or recognisable term to use – a person, in all his/her/its singularity and denial of singularity) who represents most clearly, most starkly, the status of the outlaw, the irreducibility of personal desire to social framework, the occlusion of the Other? Well, we may well wish to 'entertain' this hypothesis, to give it houseroom, to exercise some hospitality; but we shall end up on the wrong side of the law: incarcerated, imprisoned, abandoned in the course of our rapture to the forces which (sadistically, violently) seek to repress this finally inadmissible freedom. Perhaps none of us readers is truly a 'consenting adult'.

However. If you can't beat them, join them: and so, 'Love, love,/I have hung our cave with roses,/With soft rugs – /The last of Victoriana', and here in this haven of domesticity, in this rebuilding of the household, we will find our refuge, our shelter, our recourse from the debt, from *Schuld*,[24] and we will hug each other close, will we not, and not even suffocate, although we shall know – or at least the 'I' shall know – that in doing this we are living out a myth, the underside of which we have always already known and which may yet still rise again to 'engulf' us. For this is after all the *last* of Victoriana; and if it is at one level Victoriana's trade, its great and signifying skill ('last'), then it is also a refuge at the end of the world; whither I have come, such is my love, or so *you* must believe, to re-gather you from my previous scattering of your identity, to bring you back together, baby, and back to me, as a comfort closer than death; or *as* the problematic incarnation of death, as figure for the ('Victorian') repression which looms larger in its fascination than the very thing it purports to quell, and thus brings into the very home, brings into a soft chair by the very hearth, precisely the array of rapturous feelings and fears it wished to leave shivering on the porch outside.

## Why do Ghosts Limp?

But this, again, is undecidable. All will be saved, all shall be well, and this consummation, even with the ironically implicit secondary knowledge of all the primary knowledge which is hidden away behind these soft rugs which have been woven with care from the remains of certain raggy shawls whose existence we prefer now to forget – this consummation will be such that we shall neither see nor hear the stars plummeting, although we may at some other level appreciate and sigh over the parallels between this evidence of their precariousness and the precariousness of our own psychic plight, still and always on the threshold of the world, never quite moving into it, covering the walls of the caves with the soft and the already inscribed.

> Let the mercuric
> Atoms that cripple drip
> Into the terrible well

We can best read these lines in terms of an oscillation between the decidable and the undecidable, evidenced in features of form; and we can begin from the first of them, 'Let the mercuric', and allow this *line* (a line of beauty, perhaps[25]) itself to expand and yield meaning. A set of tricks informed and circumscribed by a double doubt: the first doubt summarised in the ambiguities of the term 'let', allow or prevent, the second always present when we are speaking of the mercuric, the mercurial, the hermetic, that which flows and yet stays the same, that which proffers beauty and also offers poison, that which promotes communication and always keeps secrets – we are here in the realm of Hermes, which is inevitable, for this is the world of the trickster, although probably what the narrator is up to here is a self-trickery which is redoubled as we, the readers, try to make up our mind about our status as co-conspirator or as butt of these tricks.[26] Are we to prevent all from sliding away into the realm of Hermes, where nothing will ever be the same again; or are we to allow this to occur, to connive at this slippage, on the grounds that even this is better than a cold-turkey confrontation with the coming night?

And is one of the principal illusions to which we are here being subjected by a 'master' conjuror the illusion that we have any choice in this matter anyway? There are no real bodies and no real psyches, only atoms: this has been the burden and heresy of atomism down the ages.[27] The very thought of atoms is crippling; alternatively, in order to cripple (others or ourselves) we may need to think of atoms, to think of the body or of the Other *as* 'mere atoms'; and then we might find that many of these knots of pain go away, are decently covered over and we can no longer hear the drip into the well, the 'well of death' into which the misplaced canal may lead us but from which we can perhaps be saved by the operations of the heart and by the full investiture of another with human dignity, even if this involves making over all body to the Other and abandoning liquidity for the 'one/Solid'; and there is of course a financial metaphor here again which follows from the cave as a conversion into a kind of tax shelter, so that if we leave ourselves with no personal reserves, if we have always already avoided paying death duties by passing on our wealth (and avoiding even salvaging the body), such as it is, to our child, then we cannot be in debt and we have in any case no 'liquid' capital left with which to repay if we are summoned. After that, there may be continuing life, but it is elsewhere; for us, there is only bankruptcy, the rapture of total evasion; and/or suicide.

> You are the one
> Solid the spaces lean on, envious.
> You are the baby in the barn.

Much could be said, and much has been said, about this ending, with its intensification of Christian imagery and the confusing blankness/bleakness which cohabits in the final line with a rhetorical certainty. I want to use it only to return, as I promised above, to the question of the threshold and what secrets lie buried beneath it. It is in passing interesting to note that the *OED*, as well as sharing (or originating?) the customary uncertainty about the derivation of the second component of the word 'threshold' and thus of the word itself, also deems the number of times on which it has been used mistakenly to mean not threshold but lintel, not that *over* which we putatively pass but that *under* which, sufficient to warrant a separate entry; and so we are here also perhaps in the presence of the lintel, the great beam over the barn-door on which the spaces lean, the taker of weight which is also that which comes down on our head if the door-gods have not been placated and ruins family, household, dynasty.

What lies beneath the threshold, what signifies the real-because-hidden entrance to the barn, what underpins, underlies, underscores our attempts at linear progression from outer to inner? Many things. A hank of hair, fetishised or totemised, signifying a bar on the approach route, a family not to be admitted. A relic of the grandfather, which sanctifies the approach, which ensures the transformation of all who pass over it but also ensures that they are never the same again. A double activity of 'letting', a prevention and a permission, thus a separation, like the signs daubed on the lintels of the Jews, a salvation predicated against the dark background of slaughter. But outward signs can so easily be confused, repainted, substituted; to dig up the threshold is altogether a more difficult and serious matter and might even result in an accident involving a fallen lintel . . .

So what gets buried under the threshold is the past rapture, and here we are between the realms of psychopathology and homeopathy; which is a disturbing and uncomfortable place to be, for it is not clear whether these particular burials have to do with the continuation of memory (stasis, no change, the cold pathic) or with the will to forget (curing, healing, inoculation); and we sense that this will never become clear. Under the stone lie the lusts, greeds, angers towards which we have to rearrange our feelings each time we pass them; and how can we avoid passing and repassing them when they lie beneath our front door, when they bar our approach road, when they mark our passage as securely as any other *rite de passage* does on our journey through life, guard us as securely and ambiguously as Cerberus or any other cemetery guard – and perhaps we can now see a little more clearly who this cemetery guard really is. No, he is not Cerberus, he lacks the mythic backdrop, and the graveyard he guards really leads almost nowhere, out here in the chill and the rain; neither is it a *she*, the nanny or the governess, although their occupancy of the midway position (Nelly

Dean, or the 'guardian' of Miles and Flora) frequently gives them too much, and the wrong kind of, acquaintance with the family burial plot for their own good. Instead he is the zombie we have come across before, the addict, pure body without soul, the derepression of all the repressed within his care, and he is thus quite alien, quite foreign, beyond mania and melancholy alike, the soul of *différance* or the *différance* of soul, quite mad and dangerous out there in the open night; as are our own late-night and sleeping memories when those ancient passions seep up from under the threshold and remind us how shaky are the patterns with which we surround our lives, how thin the borderline between the Vedic and Tantric gods, how important it seems to have been to so many peoples that there be door-gods *but also* that those door-gods be not strong, that they permit some movement, some interplay, some transgression between within and without, some transgression (perhaps in the end based on gender) – but how much is enough? How often will (the boy) Nick jump over the candlestick and when will he be burned? How many times can we perform the trick, take on the unequal contest with our own passions and addictions and survive? Where will the (female/sacrificial) suicide be buried except under the threshold, at the undecidable point at which all human life is opened and closed and displays the ineradicable possibility of its own abhuman opposite?

# 12

# Rapt

We are beckoned towards an ending; a thought which is inexplicable, even if devoutly to be wished. In the course of his discussion of the later work of Hans-Georg Gadamer, Timothy Clark writes that 'there are places where understanding stops – something is reached which we can neither unthink nor explicate further. The English term "the undefinable" seems a good basis on which to think about what Gadamer is discussing here'.[1] The German word alluded to is *das Unvordenkliche*, but I would suggest that 'the unnameable' might be at least as useful a translation (if such a translation were at all possible), reaching out as it does to two other textual fields. One is that of Beckett, most aptly summarised for this purpose in the title of his 'novel' *The Unnamable* (1958) (*L'Innommable* [1952]); the other is Lovecraft's frequent textual play on the notion of the unnameable, the nameless.[2]

And these textual fields perhaps tell us something about that which resists naming, that which approaches yet always, in the recounting, falls short of the state of rapture. For the first field, the field of Beckett's prose and drama, is characterised throughout by a falling short and also by a brevity, a clippedness, a sense of the ever-present possibility that the ocean of language might dry up altogether, be reduced to an inexplicable and withered tree. Here there is the threat of an end to fecundity, a relapse into a discourse which provides continuing evidence of how little can be brought back, of how great is the size of the gap or wound which intervenes between language and its object; in Beckett's textual world, everything is held in unwilling, unwitting secrecy, is reduced to the shards and fragments which we might rescue from the dustbin or from the isolated mouth, talking, crying, screaming in the wilderness.[3]

## How Many Junkies does it to take to . . . ?

Lovecraft's world moves us to the opposite extreme, to a mad and maddening plethora of experience which presses in on us with the utmost density and yet which still resists explanation, refers us only further and further back into a set of myths of origin which do, in the end, nothing to reassure us as to the sense of the world, its credibility. In Lovecraft's world there are always other, older gods, secreted away behind the curtain, hidden in the stones of the building of the present; names abound, but they only refer us back to other names, other attempted namings. Lovecraft's virulent racism can be seen, from one angle (and to attempt to understand is not to forgive) as a desperate sequence of attempts to secure a 'home base', a space which can be protected from intrusion; yet the intrusions continue, for without those intrusions there can, it would appear, be no narrative. Nothing can happen unless things happen.

Yet rapture is not a happening, it is not an 'event'; rather, it is the horizon, the ground on which events take place, while it is also the hidden fullness, plenitude which is continually hidden from us as events take place; it is the sense that every event is in fact an interruption, a deflection from something which might be perceived as more pure, even, one might say, more innocent than the experience with which we are constantly surrounded. Rapture is always of the present; yet rapture is also always of the past or of the future, never of the present. To refer to Clark again, in the context of Gadamer's mention of 'the whole radiation and the multiplicity of directions contained in its power to mean' he comments that 'since a text's readability is not confined to the time of its inscription, this "radiation" of connotations and inflections of possible contexts is continuously shifting: it projects itself into a future that always transcends the time of any one reading'.[4]

The text, we might say while shifting the metaphor just a little, is radioactive: it gives off an energy which warms, even heats, while at the same threatening us (constant readers) with a contamination, with a being in the presence of a force that is all the while irreducibly colouring our outlook, changing the contours of the world we confront. And this, of course, is why the provision of the inadequate, even poisonous reading matter to be found, for example, in the tabloid press is a problem not only of taste: it is also a problem of radiation, of sealing its readers into an airtight compartment where there is no possibility of refreshment, where, as in an echo chamber, contaminated particles are in a continuous process of collision and the reader is reduced to a mere node of the 'doped' fare on offer. In place of a 'radiation' which might effect some contact between inner and outer, the outer is totally removed: the possibility of rapture is taken away and replaced by the simulacra of desire, the violent reduction of words to a series of gestures which invite only Pavlovian acceptance or rejection.

But it is insufficient to mount against this flood the dyke represented in mere narrative: narrative as such is – as we have seen when we last visited Bali – itself a deflection, protective up to a point but ultimately without meaning; it is the wide projection of event, which obscures the ground on which event is built. We are, as readers in the early twenty-first century, in the constant presence of narrative: stories abound, through all the media, on all the billboards, flowing through the ether, reproducing themselves virally through technology.[5] There is, of course, a richness to this, albeit a confusing one: but that richness is not in itself rapturous, although it may gesture towards the delayed possibility of rapture, of total immersion in 'another scene', in a realm where words dissolve, move behind the curtain, where language demonstrates its full force of gesturing towards something other than itself. Rapture, in one recounted form, consists in the expansion of the word, in the striking of the 'human chord' in the limitless exploration (through the labyrinth) of that which resists exploration, that which, on the surface, is composed only of letters, signs, hieroglyphs, the heresy of atomism 'writ large'.

And so, a final attempt to explore this rapture: and it can only be done through attending to voices, and in this case a series of voices which have 'come back' to us, which are always in a state of 're-turn', and perhaps attendant on this an attempt to set them in motion, to encourage a dialogue of the dead (for it is only thus, so the myths tell us repeatedly – for, of course, myth is the soul of repetition, the repetition of soul – that wisdom can be attained, old-fashioned thought though that might seem to be). And the first voice at the end, as it were, is (necessarily) that of De Quincey, who knows, so he tells us, something about the rapture. What does he know (what can he know, what can we know he knows)? Well, one thing he appears to know, or at least suggest, is this:

> But now, at last, came over me, from the mere excess of bodily suffering and mental disappointments, a frantic and rapturous re-agency. In the United States the case is well known, and many times has been described by travellers, of that furious instinct which, under a secret call for saline variations of diet, drives all the tribes of buffaloes for thousands of miles to the common centre of the 'Salt-licks'. Under such a compulsion does the locust, under such a compulsion does the leeming [*sic*], traverse its mysterious path. They are deaf to danger, deaf to the cry of battle, deaf to the trumpets of death. Let the sea cross their path, let armies with artillery bar the road, even these terrific powers can arrest only by destroying; and the most frightful abysses, up to the very last menace of engulfment, up to the very instant of absorption, have no power to alter or retard the line of their inexorable advance.[6]

'Such an instinct it was, such a rapturous command', our friend the opium-eater continues, that it 'suddenly transfigured my whole being'. There is, of course, what might be considered to be a certain bathos about this particular instance of rapture, for it transpires that the 'adamantine resolution' which results from this experience is to 'elope from Manchester'; however, this if anything only strengthens the force of the discourse, and it touches at many points on what I have been trying to depict in rapture. First and perhaps most obvious, there is the interesting comparison of this overwhelming drive, this source of transfiguration, with the realm of the animal: of the buffalo, the locust, the lemming.[7] There is that in this experience which undercuts the human, which suggests a level or stratum of being where the writ of humanity, and by extension of the moral law, fails to run.

## Gulf States

We are here in a realm instead of 'compulsion', 'engulfment', 'absorption'; these may be literal dangers to be encountered on the route out of Manchester, but here they figure – or rather, prefigure – the relapse which rapture brings into the condition of the addict. The customary measurements, the 'risk assessments' according to which we order our rational life, have ceased to count, have demanded, as it were, a recount: even the possibility – indeed the likelihood – of rushing over the edge of the abyss does nothing to temper the onrush of conviction. Indeed, it would be impossible to read this passage without sensing that something more is in play, something we have come across before: namely, the *desire* to participate in this onrush to abandon the self to the wild winds in the name of participating in some greater whole – the herd, the swarm, the wider group – which is seen as taking over responsibility.

What we might also notice is that, counter-intuitively, it is not opium or any other drug which in any sense 'causes' this moment of rapture; that will all come later. Rather, it is that the text is suffused, soaked, drenched in the rhetoric of the unstoppable. Words are used, of course, to recount this experience: but the experience itself points beyond words, to a realm where words point towards a transfiguration, a transmigration. Here the writ of words does not run; it is the buffaloes who run, obedient to a command which must be enacted even if – and specifically because – it is *not understood*. It is *onto* this scenario, this already painted backdrop, that opium and its many derivatives, medical and psychological, will make their appearance: the scene has already been prepared, the die is cast – even if, at the same time, the cast (of thousands in this nightly theatre) is running mortal risk, the risk of dying.

Yet at the same time, thinking of the rhetorics of Deleuze and of Paul Virilio, we can see here the curious affiliation between this portrait of a soul come unhinged and the mechanisms symbolised by the apparatus of war, of the military machine.[8] Buffaloes and artillery? Locusts and the 'trumpets of death'? What is all this to Hecuba, or Hecuba to TDeQ? In this transfigured world, proportion and appropriateness are gone, plunged into the abyss ahead of the animals, seized away by the rapture, wrapped in a mystery which can only seek the vaguest but at the same time the most startling analogies, ones which challenge our sense of causality, which threaten us with a monstrous mismatch between apparent cause and apparent effect.

Ah, but perhaps I make too much of this; perhaps there is a certain strain in treating this version of 'loving you and leaving Tennessee' as a full account of rapture.[9] Yet maybe this is as it should be: for no 'full account' of rapture, we know by now, is possible. What we have instead are moments, moments of the inappropriate, moments within which can be conjured up the 'most frightful abysses', abysses within which the nature and continuity of narrative will dissolve, as might also our sense of what is serious and what is playful. 'Whence came the indignation', Thomas the future junkie, the past junkie of the future, asks: 'and the hope'?[10] Whence indeed. Not, he intimates, from 'what/We think truest, or most want to do', but from something else which Larkin refers to, in a constantly present aporia, as 'habit':[11] to be non-habitual, to seek an absence of habituation, or even habitat, this is, it would appear, our habit, the habit in which we are clothed, the habit we pick up on the road, the habit which stays with us for life and which turns clothing into a shroud.

And who could be a better commentator on the habits of a lifetime, on what they conceal and what they reveal, than that great addict of words, Nietzsche; who also experienced his moments of rapture. Here is one:

> The buffalo looks on insolently, his soul like the sand, yet more like the thicket, but most like the swamp.[12]

No no, that is not it, that is not it at all: here we are again with the buffaloes – or is the plural of 'buffalo' 'buffalo', are they creatures of an overweening and problematic singularity? At any rate, I did not intend to return us to the onrushing herd, I meant an entirely different quotation – but wait, perhaps that is not so, for what is this about 'his soul', this intricate latticework of images pertaining to the putative soulstuff of the buffalo? In what way can the soul of a buffalo (*the* buffalo – plural or singular?) be possibly compared with these 'natural' features, what would it mean to have a soul like a thicket or a swamp? And again, what could the relation possibly be between the buffalo and rapture? None. None at all, we are tempted to say. Except. Except that Nietzsche's previous sentence, I now notice, is about peacocks, and how the peacock 'unfurls its tail even before the ugliest of buffaloes, it never wearies of its lace-fan of silver and satin'.

Ah well. It would seem that, against all odds, the soul of the buffalo is itself enraptured, although it would also appear that it is doing its best (like sand, like a thicket, like a swamp) to resist this identification, to summon some (anthropomorphic) 'insolence' against the hallucinogenic presence of the peacock, to summon an attitude which might protect it from springing into the abyss. But, as I have said, this is not the point: buffaloes (or buffalo) are a side-issue, they may provide a momentary dumb commentary on rapture but they do not go to the soul of the matter – even if, when we go to the soul of the matter ourselves, what we might find there, in the shape of the Minotaur, is curiously reminiscent of the buffalo, but shorn, shorn of its herd, shorn of its plurality, shorn of one of its eyes, existing in a darkened, dreamlike world to which it has been consigned by an anthropocentric imagination, waiting to be enraptured so that it can be deflected from its fell purpose, a purpose of which it is entirely unwitting . . .

I am struggling here, hallucinating vast plains of buffalo, struggling to return, to grasp again what the point might have been. It might have been this, it might have been a moment when Nietzsche writes of rapture, in the following terms:

> Whenever your spirit wants to speak in images, pay heed; for that is when your virtue has its origin and beginning.
>
> Then your body is elevated and risen up; it enraptures the spirit with its joy, that it may become creator and evaluator and lover and benefactor of all things.
>
> When your heart surges broad and full like a river, a blessing and a danger to those who live nearby: that is when your virtue has its origin and beginning.[13]

Here is what is, perhaps, more important; here is a moment when the spirit (soul, I seem to have been calling it) is captured, seized away, by the body, when spirit becomes a recipient, a receptacle, for rapture, when it is 'enraptured', 'wrapt' in a physical housing in a 'transfigured' way, no longer 'struggling' against material swaddling bands but suffused with a joy which can come only from the body. The peacock and the buffalo; the complex organism which is made between them – made, perhaps, only on the body of the text, since the capacity of the buffalo to observe the peacock's display is surely limited unless under conditions of hallucination. But man, we have heard it suggested, is the only species which hallucinates; again, how do we know? We know (although we still cannot understand) how humanity has depicted the buffalo from ancient cave paintings onwards; what do we know of how the buffalo has depicted man?

## Trampolines of Desire

But let us again try to escape from the buffalo, before we fall into an abyss: the heart 'surges broad and full like a river', there are no longer any boundaries, any tidal restrictions, which cannot be overcome, whether we will this overcoming, this transcendence, this transfiguration or not. There is instead a predestined slow movement (of rapture), a movement which is beyond control, and thus of course it is both a 'blessing' and a 'danger': the soul of risk, the risk of soul. And this is all to do with 'images' – with, one might say, the birth ('origin and beginning') of the image, with what happens when an image comes to us, takes us over, when, instead of being readers, we sense that what is happening is that we are being read, that the creativity which we sensed coming to birth inside us has instead overwhelmed us, that we are now servants rather than masters, that we are obeying different laws, even if they are ones which we can neither understand or love.[14]

It would be good, it would be attractive, to reside here with Nietzsche on the banks of this ever-flowing, over-flowing river; but we are, are we not, enraptured, and we cannot therefore avoid seeing where the stream will take us. If we were talking in terms of the law, we would say that we need to call other witnesses; but out here where the river and the buffalo run, the writ of the law does not, and so we are entitled to doubt whether 'witness' is the right word when we are, in fact, out of our wits, drunk or doped on reading, rushing onwards, comically or tragically, towards . . .

Well, in this case towards a crack-up, the crack-up of F. Scott Fitzgerald (does his cracking up, his breaking down, make us 'crack up' in the other, linked sense, become hysterical with laughter, find comic *Schadenfreude* in a life, and death, which so uncannily replicates its own textuality?[15]). But I prefer to pause before *The Crack-Up* (1945) and its odd (posthumous) take on autobiography, and to come to rest instead in a different text of addiction and rapture, *The Beautiful and Damned* (1922). What comes to my mind in particular is a scene where Anthony and Gloria are confronting their wedding presents (and simultaneously the problematic, puzzling – at least to Anthony – presence of their wedding). They are on a threshold, but:

> To most of the presents Anthony was cold. It seemed to him that they would necessitate keeping a chart of the marital status of all their acquaintances during the next half-century. But Gloria exulted in each one, tearing at the

> tissue-paper and excelsior with the rapaciousness of a dog digging for a bone, breathlessly seizing a ribbon or an edge of metal and finally bringing to light the whole article and holding it up critically, no emotion except rapt interest in her unsmiling face.[16]

A scene, obviously, of 'unwrapping', of bringing – or rather, in this case, perhaps of dragging – into the light what had been hidden. But also a scene of rapaciousness, rapacity, words also etymologically connected with rapture, in the sense at least of a seizing away, even a sequestering, a greed to know that which has hitherto been unknown, although also with the connotation of ownership, of the now known becoming also 'my own', the 'owned', 'mine'. But all of this, of course, moving on to the 'rapt', and this is indeed a curious kind of rapture, which consorts not only, perhaps, with the inexpressible, but, more certainly, with the expressionless; typical, of course, of Gloria, who is the novel's enigma, the secret which is also simultaneously laid out for us through the most thorough acts of display, but it also points us toward the point where rapture cannot be decoded according to conventional descriptions of expression, where the face absorbed in rapture resists interpretation, becomes bland, flat, drained of the gradations of expression by which we conventionally judge 'the Other'.

'Rapt interest in her unsmiling face'; this, taken out of context, also refers to Anthony's 'interest' in Gloria, which is an interest combined of a certain rapaciousness, a will or need to break down, to break apart, to crack open or indeed to crack down on, this resistant face which betrays no emotion, which resists having its secrets opened up (like presents, ripped open in a parody of generosity, of participation), and an absorption whereby Anthony's whole personality becomes temporarily submerged in Gloria, in an inexpressible (but hallucinated) glory which cannot be grasped, cannot be seized and instead evaporates as it is approached. Would he be interested in her face if she smiled? Or would this break the spell, crack open the fantasy, ruin the *folie à deux* which will from this point on, from the point of the wedding, build to the terrible climax where everything is drowned, spent in the aftermath of rapture, the coming down which follows the cracking up?

But Gloria, of course, is not entirely a mute object of desire. On the contrary, she is herself keenly absorbed in her own predicament, as she says a little later when she defines her own version of jealousy, or of what would spoil the rapture:

> 'You see . . . it doesn't matter to me how many women you've stayed with in the past, so long as it was merely a physical satisfaction, but I don't believe

> I could endure the idea of your ever having lived with another woman for a protracted period or even having wanted to marry some possible girl. It's different somehow. There'd be all the little intimacies remembered – and they'd dull that freshness that after all is the most precious part of love'.[17]

Something here would break, crack open, a perfect surface, or the fantasy of a perfect surface: the sublimity of rapture would be reduced to a mere catalogue of 'little intimacies', objects and moods (and events, indeed) from the real world would intervene and threaten to reduce rapture to a merely human timescale, to merely human proportions. Gloria cannot have this: but it is Anthony's reaction which is perhaps more interesting, as 'rapturously, he pulled her down beside him on the pillow'. Why 'rapturously': because, of course, her words signify that he is the prime object of her desire; but also, presumably, because what she has revealed is that her needs – to elude the constrictions of life, to relegate the pettiness of 'real intimacy' to some place which the addict need not inhabit, which s/he has always already transcended – are, or appear to be, the same as his own, that here there is the potential for a true and terrible meeting of minds.

And yet, we are entitled to ask, what else is going on behind this mutual, and mutually reinforced, mask? A further clue comes a few lines later, when Anthony has gone out into the hall on his way to provide his loved one with the all too mundane sustenance of water, a cracker and some marmalade: 'Oh, gosh!', he sighs, 'in rapturous slang': 'she's wonderful, that girl! She *has* it!'. 'Rapturous slang': a point where, under the pressure of an apparent yet curiously inexpressible meeting of minds, conventional language breaks down, cracks up: but this does not point in the direction of a poetics of transcendence, but rather towards slang, stereotype, a love which, certainly, is incapable of speaking its name but which also, as in the words of any conventional love song, whether of the 'jazz age' or not, can only adopt an already used, soiled language, can only seek expression in the lowest common denominator, perfecting a joy in debasement, allowing words to crack under the pressure . . .

As, of course, Anthony and Gloria crack under the pressure; as Fitzgerald cracked under the pressure. And as, in this sad litany addressed to, and by, the saints of addiction, William Faulkner (like his characters) was in constant danger of cracking under the pressure, as Faulkner's texts offer us, his privileged and debased audience, ambiguous moments of rapture.

It is, of course, well known that Faulkner's disappointment with *The Sound and the Fury* (1929) felt to him specifically as though, in writing it, he had not attained to the 'state of rapture' which he had experienced in the writing of his previous novels:[18] as though something had fallen short, some disunion had occurred which he later found himself trying to repair in a series of attempts to sew the book back together, or to rearrange its disparate sections, or to provide some overview – because the monstrous body of bits and pieces had, it appeared, not attained to life, had not been fully born into the realm of organic being. Yet, it is equally well known that it was precisely that approach to rapture, and the textual dislocations it necessitated, which grated most on the nerves of contemporary critics. To take but one example: 'In book after book now [Faulkner] has dropped tears like the famed Arabian tree, in a rapture of sensibility amounting to continuous orgasm'.[19]

## The Spoon and the Powder

There can be no hierarchy in the textuality of rapture; but within the pantheon Faulkner obviously occupies a specific place, if only because of the ways in which text continually threatens to overflow its allotted boundaries ('the kind of "explosion" of words by whole pages', as another critic puts it[20]). Conrad's comrade, opposite and nemesis, Faulkner certainly has the haze; the question is about whether the kernel still retains any kind of life, or whether it has been wholly absorbed, consumed in the fire, and here, of course, *The Sound and the Fury* is emblematic. Partly this may be because of the way in which the sermon in the final section has been seen as a major avatar of the neo-Christian rhetoric of 'the rapture', as emblematic of its roots in the southern USA;[21] but it is more to do with the ways in which the words of the characters, particularly Quentin as he prepares for death, shoot off in all directions, threaten all the time to 'crash and burn' – a later equivalent would be the film *Two-Lane Blacktop* (1971), where the rapture, the ecstasy of the riders reaches its apotheosis as the film itself burns out at the end.

But the key to the rapture in *The Sound and the Fury* is Benjy, the largely inarticulate heart of the novel, the anomalous being who is 'wrapped up' within the text as he is wrapped up in the heart of the dying household, wrapped up against his endless wound, 'rapt' also in his mute contemplation of a world which is forever a puzzle to him:

> In the midst of the voices and the hands Ben sat, rapt in his sweet blue gaze. Dilsey sat bolt upright beside, crying rigidly and quietly in the annealment and the blood of the remembered Lamb.[22]

Here there is a matching of raptures: the rapture of which the pastor is speaking in his sermon, the other, untouchable rapture which is Benjy's and Benjy's alone – reminiscent again of Conrad, of the strange rapture of the sacrificed boy-hero of *The Secret Agent* (1907), as he sits in the kitchen drawing ever more complex series of concentric circles which are unsusceptible of explanation or interpretation.[23]

'The sound and the fury', as we well know, signify nothing. That is not merely to say that they 'do not signify'; it is equally that *what* they signify is 'nothing', is an ineluctable reduction to a place before, or outside, language, a place to which language is condemned endlessly to gesture without having the power to bring it to incarnation, lacking the power to 're-member' the lamb, to put back together that which has been sacrificed, sundered. Dilsey may sit 'bolt upright'; Benjy's posture is the reverse, an entire unthought concentration on the within, on a saintlike purity of spirit which others can only approximate but which also draws down upon Benjy the dreadful vengeance, already located in the past, which will forever prevent him from growing into conventional adult shape.

Thus, in the shape of Benjy, a terrible connection between rapture and mutilation: the attainment of rapture can only be predicated on a thwarting, or at least a stepping aside from, the processes of maturation. Benjy's is a kind of innocence, to be sure, but it is one which cannot be protected from man's inhumanity to man, even if it serves precisely to bear a kind of witness, a witness which will always be inarticulate, which will never be able to prove itself in its own defence before a court of law. Everything in *The Sound and the Fury* happens, we might say, after the trauma (or on the point of the descent into an alcoholic haze); the knot which binds rapture to sacrifice is drawn tight, the family ties which bind even as the family itself lingers on the precipice, running through past glories, reflecting on the descent, the collapse – rapture arises on a scenario of the abandonment of hope, the imminence not only of death but of a forgetting, precisely that rewriting of the story which we have now come across on numerous occasions and which is both the fate and task of narrative and the site of its inevitable betrayal of anything we might take for truth.

As the spirit ascends, the body goes down to desuetude and collapse: the perennial story of the addict, the alcoholic trying to re-member, trying to fit back together, the bits and pieces of an already shattered experience, trying to 'bring home' from another realm a set of materials which are untranslatable, unrepeatable even as they condemn to an endless cycle of repetition: every hallucinated event is different, every hallucinated event is the same; every sense of where the same and the different might intersect is hallucinated. As also, we can now add (reverting to the trials of the body, to its transmutations and sufferings in the name of vision), in the case of Genet, thief and saint, incarnation of 'our lady of the flowers' even while also the emblem of our dealings with all that drags the body down through changes to a pit from which resurrection is no longer possible.[24]

Where are we with Genet? Are we still with Genet at all, with that name which signifies generation, regeneration, the omitted name on Derrida's list of geneses, genres, genius, but also a series of acts of transmutation, sliding, the collapse of gender, the omitted letter, reminiscent of a time when perversion could signify vision and insight, a time (mythically) before the interceptions of the law, the intervention of the rigid body, the body rigid with grief, the body which can do nothing but await, passively, the rapture which it hopes (against hope) will overtake it, despite itself, in spite of itself, spiting its self in the name of something larger, greater but also congenitally malformed, a spirit or soul within a body which is not its own, not its home, before the emergence, the emergency, of the rhetoric of 'gender reassignment', yet also succeeding to the transgender excesses of, to take a resonant example, the French revolution (re-membering Charles Dickens and the tale of two cities, opposed in many more ways than one, or even two), that turn of the wheel which was also the drop of the guillotine, the castration of Benjy, the violent irruption of the forces of control which seek to protect us against rapture by ensuring that we stay within our recognised boundaries, that we do not stray over the fatal threshold, that we remain available at all times to the alternative, reductive vision of the panopticon of power, which operates at its strongest in its surveyal of those whose addictions have driven the sources of crime and terror of which all just men should be rightly afraid . . .

But I digress. Genet, of course, is enraptured: enraptured constantly. He is enraptured by evil, or by his own singular definition of evil. He is enraptured by betrayal, and by the infinite possibilities it appears to offer for changes in the *status quo*, for revelations of a hidden script which lies at, or below, the heart of things. He is enraptured by cowardice, by the sliding away from confrontation, by the consequent need for hierarchy and protection. He is enraptured by the (male) body, by its hardnesses and softnesses, its strength and its weakness. He is enraptured by prison and by the strange ways in which beauty can flower (or so it seems to him) under conditions of harshness. He is enraptured by abjection, by the unrecountable feelings which emerge under circumstances of the grossest of deprivations. He is enraptured by dirt, by roses, by miracles, by fear, by hope, by the coming of the thief in the night to disturb and enliven our otherwise endless days. Above all he is enraptured by words, by the power of language to transform, by its powerlessness to reveal, by the endless layers of mutation and perversion which it places – tenderly, like a quilt or like a jailhouse blanket – over the unyielding edges of the world.

He is, in *Miracle of the Rose* (1946), enraptured by song:

> We learned *My Paris*, *Two Loves Have I*, *Place Blanche*, *Strawberries and Raspberries*, *Hallelujah*. But the favourites were the soulful and violent ones that spoke of love, leave-taking and rapture.[25]

By this means, we learn, the protagonist of *Miracle of the Rose* – whoever, in Genet's hall of mirrors, he may be – pays his dues at the entrance gate to hell: 'thanks to my singing the first evening, I was at first spared the shame of prostitution', even though we as readers are spared, if that is the right word, details of these songs of 'love, leave-taking and rapture', seeing them instead replaced by other songs, lesser songs, perhaps indeed the wrong songs. But it is rapture, or a species of rapture, which paves the way: a sense of being seized away, of being 'transported' (although one would not lightly use the word 'transported' before the assembled gang of thieves, pimps and murderers who are his textual audience, an audience so like ourselves) which means he can bypass the more commonplace initiation rites: a reminder of violence which protects, at least for a time, from a greater, or at least more intimate and physical, violence.

And, of course, Genet is enraptured by perversion, by role-changing, by the gift of the gods which is to enable men to be women, to be free from the established weight of masculinity and to find an inner freedom which can challenge physical constraint. He is constantly involved in situations of complex jealousy – and yes, again, betrayal:

> He knew that what I said was right and that my love would be stauncher, but he was already abandoning me, forgetting my love which would not fulfil him. Enraptured by the men, he ran to them. I dared not reproach him.[26]

The 'I' here has slipped out of role, out of focus, is 'rapt', 'wrapped' in a different perspective, which also abuts onto one of Genet's main preoccupations, which is the path of saintliness, an abjection of self so that something other can flow in and wrap the subject, frail and pitiful as it is, constantly forced to bow down and perform acts which can be saved only through inversion, in the ragged robes of a transcendence which is itself always aware of its own fragility, its vulnerability to shiftings of power and obeisance.

## Gold, Marble, Flesh

In *The Thief's Journal* (1949), a reverie on the physicality of Armand, on his ability to position himself in the world and on the impossibility of deducing whether this positioning is by force of chance or chosen arrangement, is interrupted – or continued? – by a further reverie on the narrator's own position:

> No meditation, whether rapt or casual, on the planetary systems, the suns, nebulae and galaxies will ever enable me to contain, will ever console me for not containing, the world: confronted with the universe I am lost, but the simple attribute of a potent virility reassures me. Disturbing thoughts and anxiety cease. My tenderness – the finest gold or marble figure is inferior to a model in the flesh – arrays this power with bracelets of wild-oats.[27]

'Whether rapt or casual': the opposition is significant, as significant as the assertion of a 'potent virility' even though we as (by now inconstant?) readers know that this virility manifests itself as much in subjugation as in control. But what is perhaps most significant here is the reflection on the containment of the world, the outward extrusion of a life (so far) spent entirely 'contained', 'banged up', stripped of freedom and movement, at the whim of others even when the expression of that whim can be converted through an act of the enraptured imagination into the presence of flowers, roses, miracles, a transformation of the world through a shift of perception which is, in the end, involuntary, a gift which is simultaneously a curse; a sacrifice; a dealing with a guilt which is beyond the individual, under the shadow of which one has a perverse freedom to remake one's life.

> If he has courage – please understand – the guilty man decides to be what crime has made him. Finding a justification is easy; otherwise, how would he live? He draws it from his pride. . . . He wraps himself up in his shame out of pride, a word which designates the manifestation of the boldest freedom.[28]

'Wraps himself up'; and simultaneously seizes himself away, removes himself to another terrain, beyond the scope of the law, the terrain of the addict whose guilt will be forever contestable since his subjectivity has already, and for ever, been called into question, whose responsibility will batter at the gates of the prison, will challenge the forces of order to establish, once and for all, who here is the guilty party, whether there are recognisable motives (besides the simple, unassailable ones of greed and fear) which can be put forward as explanation of the uncanniness of these happenings (which are in any case always in the past, that past which is a closed book to the consciousness which has moved away from its rational axis).

And from Saint Genet we can move in two directions (both of which he clearly indicates for us): we can move down, and/or we can move up: down into the depths of addiction, up into the soul of the rapture. We will move down first; because that is the more satisfying trajectory: we would prefer not to be left in hell, we would prefer to be, at least in hallucinatory fashion, attempting to scale the heights of the soul mountain. And so we shall, so we shall; but first, we need to follow the primrose path. Our company will be a writer called John Rechy, one of those authors – far from unique or singular – who has written several books but only one which carries resonance: *City of Night* (1963), which is about a young man who becomes part of the world of male hustling: in New York, in California, in the climactic scenes in New Orleans at Mardi Gras. This, we are constantly told (the author lies, but I hope we no longer have a problem with that), has nothing to do with homosexuality, perversion[29]: it is far more problematic than that, but largely economically driven. So goes the reasoning, which (like so much other reasoning) leaves the book unexplained and inexplicable: at any event (at all events) the protagonist finds an uncanny fascination in desire – but not, as he keeps protesting, his own desire, rather his experience of being desired by others, especially by men, even more especially by men who are themselves tremulously unwilling to admit to their own desires. It would be no exaggeration to say that *City of Night* undoes patriarchy from the inside: partly through the endless parade (and this book is repetitive like nothing else) of disappointed, disavowed, middle-class men looking for cheap male sex, but far more urgently through the more glowing, rapturous parade of men who need to disavow their sexual insignia, the fairies, the queens, the hustlers, those who stand athwart the conventions and who seek to possess – and in some cases do – the sublime dignity of pathos, the pathetic dignity of the sublime.

Condemned to outlaw status, as well as revelling in the temporary exemption their 'new' status brings, they swirl and eddy through a transformed USA, a night country where straight existence, straight sex, hardly exists; or if it does, it is only on the periphery of the real scene, a marginal footnote to the real history of the times. Here paraphilia, perversion (the thoroughgoing version, the real version, the story which is constantly being told and which gains added, indeed supernal strength from being constantly ignored by the inconstant reader) is the centre, and all else is consigned to a drab margin. But more than this: repetition, the constant repetition of sex acts devoid of meaning, feeling or indeed recognisable ownership, attains to its own state of rapture. Persons, usually in any case masked, concealed, cross-dressed, seeking an unachievable and non-viable different identity which is constantly betrayed in the very act, as it were, are no longer the issue: they have ceased to issue, they have ceased to have issue, the issue has altered, the case is altered, as has the very tissue of the drag queens and super-male fake idols of the text. The rapture is in the forgetting, the transmutation, which calls into question any simple structure of belief: what one believes in is what one wants to believe in before night falls; or, as in the closing scenes of Mardi Gras, when night comes to reveal and conceal all change.

Rapture:

> And while the preachers dash out their damning messages, the winos storm Heaven on cheap wine; hungry-eyed scores with money (or merely with a place to offer the homeless youngmen they desire) gather about the head hunting the malehustlers and wondering will they get robbed if – . . . Pickpockets station themselves strategically among the crowds as if listening in rapt attention to the Holy Messages.[30]

Or, at the very least, 'rapt attention', but here, obviously, an attention which is invariably fake, a deflection from a quite different kind of attention. Rapture as a melting into the crowd, as the convergence between the unnoticeable and that which is noticeable to the point at which credulity is strained and all attempt at gender assignation is broken beyond repair, the apotheosis of the impossibility experienced by the *flâneur* as he tries to make sense of an experience which is all the time seizing him away, preventing him from bringing back a true account of what he claims to have seen.

And so through rapture and its suspect cognates we can come down to an apparent nadir of human experience:

> Wrapped around a post near the Bourbon House, a drunk man is proclaiming: 'This is my true love!' as he hugs the post passionately. An outraged woman pulls at him insistently. 'Get away from me!' he commands her, 'I found My True Love!' – as one leg curls about the post like a dog's.[31]

Rapture and abjection; rapture under conditions of hallucination which constantly invoke abjection, which permit no dignity; the condition of the alcoholic, the junkie, the addict, wrapped in a miasma – which can also be seen, perhaps by mistake, as a halo, as saintly garb – that cloaks all possibility of return. A narrative which is not a narrative, which tells no story, which is merely – and grandly – a wall of words which prevents intrusion, which absorbs all interference from the outside and remains in the heart of darkness.

## Onwards; Down the Line

But of course rapture, as we have seen, is not always seen: it also moves us forward to great heights, indeed it challenges us – lingeringly, painfully – to explain why we choose to exist in any other world; as the addict asks – plaintively, seekingly – how it is that we (others, if that is what we are) can abide to live in a world where rapture and transcendence are forbidden. And, indeed: how do we do that? How is it that we adopt and relish the mind-forged manacles? How is it that we permit ourselves to remain exiled from the world just around the corner, down the rabbit-hole, through the green door, within the syringe? Why do we not try all the time to climb soul mountain – for here, at the end, is where soul comes into its own.

And it does so, emblematically, in Gao Xingjian's *Soul Mountain* (1990). Here the protagonist struggles throughout with the knowledge that somewhere – perhaps close by, perhaps not, flickering in and out of vision – there is a way of ascending to rapture; but he is also more than aware that this is not a matter of a retreat from human, even historical, concerns, rather it necessitates a continuing re-engagement with the facts of a life lived in the shadows, under the pressure of repression, dreading unexpected violence (the text is a constant reflection, dear reader, on China's Cultural Revolution). Under these conditions, the subject shatters: the text has many protagonists – 'I', 'you', 'he', 'she' – and even a more overarching narrator who is able, on rueful occasions, to discuss the very shattering or splintering which has given birth to this plethora of selves.

Perhaps Soul Mountain, *Lingshan*, will be reached; perhaps not; perhaps it is not even there, but marks a place on the map where other geographical markers run out, or run endlessly into one another. Perhaps in any case, even if Soul Mountain is reached, it will not be apparent who or what has reached it. At all events, 'something happens': 'a never before experienced limpidity, a totality of purity and freshness'. On the verge of vision, 'your whole body is cool, your body and mind listen intently, your whole body and mind hear this soundless, billowing music'. And then:

> As a mass of long notes takes shape, there is a vigorous middle note, you can't catch the melody but can perceive the richness of the sounds. It links up with another mass of sounds, intermingles, unfolds, turns into a river

> which disappears and appears, appears and disappears. A dark blue sun circles within an even darker moon, you hold your breath enraptured, stop breathing, reach the extremity of life.[32]

And so, once again, rapture and death are intertwined, an 'even darker' moon around a 'dark blue' sun, the culmination of an ascent in which the self has been purged – indeed in this case evacuated to make space for the birth of the 'you', for a final meeting point of narrator and audience, where it is the ghost of the reader which is lifted to the highest level. We no longer need to leave the theatre; we can stay all night.

And so, also, something is 'seized away', 'transported', moved over a threshold into a realm where the writ of law does not run and where, therefore, we cannot be pursued through the evil forest. Is the journey of *Soul Mountain* a quest or a flight? By this point, at the end of the book, the question no longer makes any sense: in one way, the source of all secrets has been revealed, while in another everything remains secret, hidden, just as the location of Soul Mountain remains a mystery, the paths to it never meeting, never making any credible sense. The journey is one of constant errors, misprisions, misdirections; adjuvants and guides are constantly unreliable, reliable only in their inconstancy.

And so, at the final, the closing moment of rapture, in the course of the rapture of simultaneously attaining and evading closure, of being lost within a process which, as we have seen, is endlessly repetitive and yet also carries the ineradicable hallmark of the new, there is a radical forgetting, an incomprehension, a clear statement – as clear as a statement can possibly be – of the impossibility of recounting the experience of rapture, the rapture of being immersed in experience, the impossibility of returning and bringing anything back from the realm of narrative, the realm of the dead, the realm of the – perhaps terminally – hallucinated where shapes flicker and warp, where it is impossible to tell shadow from substance, use from abuse, joy from the mundane:

> I don't know where I am at this moment, I don't know where this realm of Heaven comes from, I look all around.
>
> I don't know that I don't understand anything and still think I know everything.
>
> Things just happen behind me and there is always a mysterious eye, so it is best for me just to pretend that I understand even if I don't.
>
> While pretending to understand, I still don't understand.
>
> The fact of the matter is I comprehend nothing, I understand nothing. This is how it is.[33]

Rapt.

# Notes

## 1 Enraptured

1 A good starting-point for thinking this connection is in Jung's remarks on volition, numinosity and rapture in 'On the Nature of the Psyche' (1954) in *The Structure and Dynamics of the Psyche*, trans. R. F. C. Hull (2nd edn, London, 1969), p. 186; see also John Weir Perry, *The Far Side of Madness* (Dallas, TX, 1989).

2 Eliot's 'ecstasy of the animals' figures, perhaps inevitably, as one of the four routes to (spiritual?) death. Another is that taken by 'those who sharpen the tooth of the dog' (see Eliot, *Collected Poems 1909–62* [London, 1963], p. 115).

3 Derrida, 'Che cos'è la poesia?', in *Points . . . Interviews 1974–1994*, ed. Elisabeth Weber, trans. Peggy Kamuf *et al.* (Stanford, CA, 1995), p. 298.

4 Weber, Notes, in Derrida, *Points*, p. 475.

5 Derrida, 'Che cos'è la poesia', in *Points*, p. 299.

6 Derrida, *Without Alibi*, ed., trans. and introd. Kamuf (Stanford, CA, 2002), p. 160.

7 See, e.g., Megan Stern, 'Imagining Space through the Inhuman Gaze', in *Inhuman Reflections: Thinking the Limits of the Human*, eds Scott Brewster, John J. Joughin, David Owen and Richard J. Walker (Manchester, 2000), pp. 203–16.

8 J. H. Prynne, 'On the Anvil' (1969), in *Poems* (2nd edn, Tarset, Northumberland, 2005), p. 42.

9 Punter, 'Interlocating J. H. Prynne', *The Cambridge Quarterly*, 31.2 (2002), 124.

10 Derrida, '"The Almost Nothing of the Unrepresentable"', in *Points*, p. 82. Or:

> . . . certain modern literary practices, rather than being founded by their representational function, can be understood as a profound experimentation that reveals the positivity and the limits of our language-habits (our addiction to saying 'I').

(Gregg Lambert, 'On the Uses and Abuses of Literature for Life', in *Deleuze and Literature*, eds Ian Buchanan and John Marks [Edinburgh, 2000], p. 159)

11 Derrida, '"Dialanguages"', in *Points*, p. 142. Timothy Clark remarks that for Heidegger

> the space of the leap inherent to the poetic is necessarily one which puts into abeyance saying 'I' in terms of some given cultural, familial or national identity. Uncertainty, impersonal insecurity and psychic dislocation or rapture [*sic*] may beset the artist in the holding open of a space against the vast pressure of given ways of perception.

(Clark, *The Poetics of Singularity: The Counter-Cultural Turn in Heidegger, Derrida, Blanchot and the later Gadamer* [Edinburgh, 2005], p. 43).

12 Derrida, '"There is no *One* Narcissism"', in *Points*, p. 201.

13 Prynne, *Stars, Tygers and the Shape of Words* (London, 1993), p. 3.

14 Bob Dylan, 'Ballad of a Thin Man' (1965), in *Lyrics, 1962–1985* (London, 1987), p. 303. But salvation may nonetheless be at hand: Mr Jones has 'been with the professors'; they have all liked his looks; and he has read, as we may have done by the end, 'all of F. Scott Fitzgerald's books' (p. 304).

15 The relevant literature, from Socrates to Freud, is enormous and well-known. Additional sources include Katherine M. Briggs, *An Encyclopaedia of Fairies, Hobgoblins, Brownies, Bogies, and other Supernatural Creatures* (New York, 1976); Hasan M. El-Shamy, *Folktales of Egypt* (Chicago, 1980); and the often violent fantasies of the Brothers Grimm.

16 Prynne, *Stars, Tygers and the Shape of Words*, p. 19.

17 Derrida, 'Unsealing ("the old new language")', in *Points*, p. 118.

18 See Maurice Blanchot and Derrida, *The Instant of my Death/Demeure: Fiction and Testimony*, trans. Elizabeth Rothenberg (Stanford, CA, 2000), pp. 13–103.

19 Prynne, from *For the Monogram* (1997), in *Poems*, p. 431. Perhaps relevant is a comment of Norman O. Brown's quoted by Eric Mottram:

> The human body is not a thing or substance, given, but a continuous creation . . . The human body is an energy system . . . which is never a complete structure; never static; is in perpetual inner self-construction and self-destruction . . .

(Mottram, *William Burroughs: The Algebra of Need* [London, 1977], p. 197)

20 The echoes here, of course, are of Samuel Beckett, *Krapp's Last Tape* (1958) and David Rudkin, *Afore Night Come* (1962).

21 Donne, 'The Relique', in, e.g., *The Poems of John Donne*, ed. Herbert Grierson (London, 1933), p. 56.

22 See Punter, 'Shape and Shadow: On Poetry and the Uncanny', in *A Companion to the Gothic*, ed. Punter (London, 2000), pp. 193–205; also, more generally, Royle, 'Foreign Body: "The Deconstruction of a Pedagogical Institution and all that it implies"', in *After Derrida* (Manchester, 1995), pp. 143–58.

23 Derrida, '"Dialanguages"', in *Points*, p. 145.

24 See Freud, 'Creative Writers and Day-Dreaming' (1908), in *The Standard Edition of the Complete Psychological Works of Sigmund Freud*, eds James Strachey *et al.* (24 vols, London, 1953–74), IX. 141–53.

25 See, e.g., Olga Bogdashina, *Sensory Perceptional Issues in Autism and Asperger Syndrome: Different Sensory Experiences, Different Perceptional Worlds* (London, 2003); Uta Frith, *Autism and Asperger Syndrome* (Cambridge, 1991).

26 See Punter, 'A Voyage through the Phantom Museum', in *Le Gothic: Influences and Appropriations in Europe and America*, eds Avril Horner and Sue Zlosnik (London, 2008), pp. 219–41, as well as the references (and illustrations) therein.

27 Derrida, 'Passages – from Traumatism to Promise', in *Points*, p. 373.

28 Derrida, 'Between Brackets I', in *Points*, pp. 24–5.

29 As it is also a question about the proper name and the signature, both themes to which we shall return; see Derrida, 'Between Brackets I', in *Points*, p. 25.

30 W. S. Graham, 'The Nightfishing', in *New Collected Poems*, ed. Matthew Francis (London, 2004), p.109.

31 Eliot, 'Marina', in *Collected Poems*, p. 115.

32

> What I needed was something easily seen, a piece of paper, which I could throw overboard and watch. I had nothing on me. To run down for it I didn't dare.

(Conrad, 'The Secret Sharer', in *'Typhoon' and Other Tales*, ed. Cedric Watts [Oxford, 1986], p. 294). The day (or rather the night) is of course saved by a hat.

33 Derrida, 'Demeure: Fiction and Testimony', in Blanchot and Derrida, p. 45.

34 See Dylan, 'Mr Tambourine Man', in *Lyrics*, p. 270.

35 An interesting historicisation of angina can be found in Leon Michaels, *The Eighteenth-century Origins of Angina Pectoris: Predisposing Causes, Recognition and Aftermath* (London, 2001).

36 Derrida, 'Demeure: Fiction and Testimony', in Blanchot and Derrida, p. 72. See also Charles Altieri, *The Particulars of Rapture: An Aesthetics of the Affects* (Ithaca, NY, 2003) and bell hooks, *Remembered Rapture: The Writer at Work* (London, 1999).

37 Derrida, *Without Alibi*, p. xxxiv.

38 See especially Gaston Bachelard, *Psychoanalysis of Fire* (London, 1977); Johan Goudsblom, *Fire and Civilisation* (London, 1992); Stephen J. Pyne, *Fire: A Brief History* (Seattle, WA, 2001).

39 Prynne, 'A Dream of Retained Colour' (1969), in *Poems*, p. 103.

40 The echo is of Ezra Pound's 'petals on a wet, black bough' in his 'In a Station of the Metro'; although perhaps this too is merely an echo of the 'petals' that 'fall in the fountain' in 'Ts'ai Chi'h', a poem which immediately precedes it (see Pound, *Selected Poems*, introd. T.S. Eliot [London, 1948], p. 113).

41 Derrida, '*Ja*, or the faux-bond II', in *Points*, p. 45.

42 Prynne, from *The Oval Window* (1983), in *Poems*, p. 322.

43 Derrida, 'Between Brackets I', in *Points*, p. 21.

## 2 Romanticism and the Open Secret

1 The best introductory guide to literature and secrets is in Andrew Bennett and Nicholas Royle, *Introduction to Literature, Criticism and Theory* (2nd edn, Hemel Hempstead, 1999), pp. 222–30. See also Esther Rashkin, *Family Secrets and the Psychoanalysis of Narrative* (Princeton, NJ, 1992).

2 See Nicolas Abraham and Maria Torok, *The Wolf Man's Magic Word: A Cryptonymy*, trans. Nicholas Rand (Minneapolis, 1986), and particularly Derrida's 'Foreword' to the book.

3 See Jean Laplanche, *Essays on Otherness*, trans. John Fletcher (London, 1999), esp. pp. 70, 73, 78, 111–12, 179–83.
4 See Blake, *Complete Writings*, ed. Geoffrey Keynes (Oxford, 1966), pp. 424–7.
5 The reference is, of course to, Žižek, *Looking Awry: An Introduction to Jacques Lacan through Popular Culture* (Cambridge, MA, 1991). Like many other readers and reviewers, it is not clear to me that Žižek's ideas and insights stand or fall via their relation to Lacan.
6 See Bennett, *Ignorance: Literature and Agnoiology* (Manchester, forthcoming 2008); also his 'Poetry and Ignorance', *Angles on the English-Speaking World*, 3 (2003), 77–92.
7

> The cultural message, the artistic 'creation', is situated beyond a purely pragmatic aim (to produce such and such an effect on an addressee, by using some particular means). It is, in its depths, provoked by the 'nameless public', 'scattered into the future', who will receive (or not) this message in a bottle.

(Laplanche, *Essays on Otherness*, p. 111)
8 Blake, *Complete Writings*, p. 440.
9 See Murdoch, *Metaphysics as a Guide to Morals* (London, 1992), pp. 498–503. This chapter, Murdoch says, 'could also be called "despair" or "affliction" or "dark night"' (p. 498), although it ends with the tantalising suggestion that 'in the more obscure labyrinths of personal relations it may be necessary to make the move which makes the void appear' (p. 503).
10 Frances Burney (writing as Madame D'Arblay), *Camilla, or a Picture of Youth* (London, 1796), IV.337.
11 *Le Sage's (A.R.) Adventures of Gil Blas of Santillane*, trans. Benjamin H. Malkin (London, 1809), VII.xiii.16.
12 William Sewell, *The Domestic Virtues and Manners of the Greeks and Romans* (London, 1828), p. 45.
13 Cf. Derrida's extended remarks on the secret in 'Passions: "An Oblique Offering"' (1993); see *On the Name*, ed. Thomas Dutoit (Stanford, CA, 1995), pp. 24–7.
14 Blake, *Jerusalem*, 79.33–44, in *Complete Writings*, p. 720.
15 See, e.g., Freud, 'Fragment of an Analysis of a Case of Hysteria' (the Dora case history) (1905), where he is much more inclined to speak of infantile 'sympathetic excitement' (*Standard Edition*, VII.79–80).
16 See Blake, *Jerusalem*, 69.44, 43, in *Complete Writings*, p. 708.
17 Blake, *Vala, or, The Four Zoas*, Night the Second, ll. 308–21, in *Complete Writings*, p. 288.
18 On *Travelling Wilburys*, Vol. 3 (afficianados will be aware that there is no Vol. 2). 'These popular songs, laments and heroic tales fuse together into a rhythmic and harmonic trifle . . . (Ted Ashenbecker [M.A. Berlin University, 1988], sleeve note).
19 Blake, *Vala, or, The Four Zoas*, Night the Eighth, ll. 140–2, in *Complete Writings*, p. 344.

20 These lines of thinking are brought together most strikingly in Derrida, '*Istrice 2: Ick bünn all hier*', in *Points*, pp. 300–26.
21 See *Complete Writings*, pp. 434–6. Like 'The Mental Traveller', 'William Bond' is a poem from the Pickering Manuscript, which represents some of Blake's most extraordinary and enigmatic work.
22 Derrida's most interesting reflections on the signature effect, the proper name and related matters occur in *On the Name*, ed. Dutoit.
23 Heidegger, 'Letter on "Humanism"', in *Pathmarks*, ed. William McNeill (Cambridge, 1998), p. 240.
24 Hölderlin, 'Sunset', in *Poems and Fragments*, ed. Michael Hamburger (4th edn, London, 2004), p. 103.
25 See, e.g., George Mills Harper, *The Neoplatonism of William Blake* (Chapel Hill, NC, 1961) and Kathleen Raine, *Blake and Tradition* (2 vols, London, 1969).
26 'Novalis' (Friedrich von Hardenberg), *Schriften*, ed. Johannes Minor (5 vols, Jena, 1923), II.178; see also Hamburger, *Reason and Energy: Studies in German Literature* (London, 1970), p. 74.
27 See Hamburger, *Reason and Energy*, p. 66.
28 Hölderlin, 'Bread and Wine', in *Poems and Fragments*, p. 323.
29 See, e.g., Deleuze and Guattari, *A Thousand Plateaus: Capitalism and Schizophrenia*, trans. Brian Massumi (London, 1988), *passim*, but, e.g., p. 8 on the relations between multiplicity, the rhizomatic and the subject.
30 Hamburger, in Hölderlin, *Poems and Fragments*, p. 45. Hölderlin was discharged as an 'incurable case' and lived for a further 37 years, in what at least some critics regard as a poetical living death; or at least a relative silence from which no account could emerge.
31 Constantine, *Hölderlin* (Oxford, 1988), p. 306; although as he also remarks, 'John Clare, certified insane for almost as long as Hölderlin, wrote more and better in his alienation'.
32 See Blake, *Vala, or, The Four Zoas*, Night the First, ll. 94–6, in *Complete Writings*, p. 266:

> There is from Great Eternity a mild and pleasant rest
> Nam'd Beulah, a soft Moony Universe, feminine, lovely,
> Pure, mild and Gentle, given in Mercy to those who sleep . . .

33 See Blackwood, 'The Pikestaffe Case', in *Tales of the Uncanny and Supernatural* (London, 1962), pp. 316–48.

> It was when Mr Thorley looked at her with his brilliant eyes and blazing smile that her heart gave its violent jump, missed a beat or two, then began hammering against her ribs like released machinery that has gone beyond control. She was aware of the happy glory in the face, a face that was thin to emaciation, almost transparent . . . (p. 345)

Rapture; angina; anorexia.
34 'I wish I was like that earth person who just left the bar with her drink glass still half full' (<www.urbandictionary.com>).

35 Heidegger, 'The Nature of Language', in *On the Way to Language*, trans. Peter D. Hertz (New York, 1971), p. 69.

36 See Blake, *The Marriage of Heaven and Hell* (c. 1790–3), 8.15, in *Complete Writings*, p. 151: 'The cistern contains: the fountain overflows'.

37 Except, of course, that this is now possible, albeit at a price high in toxicity; see, e.g., Warren E. Leary, 'Mislabelling and Health Risks tied to Skin Lightener Creams', *New York Times* (26th Feb. 1992), as also the obscene current internet advertisements for 'anal and vaginal bleaching' from South Beach Skin Solutions.

38 The author of peace and lover of concord, in knowledge of whom standeth our eternal life, whose service is perfect freedom.

(*Book of Common Prayer*)

39 The rhetoric of singularity will become, I hope, clearer later on; see Derek Attridge, *The Singularity of Literature* (London, 2004), as well as Clark, *The Poetics of Singularity*.

40 One of the poems in which this is at its most intense is 'The Blind Singer', which is suffused with a remarkable harmonic density of echo and counter-echo (see *Poems and Fragments*, pp. 245–7).

41 See, e.g., *Essential Psychiatry*, ed. Nicholas D.B. Rose (2nd edn, Oxford, 1994), pp. 9, 59; Andrew Sims and David Owens, *Psychiatry* (6th edn, London, 1993), pp. 24–50.

42 The reference is to Ronell, *The Telephone Book: Technology, Schizophrenia, Electric Speech* (Lincoln, NE, 1989); I will give some more detailed account of Ronell's arguments and imagery later.

43 See, e.g., Alan Richardson, 'Apostrophe in Life and in Romantic Art: Everyday Discourse, Overhearing, and Poetic Address', *Style*, 36 (2002), 363–85.

44 Heidegger, 'The Nature of Language', in *On the Way to Language*, p. 75.

45 Chomsky, *Syntactic Structures* (The Hague and Paris, 1957), p. 15.

46 'Novalis', *Heinrich von Ofterdingen: A Novel*, trans. Palmer Hilty (Prospect Heights, IL, 1990), pp. 16–17.

47 On *Travelling Wilburys*, Vol. 3: 'The original Wilburys were a stationary people who, realising that their civilisation could not stand still forever, began to go for short walks' (sleeve note). This was the origin of nomadry.

48 The most obvious of the many Poe references would be to 'The Facts in the Case of M. Valdemar', in, e.g., *Tales of Mystery and Imagination* (London, 1919), pp. 345–53, with its famous line: 'Yes; – no; – I *have been* sleeping – and now – now – *I am dead*' (p. 351).

49 The background to this kind of thinking can be found in James Hillman, *The Dream and the Underworld* (New York, 1979).

50 Freud, 'Psycho-analytic Notes on an Autobiographical Account of a Case of Paranoia', in *Standard Edition*, XII.23. The text goes on to mention the language in which souls converse in this 'state of bliss' or rapture.

51 Freud, *Standard Edition*, XII.30.

52 See, e.g., *Psychotic States in Children*, eds Margaret Rustin, Maria Rhode, Alex Dubinsky and Hélène Dubinsky (London, 1997).

53 Freud, *Standard Edition*, XII.53. But we might be equally interested in Schreber's 'miracled birds' or 'talking birds' (XII.35); is talking, perhaps, a miracle? Or would these be birds, as might become clear later, that can only be seen through a ceiling of alabaster?

54 I am going to refer at many points to the moral law as the limit of addiction, as what is limited by addiction. There cannot be better descriptions of it than those of Blake in, e.g., the short poem 'I saw a Monk of Charlemaine', *Jerusalem*, 52.1–28, in *Complete Writings*, p. 683.

## 3 The Scene of Addiction

1 See, e.g., Jacqueline Labbe, *The Romantic Paradox: Love, Violence and the Uses of Romance, 1760–1830* (London, 2000), which includes detailed consideration of how 'the Romantic romance disorders itself; it commits crimes against genre, impairing the cliché of plot' (p. 3).

2 Some of the most obvious examples of this occur in Poe; see, e.g., 'Eleanora' and 'The Black Cat', in *Selected Tales*, ed. David van Leer (Oxford, 1998), pp. 123–8, 230–8.

3

> For example, a death virus could be created that carries the coded message of death. A death tape, in fact. No doubt the technical skills are complex and perhaps a team of sound and camera men working with biochemists would give us the answer (see Mottram, p. 158).

4 The presence of the doctor in literature is obviously far too vast a topic to review here; but the more limited figure of the addicted doctor, the madman loose in the pharmacy, would appear to be a more specifically modern image.

5 See Punter, *The Literature of Terror* (2nd edn, 2 vols, London, 1996), I.114–39 and II.131–3.

6 Burroughs, *Nova Express* (London, 1966), p. 90.

7 See Barry Miles, *William Burroughs: El Hombre Invisible* (London, 1992), pp. 56–8. On p. 57 Miles quotes Burroughs: 'I am forced to the conclusion that I would never have become a writer but for Joan's death, and to a realisation of the extent to which this event has motivated and formulated my writing'.

8

> The new school is located universally in a network of fluid, often short-lived, institutes and foundations which teach a variety of possible counter-fascist activities, from karate to the writings of Reich on D.O.R., with courses on virology, linguistics, general semantics, assassination techniques, improvised weapons, and riot.

(Mottram, *The Algebra of Need*, p. 150)

9 Cf. Keith Ansell Pearson, *Viroid Life: Perspectives on Nietzsche and the Transhuman Condition* (London, 1997).

10

> Technical progress, extended to a whole system of domination and coordi-

> nation, creates forms of life (and of power) which appear to reconcile the forces opposing the system and to defeat or refute all protest in the name of the historical prospects of freedom from toil and domination.

(Marcuse, *One Dimensional Man: The Ideology of Industrial Society* [London, 1964], p. 11)

11 *Nova Express*, p. 46.

12 See Zygmunt Bauman, *Modernity and Ambivalence* (Ithaca, NY, 1991); Matei Calinescu, *Five Faces of Modernity: Modernism, Avant-Garde, Decadence, Kitsch, Postmodernism* (Durham, NC, 1987); *The Modernity of the Eighteenth Century*, ed. Louis T. Milic (Cleveland, OH, 1971); and Punter, *Modernity* (London, 2007).

13 The pharmacological literature is surveyed in Andre Lees and Kirsten Turner, 'Apomorphine for Parkinson's Disease', *Practical Neurology*, 2 (2002), 280–7.

14 *Nova Express*, p. 67.

15 See, e.g., Punter, *Gothic Pathologies: The Text, the Body and the Law* (London, 1998); Fiona Robertson, *Legitimate Histories: Scott, Gothic, and the Authorities of Fiction* (Oxford, 1994); and Dale Townshend, *The Orders of Gothic: Foucault, Lacan, and the Subject of Gothic Writing 1764–1820* (New York, 2007).

16 Or of the 'grim Gothic Foreman': see *Nova Express*, p. 93.

17 To speak of the cyborg in connection with the addict is complicated and raises the necessary question of what the organic is or continues to be in a realm where its very definition is under threat or erasure.

18 *Nova Express*, p. 79.

19 Not all, of course, are *papaver somniferum.*

20 *Nova Express*, p. 103. Cf., of course, Eliot, *The Waste Land*, ll. 141–72, in *Collected Poems*, pp. 68–9; but also, earlier, 'Those are pearls that were his eyes' (l. 125, p. 67) and, later, 'the violet hour' of Tiresias, 'old man with wrinkled female breasts' (ll. 215, 218, p. 71).

21 When it is always 'dusk through narrow streets, toilet paper, and there is no light in the window – April wind revolving illness of dead sun . . . Departed have left used avenue . . . Dream of the dead' (*Nova Express*, p. 145).

22 See, e.g., Alethea Hayter, *Opium and the Romantic Imagination* (London, 1968).

23 See Mottram, *The Algebra of Need*, pp. 130–1.

24 The reference is to Maturin, *Melmoth the Wanderer* (1820), ed. Douglas Grant, introd. Chris Baldick (Oxford, 1989); see also Kathleen Fowler, 'Hieroglyphics in Fire: *Melmoth the Wanderer*', *Studies in Romanticism*, 25 (1986), 521–39.

25 See Karl Marx and Friedrich Engels, *The German Ideology*, ed. C.J. Arthur (London, 1970); Althusser, *For Marx*, trans. Ben Brewster (London, 1969) and *Reading Capital*, trans. Brewster (London, 1997).

26 This, of course, is the repeated refrain of William Dunbar's magnificent 'Lament for the Makaris' (1505); see *The Poems of William Dunbar*, ed. Priscilla Bawcutt (2 vols, Glasgow, 1998), I.94–7.

27 See Wordsworth and Coleridge, *Lyrical Ballads*, eds R. L. Brett and A. R. Jones (London, 1965), p. 249, where we hear of a culturally prevalent 'degrading thirst after outrageous stimulation'.

28 Which mirrors cultural movement:

> . . . formal acculturation by schooling is increasingly lengthy and gets increasingly audited according to standards. A person's performance in one subject or at one time can be compared to her performance elsewhere or to another person's, with increasing precision . . .

(George Ainslie, 'The Dangers of Willpower', in *Getting Hooked: Rationality and Addiction*, eds Jon Elster and Ole-Jørgen Skog [Cambridge, 1999], p. 82)

29 'For Lacan, perversion designates a very precise subjective attitude that is an attitude of auto-objectivisation or autocephalopodisation'; this comes from a hysterically funny interview with Žižek about squid theory by Ramon Benitez at <www.eyeshot.net/squid1>. Andrea Dworkin, *Pornography: Men Possessing Women* (London, 1981), is less amusing.

30 See Sedgwick, *Between Men: English Literature and Male Homosociality* (New York, 1985); also Jason Edwards, *Eve Kosofsky Sedgwick* (London, 2008).

31 But not really Crowley's of course; 'Nothing is true, everything is permitted' can be traced back, if phantomatically, to Nietzsche and to the 11th-century Ismaili Hassan-i-Sabah. But is the crucial word 'true'; or 'real'; or 'forbidden'? And what would the relations be among that intriguing triplicity?

32 Helge Waal, 'To Legalise or Not to Legalise: Is That the Question?', in *Getting Hooked*, eds Elster and Skog, p. 143.

33 Ann Dally, 'Drugspeak', in *Addiction Controversies*, ed. David M. Warburton (London, 1990), p. 1.

34 For commentary, see Mottram, *The Algebra of Need*, pp. 206 ff.

35 Eliot L. Gardner and James David, 'The Neurobiology of Chemical Addiction', in *Getting Hooked*, eds Elster and Skog, p. 104.

36 See Donna Haraway, *Simians, Cyborgs and Women: The Reinvention of Nature* (London, 1991), pp. 203–30.

37 One of the most extraordinary descriptions of this process concerns the relationship between the 'K-ship' and its commander in M. John Harrison, *Light* (London, 2002); see also Punter, *Modernity*, pp. 193–207.

38 For a radical and disturbing take on what it might be like for humans to be battery farmed on the grounds that they have little in the way of valuable or sophisticated senses, see Michel Faber, *Under the Skin* (Edinburgh, 2000).

39 Wall, 'To Legalise . . . ', in *Getting Hooked*, eds Elster and Skog, p. 143.

40 See the continuingly relevant arguments of Denis de Rougemont in *Love in the Western World*, trans. Montgomery Belgion (Princeton, NJ, 1983). I have used de Rougemont's arguments so exhaustively in *Writing the Passions* that I will not try to develop them further here.

41
> When I but think upon the great dead days
> And turn my mind upon that splendid madness,
> Lo! I do curse my strength
> And blame the sun his gladness;
> For that the one is dead

And the red sun mocks my sadness.

(Pound, 'Pier Vidal Old', in *Selected Poems*, p. 55)

42 I am thinking of some of the rhetoric of Giorgio Agamben's *Homo Sacer: Sovereign Power and Bare Life* (Stanford, CA, 1998).

43 I have already alluded to Mottram's book on a number of occasions, since it forms a complex and, I think, still vibrant intertext with Burroughs' own writings. But nothing here, we may suspect, is truly to be relied upon.

44 Ronell, *The Telephone Book*, p. 180.

45 Ronell, *The Telephone Book*, p. 180.

46 Ronell, *The Telephone Book*, p. 361, partially repeating what has already been said (to an answering machine, or a tape recorder?) at least once before, on p. 353.

47 See Punter, *Gothic Pathologies*:

> . . . the law is not absolute, it is a way of seeing things. . . . We may here hazard an illicit thought: which is that the body of the addict is not under the control of the law. Further: the body of the addict represents, perhaps incarnates, a limit of the law . . . (pp. 3, 8)

48 Ronell, *The Telephone Book*, p. 353.

49 Ainslie, 'The Dangers of Willpower', in *Getting Hooked*, eds Elster and Skog, p. 65. The passage continues to worry about how 'attractiveness does not explain the sense of slavery'; but perhaps, according to a logic of perversion, it does.

## 4 Imagining Animals

1 It is also the title of a book by my wife, Caroline Case (*Imagining Animals: Art, Psychotherapy, and Primitive States of Mind* [London, 2005]).

2 Which might cause us to think further about a remarkable moment in Deleuze and Guattari's *A Thousand Plateaus*: 'Anyone who likes cats or dogs is a fool' (p. 240). Cf. Luce Irigaray, 'Animal Compassion', trans. Marilyn Gaddis, in *Animal Philosophy: Ethics and Identity*, eds Peter Atterton and Matthew Calarco (London, 2004), pp. 195–201.

3 Calvino, *The Literature Machine: Essays*, trans. Patrick Creagh (London, 1987), p. 329; the original edition of Pliny was published in Turin in 1982.

4 Calvino, *The Literature Machine*, p. 330.

5 As he does, of course, in *Invisible Cities*, trans. William Weaver (London, 1974); the city of Clarice in particular appears to be a place of rats, birds, rabbits, butterflies and chickens (pp. 86–7).

6 See, on Pliny, Trevor Murphy, *Pliny the Elder's Natural History: The Empire in the Encyclopaedia* (Oxford, 2004); Sorcha Carey, *Pliny's Catalogue of Culture: Art and Empire in the Natural History* (Oxford, 2006).

7 Calvino, *The Literature Machine*, p. 316.

8 Pliny, *Natural History*, trans. Harris Rackham (10 vols, Cambridge, MA, 1938–62), Preface, 17.

9 Pliny, *Natural History*, Preface, 13.
10 Pliny, *Natural History*, Preface, 21.
11 Pliny, *Natural History*, X.305.
12 Pliny, *Natural History*, X.399–400.
13 Pliny, *Natural History*, X.411.
14 Blake, 'The Sick Rose', *Songs of Experience* (1789–94), in *Complete Writings*, p. 213.
15 Pliny, *Natural History*, XI.475.
16 Pliny, *Natural History*, VIII.43.
17 Pliny, *Natural History*, VIII.93.
18 Pliny, *Natural History*, XI.595.
19 See Deleuze and Guattari, *Kafka: Toward a Minor Literature*, trans. Dana Polan (Minneapolis, 1986), *passim*.
20 Pliny, *Natural History*, VIII.79.
21 Pliny, *Natural History*, VIII.95.
22 Pliny, *Natural History*, VI.1.
23 Rackham, in Pliny, *Natural History*, VIII.58.
24 Pliny, *Natural History*, Preface, 21.
25 Pliny, *Natural History*, X.381.
26 Yet Pliny also warns us against any tendency to feel contempt for creatures on grounds of their size or 'primitive' mode of life: see *Natural History*, XI.433–5.
27 I have in mind Royle's chapter, 'Mole', in *The Uncanny* (Manchester, 2003), pp. 241–55. 'I hope', Royle says, 'that the uncanniness of the mole might (as it were) speak for itself, in particular in terms of the relations between the human and the animal, of the animal *as* human, and in terms of deferred action or after-effect, writing, foreign body, secretiveness, solitude and death' (p. 253).
28 Pliny, *Natural History*, VIII.3.
29 Pliny, *Natural History*, VIII.5–7.
30 This bears interesting relations to Marx's thoughts on species-being in relation to the human and the animal: see *The Economic and Philosophic Manuscripts of 1844*, ed. Dirk J. Struik (New York, 1964), p. 112, where Marx also talks helpfully about the relation between the organic and the inorganic.
31 See Freud, *Three Essays on the Theory of Sexuality* (1905), in *Standard Edition*, VII, esp. 176–9, where he speaks of latency impulses as evoking 'opposing mental forces . . . which, in order to suppress . . . unpleasure effectively, build up the mental dams [of] disgust, shame and morality [*sic*]' (p. 178).
32 See Abraham, 'Notes on the Phantom: A Complement to Freud's Metapsychology' and 'The Phantom of Hamlet *or* The Sixth Act, *preceded by* The Intermission of "Truth"', in Abraham and Torok, *The Shell and the Kernel*, ed. Rand (Minneapolis, 1994), pp. 171–6 and 187–205.
33 Rackham supplies part of the younger Pliny's account of his uncle's writing practices in his Introduction to Pliny, *Natural History*, x–xii.
34 See Elizabeth Wilson, *Adorned in Dreams: Fashion and Modernity* (2nd edn, London, 2003), esp. pp. 47–66, 91–116.

35 Deleuze and Guattari, *Kafka*, p. 13.
36 See Ralph R. Greenson and Milton Wexler, 'The Non-Transference Relationship in the Psychoanalytic Situation', *International Journal of Psycho-Analysis*, 50 (1969), 27–39.
37 Deleuze and Guattari, *Nomadology: The War Machine* (New York, 1986), p. 36.
38 Deleuze and Guattari, *A Thousand Plateaus*, p. 259.
39 Ellis, *American Psycho* (New York, 1991), p. 399.
40 Pliny, *Natural History*, IX.203.
41 Two crucial texts here are David Garnett, *Lady into Fox* (London, 1922) and Kij Johnson, *The Fox Woman* (London, 1999), which arise from very different traditions.
42 Torok, 'A Remembrance of Things Deleted: Between Sigmund Freud and Emmy von N.', in Abraham and Torok, *The Shell and the Kernel*, pp. 243–4.
43 Torok, 'A Remembrance of Things Deleted', in *The Shell and the Kernel*, p. 245.
44 '*Physis kryptesthai philei*': see Charles H. Kahn, *The Art and Thought of Heraclitus* (Cambridge, 1979), pp. 32–3, 105.
45 'Story of Fear: The Symptoms of Phobia', in *The Shell and the Kernel*, p. 178.
46 See, among other references, Barry Lopez, *Of Wolves and Men* (New York, 1995); Claire Russell and W. M. S. Russell, 'The Social Biology of Werewolves', in *Animals in Folklore*, eds J. R. Porter and W. M. S. Russell (Ipswich, 1978); Chris Powici, 'Witnessing the Wolf: The Human and the Lupine in Cormac McCarthy's *The Crossing*', at <www.dur.ac.uk/postgraduate.english/journal2 > (2000).
47 And most commonly identified as one of the accompanying symptoms of *delirium tremens*, usually caused by abstinence or withdrawal from addiction to alcohol, benzodiazepines or barbiturates.
48 Pliny, *Natural History*, X.383.
49 See in particular Hillman, *Anima: An Anatomy of a Personified Notion* (Dallas, TX, 1985) and the many works by Jung cited therein; also the chapter on 'Animus and Anima' in Bachelard, *The Poetics of Reverie* (Boston, MA, 1971).
50 Huxley, 'The Connection of the Biological Sciences with Medicine', *Nature*, 24:615 (1881), 344.
51 But other views are of course current: see Lawrence Buell, *Writing for an Endangered World: Literature, Culture, and Environment in the US and Beyond* (Cambridge, MA, 2001); *The Ecocriticism Reader: Landmarks in Literary Ecology*, eds Cheryll Glotfelty and Harold Fromm (Athens, GA, 1996); Greg Garrard, *Ecocriticism* (London, 2004).
52 The reference is to Christopher Bollas, *The Shadow of the Object: Psychoanalysis of the Unthought Known* (New York, 1987).
53 One of the more interesting roots of this concern can be found in Thomas Szasz, *The Ethics of Psychoanalysis: The Theory and Method of Autonomous Psychotherapy* (Syracuse, NY, 1989); see also Ernest Wallwork, *Psychoanalysis and Ethics* (New Haven, CT, 1992) and *Ethics of Psychoanalysis*, ed. Joan Raphael-Leff (Colchester, 2000).

54 Pliny, *Natural History*, X.377.
55 Delineated frequently in Jung's work, according to the rules of the ogdoad of elements plus qualities which he mentions in, e.g., *The Philosophical Tree* (1954), in *Alchemical Studies*, trans. R.F.C. Hull (London, 1967), pp. 278–9.

## 5 Hearing the Case

1 This chapter was originally delivered as a talk to a 'Foreign Body' seminar at the University of Stirling; in this version I have tried to negotiate the interface between that oral and this written form, in the context of hearing.
2 Cf. Royle, 'The Remains of Psychoanalysis', the title of two chapters, one on telepathy, the other on Shakespeare, in *After Derrida* (Manchester, 1995), pp. 61–84, 85–123.
3 See, e.g., Ernest van den Haag, 'Psychoanalysis and its Discontents', in *Psychoanalysis, Scientific Method and Philosophy*, ed. Sidney Hook (New York, 1959), pp. 104–16.
4 This is stated by Freud in 'Analysis of a Phobia in a Five-Year-Old Boy' (1909), in *Standard Edition*, X.5, where Freud also goes so far as to say that 'the treatment itself was carried out by the child's father'.
5 'Analysis of a Phobia', in *Standard Edition*, X.22. This is Freud's novelistically dramatic beginning to Part Two of the case history.
6 The multiple significations of the term 'legend' are developed, if often implicitly, in Samuel Weber, *The Legend of Freud* (Minneapolis, 1982).
7 Cf. Laplanche, *Essays on Otherness*:

> The messages which are the object of the first translations are not essentially verbal, nor are they 'intellectual'! They include in large part signifiers of affect, which can be either translated or repressed: a smile . . . an angry gesture, a grimace of disgust, etc. These signifiers, if they are repressed, will be designified, in the same way as are more 'intellectual' signifiers. The 'exclusion' of affect here is nothing but a general consequence of the exclusion of the signified (p. 108).

8 'Analysis of a Phobia', in *Standard Edition*, X.41.
9 'It corrupted the doctors and, perhaps, was engineered by corrupt doctors' (Dally, 'Drugspeak', in *Addiction Controversies*, ed. Warburton, p. 2).
10 'Analysis of a Phobia', in *Standard Edition*, X.141–2.
11 'Analysis of a Phobia', in *Standard Edition*, X.148.
12 'Analysis of a Phobia', in *Standard Edition*, X.148–9. Although the question of abuse must be left strictly bracketed, also interesting is Jennifer J. Freyd, *Betrayal Trauma: Logic of Forgetting Childhood Abuse* (Cambridge, MA, 1996).
13 'Analysis of a Phobia', in *Standard Edition*, X.149. We are here also referred to *The Interpretation of Dreams* (1900), in *Standard Edition*, V.120–1 (passage added in 1911).
14 See Editor's Note in 'Analysis of a Phobia', in *Standard Edition*, X.3–4, refer-

ring us to 'The Sexual Enlightenment of Children' (1907), in *Standard Edition*, IX.134–5 and fn. 1. Cows and dogs make guest appearances in this account, as well as in the case history.

15 A name (traditional in 'Novalis'/von Hardenberg's family) which is said to mean 'clearer of new land'; which, insofar as it clears away (clears up?) the old name, could appear to lead us into an infinite pseudonymous regress.

16
> . . . the secret employs inflexible violence in its petition. Having force of law, this secret is always the power of someone. There would be no secret without a pledge to the other.

(Derrida, *Geneses, Genealogies, Genres and Genius: The Secrets of the Archive*, trans. Beverley Bie Bahic [Edinburgh, 2006], p. 21)

17 Although 'communicated by' is something of a commonplace, the phrasing is considered worthy of mention in the Editor's Note ('Analysis of a Phobia', in *Standard Edition*, X.4).

18 'Analysis of a Phobia', in *Standard Edition*, X.6.

19 'Analysis of a Phobia', in *Standard Edition*, X.22, 24.

20 'Analysis of a Phobia', in *Standard Edition*, X.28.

21 'Analysis of a Phobia', in *Standard Edition*, X.24.

22 'Analysis of a Phobia', in *Standard Edition*, X.22.

23 'Analysis of a Phobia', in *Standard Edition*, X.30.

24 'Analysis of a Phobia', in *Standard Edition*, X.70.

25 See the account of rapture in H.G. Wells, 'The Door in the Wall' (*The Short Stories of H.G. Wells* [London, 1927], pp. 142–61). It is, unsurprisingly, 'very difficult for [the protagonist] to give [the narrator] his full sense of that garden into which he came' (p. 147) and, at at least one point, 'there's a gap in my memory' (p. 149).

26 'Analysis of a Phobia', in *Standard Edition*, X.85. It is indeed a wonder that Hans can work out which is or is not the 'wrong' animal, given the flood of beasts (giraffes, lions, pelicans and many others, as well as the horses, cows and dogs) in the pages of the case history.

27 'Analysis of a Phobia', in *Standard Edition*, X.121.

28 'Analysis of a Phobia', in *Standard Edition*, X, e.g., 19.

29 It is interesting to find the following comment in a clinical account of addiction:

> Attuned as we are to modern efficiency in the developed world, we do not always recognise the oppressiveness of an environment so rationalised that much of our natural idiosyncrasy has been anticipated and harnessed or selected out. Yet newcomers accustomed to more backward [*sic*] economies find our relationships superficial; and our own fictional heroes are increasingly those who rage against systems.

(Ainslie, 'The Dangers of Willpower', in *Getting Hooked*, eds Elster and Skog, p. 82)

30 'Analysis of a Phobia', in *Standard Edition*, X.31.

31 'Analysis of a Phobia', in *Standard Edition*, X.120.

32 See Henry James, *The Turn of the Screw*, ed. Allan Lloyd Smith (London, 1993); also *The Governess: An Anthology*, eds Trev Lynn Broughton and Ruth Symes (London, 1998).

33 For example, it is perhaps 'enough to say', with Wilkie Collins, one of the great psychologists of addictive behaviour, 'that at intervals almost every form of madness appeared in the family; monomania being the most frequent manifestation of the affliction among them' (Collins, *The Queen of Hearts* [London, 1925], p. 106).

34 'Analysis of a Phobia', in *Standard Edition*, X.28.

35 'Analysis of a Phobia', in *Standard Edition*, X.42.

36 'Analysis of a Phobia', in *Standard Edition*, X.12n. Cf. *Three Essays on the Theory of Sexuality*, in *Standard Edition*, VII.194 ff.

37 'Analysis of a Phobia', in *Standard Edition*, X.19, 28.

38 'Analysis of a Phobia', in *Standard Edition*, X.17.

39 See Punter, *Writing the Passions* (London, 2001), pp. 247 ff., and the references cited there.

40 On Hekate, see Hillman, *The Dream and the Underworld*, pp. 39 ff., 49 ff. But it is significant that Hekate is also in some sense the goddess of dream:

> Hekate has long been implicated in dream interpretations. Both the magical view that considers dreams to be foretellings and the nineteenth-century mechanistic view that attributes them to waste products of physiological sensations (garbage) show Hekate's influence (p. 39).

41 As well as in fiction, in more or less oblique ways: see, e.g., Jed Rubenfeld, *The Interpretation of Murder: A Novel* (New York, 2006).

42 Cf. Julia Kristeva, *Strangers to Ourselves*, trans. L. S. Roudiez (Hemel Hempstead, 1991).

43

> The search for undersense [*hyponoia*] is what we express in common speech as the desire to understand. We want to get below what is going on and see its basis, its fundamentals, how and where it is grounded. The need to understand more deeply, this search for deeper grounding, is like a call from Hades to move toward his deeper intelligence.

(Hillman, *The Dream and the Underworld*, p. 137)

44 See Punter, e.g., *Gothic Pathologies: The Text, the Body and the Law* (London, 1998), p. 102.

45 See 'Analysis of a Phobia', in *Standard Edition*, X.84.

46 Modisane, *Blame Me on History* (London, 1963), conjures it in the immediacy of death:

> Something in me died, a piece of me died, with the dying of Sophiatown . . . I was a free man, but the salt of the bitterness was still in my mouth (p. 5).

## 6 The Well of Life

1 See Lessing, *The Memoirs of a Survivor* (London, 1974); also Lessing, 'On Sufism and Idries Shah's *The Commanding Self* (1994)', at <ishk.net/Sufis/lessing_commandingself.html>.

2 See earlier work such as Andrew Crowcroft, *The Psychotic: Understanding Madness* (Harmondsworth, 1967) and Thomas Freeman, *Psychopathology of the Psychoses* (London, 1969); and more recently various essays in *Changing Outcomes in Psychosis*, eds Richard Velleman, Eric Davis, Gina Smith and Michael Drage (Oxford, 2007).

3 As in, of course, Dali's 'The Persistence of Memory' (1931), 'The Disintegration of the Persistence of Memory' (1954) or 'Soft Construction with Boiled Beans (Premonition of Civil War)' (1936). The Plath echo is from 'Nick and the Candlestick', in *Ariel* (London, 1965), pp. 40–1, which is discussed in detail below.

4 See (for convenience) *Lustful Maidens and Ascetic Kings: Buddhist and Hindu Stories of Life*, eds Roy C. Amore and Larry D. Shinn (New York, 1981), pp. 166–8.

5 See Hillman, *Re-Visioning Psychology* (New York, 1975), e.g., p.137; where Hillman also remarks that 'the enemy of *psyché* is *physis*, however it appears, concretely or abstractly. The enemy of psyche is never material things or concrete life unless we forget that these, too, are always subject to seeing through'.

6 See L. M. Vail, *Heidegger and Ontological Difference* (University Park, PA, 1972), pp. 136–8, 179–80.

7 Recommended treatments for the underlying condition behind vertigo include the benzodiazepines; withdrawal from which, as we have seen, may lead us back to zoopsia.

8 The reference, of course, is to Coleridge, 'Kubla Khan' (1798), in *Poetical Works*, ed. E. H. Coleridge (London, 1967), pp. 295–8.

9 I think here particularly of the 'cloud-sculptors of Coral D' in J.G. Ballard's story of that name, in *Vermilion Sands* (London, 1973), pp. 11–30.

10 See, e.g., Muhammad Habidullah, *The Life and Work of the Prophet of Islam* (Islamabad, 1998); Maxime Rodinson, *Muhammad, Prophet of Islam* (London, 2002); Annemarie Schimmel, *And Muhammad is his Messenger: The Veneration of the Prophet in Islamic Piety* (Chapel Hill, NC, 1985).

11 John L. Esposito, *Islam: The Straight Path* (New York, 1988). See also, intriguingly, the plethora of papers on Druze beliefs and pathology, one of which is Iulian Iancu, Baruch Spivak, Roberto Mester and Abraham Weizman, 'Belief in Transmigration of the Soul and Psychopathology in Israeli Druze: A Culture-Sensitive Psychotherapeutic Approach', *Psychopathology*, 31.1 (1998), 52–8.

12 See, e.g., *Heraclitean Fragments*, eds John Sallis and Kenneth Maly (University, AL, 1980), pp. 102 ff.

13 This reference to Balinese ritual, and others later in the chapter, are meant to point towards the discussion, in Chapter Eight, of death, story and the preservation of the soul.

14 The emblematic story of encryption here is Poe, 'The Cask of Amontillado', in *Selected Tales*, pp. 289–95, a story of which, according to the impossible secret logic of the narrator, no account survives.

15 See Chaturveti Badinath, *The Mahabharata: An Inquiry into the Human Condition* (New Delhi, 2006); Nicholas Sutton, *Religious Doctrines in the Mahabharata* (New Delhi, 2000); J. Brockington, *The Sanskrit Epics* (Leiden, 1998).

16 'The Well of Life', in eds Amore and Shinn, p. 166.

17 See Marie Louise von Franz, *An Introduction to the Psychology of Fairy Tales* (2nd edn, Zurich, 1973), and Bruno Bettelheim, *The Uses of Enchantment: The Meaning and Importance of Fairy Tales* (London, 1976).

18 And this has also to do with the whole issue of interpretation:

> The interpreter's role is to help the ego-shade adjust to his underworld milieu. The interpreter is a guiding Virgil, or a Teiresias, or a Charon; he is not a Hercules or an Orpheus. His work is in service of Hermes *chthonios* or Hermes *psychopompos*, corresponding to the one way direction downward. Hermes takes souls down; the hero standing behind the ego tries to bring them back up again.

(Hillman, *The Dream and the Underworld*, p. 108)

19 For a remarkable example, see the case of G. T. Fechner of Leipzig as recounted in Hillman, *The Dream and the Underworld*, pp. 14–15.

20 'The Well of Life', in eds Amore and Shinn, p. 166.

21 'What immortal hand or eye/Could frame thy fearful symmetry?' ('The Tyger', *Songs of Experience*, in *Complete Writings*, p. 241) when the shape of the tiger (to revert for a moment to Prynne) and the shapes of the 'forests of the night' are mutually indistinguishable, interfused.

22 The rhetoric of cross-hatching, as of latticework and grilles, looks forward to the next chapter, 'A Body of Alabaster'.

23 A curious more modern analogy, or perhaps derivative, can be found in Flora Annie Steel's short story 'The King's Well', in *The Permanent Way, and Other Stories* (London, 1898), pp. 150–64.

24 Here Blake follows an 'Angel' through a 'winding cavern . . . till a void boundless as a nether sky appear'd beneath us, & we held by the roots of trees and hung over this immensity' (*The Marriage of Heaven and Hell*, in *Complete Writings*, p. 155).

25 'The Well of Life', in eds Amore and Shinn, pp. 166–8. And cf.:

> When visceral factors overwhelm volitional choice, deviations of behaviour from perceived self-interest tend to exhibit a characteristic pattern. Not surprisingly, given their attention-focusing function, they tend to narrow an individual's perceptual and motivational focus. Hunger narrows one's focus to food, fear to options for flight, and so on. . . . Sex has little

appeal to a person who is starving; food has little appeal to a person in the 'grip' of terror.

(George Loewenstein, 'A Visceral Account of Addiction', in *Getting Hooked*, eds Elster and Skog, p. 239)

26 Recommended for further reading is Isaac D'Israeli's indispensable *Curiosities of Literature* (London, 1791–1823). Of particular interest is the essay 'True Sources of Secret History'.

27 Eds Amore and Shinn, p. 168. There are other similar structures, as for example when Kierkegaard speaks of Aristophanes' Socrates:

> Whether he is in a basket suspended from the ceiling or staring omphalopsychically into himself and thereby in a way freeing himself from earthly gravity, in both senses he is hovering.

(Kierkegaard, *The Concept of Irony*, eds Howard V. Hong and Edna H. Hong [Princeton, NJ, 1989], p. 152).

28 Eds Amore and Shinn, p. 168. Or:

> Happy then is he who reaches the musk through the scent and becomes one with the musk. Thereafter for him remains no passing away; he has become eternal in the very essence of the musk. . . . Thereafter he communicates its scent to the world, and the world is revived by him. Only the name of what he was survives in him . . .

(A.J. Arberry, *Discourses of Rūmī* [London, 1961], p. 71)

29 Via an urban equivalent, perhaps:

> The city is reached overland by a series of trails cut in stone, suspension bridges and ladders intricately booby-trapped, wrong maps, disappearing guides . . . balconies over the void . . .

(Burroughs, *The Soft Machine: A Novel* [rev. edn, London, 1968], p. 146)

30 The classic locus here is again to be found in Poe: see 'The Imp of the Perverse', in *Selected Tales*, pp. 283–8. 'We stand upon the brink of a precipice. We peer into the abyss – we grow sick and dizzy' (p. 285), and thus to the inevitable . . .

31 Arberry, *Discourses of Rūmī*, p. 55.

32 Arberry, *Discourses of Rūmī*, p. 55.

33 See Hoban, *The Moment under the Moment: Stories, a Libretto, Essays and Sketches* (London, 1992).

34 Nick Totton, 'You Can't Get There From Here (10)', in *Press When Illuminated: New and Selected Poems 1968–2003* (Cambridge, 2004), p. 157.

35

> . . . the secret is not without an affinity for the sacred, with the very genesis of that which, in a sacrifice, effects the sacred, brings forth or gives birth to the sacred and the secret in a single act of birth.

(Derrida, *Geneses, Genealogies, Genres and Genius*, p. 22)

36 See Deleuze and Guattari, *A Thousand Plateaus*, pp. 381–4, 480–2, 492–500.

37 See, e.g., Wilfred Bion, *Experiences in Groups* (New York, 1959); Barry Palmer, 'Ambiguity and Paradox in Group Relations Conferences', in *Bion and Group Therapy*, ed. Malcolm Pines (London, 1985), pp. 274–305.

38 These themes are picked up in some of Elmore Leonard's 'western' stories. See, e.g., 'Trail of the Apache' in *The Complete Western Stories* (New York, 2004), pp. 1–35.
39 See David Lewis-Williams, *The Mind in the Cave: Consciousness and the Origins of Art* (London, 2002).

## 7 A Body of Alabaster

1 In *Birds through a Ceiling of Alabaster*, eds Abdullah al-Udhari and George Wightman (Harmondsworth, 1975), p. 72.
2 *Birds through a Ceiling of Alabaster*, pp. 9–32.
3 See Punter, *Writing the Passions*, pp. 108–19.
4 See Roland Barthes, *Mythologies*, trans. Annette Lavers (London, 1972), p. 121: 'One should at least get some consolation from the fact that conceptual neologisms are never arbitrary: they are built according to a highly sensible proportional rule'.
5 See Derrida, *Geneses, Genealogies, Genres and Genius*, e.g., pp. 18–19.
6 See, e.g., Bai Juyi, 'To my Wife', 'For my Brothers in Jiangnan', 'Sending Summer Clothes to Weizhi', in *200 Selected Poems*, trans. Rewi Alley (Beijing, 1983), pp. 146–7, 151, 159.
7 See Edward Said, *Orientalism* (London, 2003), pp. 291–3; Susan Bassnett, *Translation Studies* (London, 1991), e.g., pp. 30–7; and *Postcolonial Translation: Theory and Practice*, eds Bassnett and Harish Trivedi (London, 1999), *passim*.
8 Abbas Ibn al-Ahnaf, in *Birds through a Ceiling of Alabaster*, p. 35.
9 Abdullah Ibn al-Mu'tazz, in *Birds through a Ceiling of Alabaster*, p. 87.
10 See Klein, *Envy and Gratitude: A Study of Unconscious Sources* (London, 1957), pp. 24–7, 67.
11 The references are to Graham, 'His Companions Buried Him', in *New Collected Poems*, pp. 37–8; and to Barthes, *The Lover's Discourse: Fragments*, trans. Richard Howard (Harmondsworth, 1990).
12 A particularly clear elaboration of this point can be found in Sharon L. James, *Learned Girls and Male Persuasion: Gender and Reading in Roman Love Elegy* (Berkeley, CA, 2003).
13 See, e.g., Simon Glendinning, *In the Name of Phenomenology* (London, 2007); Maurice Natanson, *Phenomenology, Role and Reason: Essays on the Coherence and Deformation of Social Reality* (Springfield, IL, 1974); Scheler, *Man's Place in Nature* (Boston, 1961).
14 Lear, 'The Dong with the Luminous Nose' (1877), in *The Complete Nonsense of Edward Lear*, ed. Holbrook Jackson (London, 1947), pp. 225–8.
15 Blake, 'London', *Songs of Experience*, in *Complete Writings*, p. 216. On the 'radioactive', see also Deleuze who, discussing Lewis Carroll, comments that

> surface nonsense is like the 'Radiance' of pure events, entities that never finish either happening or withdrawing. Pure events without mixture shine above the mixed bodies, above their embroiled actions and passions. They let an incorporeal rise to the surface like a mist over the earth, a pure

> 'expressed' from the depths: not the sword, but the flash of the sword, a flash without a sword like a smile without a cat.

(Deleuze, *Essays Critical and Clinical*, trans. David W. Smith and Michael Greco [Minneapolis, 1997], p. 22)

16 Coleridge, 'The Rime of the Ancient Mariner' (1797), in *Poetical Works*, pp. 186–209:

> And straight the Sun was flecked with bars,
> (Heaven's mother send us grace!)
> As if through a dungeon-grate he peered
> With broad and burning face.

(ll. 177–80, p. 193)

17 Apart from Turner, the references are to Derek Walcott, *Midsummer* (1984), XXIII, in *Collected Poems 1948–84* (London, 1992), p. 483, and to Blake, *Jerusalem*, 57.8–11, in *Complete Writings*, p. 689.

18 Eliot, 'Marina', in *Collected Poems*, p. 116.

19 Marion Milner, *The Hands of the Living God: An Account of a Psycho-analytic Treatment* (London, 1988), p. 184.

20 Milner, *The Hands of the Living God*, pp. 194–5.

21 See Deleuze and Guattari, *A Thousand Plateaus*, esp. pp. 149–66; also Timothy S. Murphy, 'Only Intensities Subsist: Samuel Beckett's *Nohow On*', in *Deleuze and Literature*, eds Buchanan and Marks, pp. 229–50.

22 See King, *The Shining* (New York, 1977); and on related themes, e.g., *Desperation* (New York, 2001) and *Rose Madder* (New York, 1995).

23 My earlier argument begins in *Writing the Passions*, p. 20.

24 The term 'wetware' is now in a variety of common usages, not all of them obviously linked to its neurological origins; but see Rudy V.B. Rucker, *Wetware* (London, 1997).

25 Abu al-Ala al-Ma'arri, in *Birds through a Ceiling of Alabaster*, p. 99.

26 For Blake this cleft, this opening into the deep, is an expression, a frown, in fact a

> Frown of Frowns
> Which you strive to forget in vain,
>
> For it sticks in the Heart's deep Core
> And it sticks in the deep Back bone . . .

('The Smile' [c. 1803], in *Complete Writings*, p. 423)

27 On 'The Ballad of Reading Gaol', see, e.g., Rodney Shewan, *Oscar Wilde: Art and Egotism* (London, 1977), pp. 198–202; and Peter Raby, *Oscar Wilde* (Cambridge, 1988), pp. 145–6.

28 See Blake, *Jerusalem*, 33.17 ff., in *Complete Writings*, p. 659, and 'The Clod and the Pebble', *Songs of Experience*, in *Complete Writings*, p. 211.

29 For one of the clearest explications, see Adler, 'Advantages and Disadvantages of the Inferiority Feeling' (1933), in *Superiority and Social Interest: A Collection of Later Writings*, eds Heinz L. Ansbacher and Rowena R. Ansbacher (London, 1965), pp. 50–8.

30 See, e.g., Hillman, *Re-Visioning Psychology*, p. 74, where he also reminds us that 'psychotherapy, in accordance with the root meanings of the words "psyche" and "therapy" means *to serve soul*, not to treat it'. Thus psychology 'may be fundamentally engaged with psychopathology and inseparable from the pathologising process, but it is not intended as a treatment for it'.

31 Ellmann, 'Deconstruction and Psychoanalysis', in *Deconstructions: A User's Guide*, ed. Royle (Basingstoke, 2000), p. 224; see also Derrida, 'To Speculate on "Freud"', in *The Post Card: From Socrates to Freud and Beyond*, trans. Alan Bass (Chicago, 1987), pp. 257–409.

32 Ellmann, 'Deconstruction and Psychoanalysis', p. 224.

33 Ellmann, 'Deconstruction and Psychoanalysis', p. 224, referring to Freud, *Beyond the Pleasure Principle* (1920), in *Standard Edition*, XVIII.36–8.

34 For remarkable 'accounts' of the rapture and terror of mountaineering, see M. John Harrison, *Climbers* (London, 1989).

35 See Conrad, *Heart of Darkness* (1902), ed. Paul O'Prey (London, 1983), p. 32.

36 See Derrida, 'Plato's Pharmacy', in *Dissemination*, trans. Barbara Johnson (Chicago, 1981), pp. 63–171.

37 See, e.g., Irigaray, *The Way of Love*, trans. Heidi Bostic and Stephen Pluháček (London, 2002), and Cixous and Catherine Clément, *The Newly Born Woman*, trans. Betsy Wing (Minneapolis, 1986).

38 The examples would include Crowley, *Diary of a Drug Fiend* (London, 1922); Malcolm Lowry, *Under the Volcano* (London, 1947); Eric Clapton, *The Autobiography* (London, 2007).

39 Gardiner, 'Jidohanbaiki', in *Escalator* (Edinburgh, 2006), p. 53.

40 Gardiner, 'Jidohanbaiki', p. 54.

41 Gardiner, 'Jidohanbaiki', pp. 54–5.

42 Gardiner, 'Jidohanbaiki', p. 58.

43 The references are to Ballard, *Crash* (London, 1973); and also, in terms of trauma, to *The Atrocity Exhibition* (London, 1970) and *Empire of the Sun* (London, 1984).

44 Derrida, 'The Rhetoric of Drugs', in *Points*, p. 245.

45 See Huxley, *'The Doors of Perception' and 'Heaven and Hell'* (London, 1954); Leary, *The Politics of Ecstasy* (Berkeley, CA, 1998); Robert Greenfield, *Timothy Leary: A Biography* (New York, 2006); Thompson, *Fear and Loathing in Las Vegas: A Savage Journey to the Heart of the American Dream* (New York, 1972).

46 See Welsh, *Filth* (London, 1998), e.g., pp. 315–18.

47 Boothroyd, 'Deconstruction and Drugs: A Philosophical/Literary Cocktail', in *Deconstructions*, ed. Royle, p. 54.

48 Mottram, *The Algebra of Need*, p. 197.

## **8** Death, Story and the Preservation of the Soul

1 Darnton, *The Great Cat Massacre and Other Episodes in French Cultural History*

(New York, 1984), p. 216; Carter, *Expletives Deleted: Selected Writings* (London, 1992), p. 3.

2 See Clark, *The Poetics of Singularity*, e.g., p. 9, where he speaks of a 'reading' which

> attains a space in which the text is felt to project itself so specifically that the terms of any mode of interpretation one might want to apply begin to be felt as inadequate.

3 On the inner ear, see Clark, *The Poetics of Singularity*, pp. 74 ff.; also Gadamer, 'Text and Interpretation', trans. Dennis J. Schmidt and Richard Palmer in *Dialogue and Deconstruction: The Gadamer Derrida Encounter*, eds Diane P. Michelfelder and Richard E. Palmer (Albany, NY, 1989), pp. 21–51, and 'The Truth of the Word', trans. Lawrence K. Schmidt and Monika Reuss, in *The Spectre of Relativism: Truth, Dialogue and Phronesis in Philosophical Hermeneutics*, ed. Lawrence K. Schmidt (Evanston, IL, 1995), pp. 135–55.

4 See Walter Benjamin, 'The Work of Art in the Age of Mechanical Reproduction', in *Illuminations*, trans. Harry Zohn (London, 1970), pp. 211–44.

5 The reference is to Bauman, *Liquid Modernity* (Cambridge, 2000); see especially pp. 53–90.

6 On natality, see Hannah Arendt, *The Human Condition* (Chicago, 1958), pp. 177–8.

7 See *The Tibetan Book of the Dead*, ed. W.Y. Evans-Wentz (3rd edn, Oxford, 1957), pp. 183 ff.

8 'Good King Nala's Downfall', in eds Amore and Shinn, p. 22.

9 'The Wise Old Crow', in eds Amore and Shinn, p. 60 (we shall come across another crow, if only briefly, later).

10 To get in touch with telepathy is 'to lose one's head', no more or less.

(Royle, *After Derrida*, p. 68, quoting Derrida, 'Telepathy', trans. Royle, *Oxford Literary Review*, 10 [1988], 20). As Royle goes on to say (p. 70), it is clear that 'in historical terms the word "telepathy" is part of an explosion of forms of communication and possibilities of representation'.

11 See, e.g., 'At the Mountains of Madness', in *At the Mountains of Madness, and Other Tales of Terror*, ed. August Derleth (London, 1966).

12 The reference is to Yeats, 'Long-Legged Fly', and in particular to the stanza concerning Michelangelo and, through him, the sacredness of creative activity, however mundane it might appear, and the need for a double protection, of the children and of the space itself: see *The Collected Poems of W. B. Yeats* (London, 1965), p. 382.

13 See Maturin, *Melmoth the Wanderer*, and especially the opening pages, including the Preface (*Melmoth the Wanderer*, ed. Grant, pp. 5 ff.); and Jan Potocki, *The Manuscript Found in Saragossa*, trans. Ian Maclean (London, 1995), the only modern book, as far as I know, to be prefaced by a guide to the stories within it for the reader who does not wish 'to engage with the full complexity of Potocki's interwoven narrations . . . ' (p. xxiii).

14 See Banks, *The Bridge*, pp. 281–8.

15 Such imagery is inevitably reminiscent of CERN (the European Organisation for Nuclear Research) and its Large Hadron Collider; there has recently been an interesting possibility that the opening of the LHC was to be delayed because of a lawsuit being brought by Walter L. Wagner and Luis Sancho on the grounds that it might 'rip a hole in the fabric of the space-time continuum and so destroy the Earth' (<www.theregister.co.uk/2008/03/28>).

16 In the 'case' of the 'rat-man', it is worth looking closely at the textual roles of rats and, indeed, other beasts: see Freud, 'Notes upon a Case of Obsessional Neurosis' (1909), in *Standard Edition*, X.213–16, 288–9, 296–7.

17 In all classical, and in almost all visual, representations of the Minotaur there are two eyes; the alternative legend of the one-eyed monster, potent though it is in terms of blinding and 'blind rage', is almost certainly the result of overlaps with the myths of Polyphemus.

18 See Bradbury, *Fahrenheit 451* (London, 1954), pp. 157–61.

19 See Blake, e.g., *Jerusalem*, 12.25, in *Complete Writings*, p. 632.

20 See Anna Freud, *The Ego and the Mechanisms of Defence*, trans. Cecil Baines (rev. edn, London, 1968).

21 See, e.g., *Textual Sources for the Study of Hinduism*, ed. Wendy Doniger O'Flaherty (Manchester, 1988), pp. 130–8.

22 See Brockden Brown, *Wieland, or, The Transformation: An American Tale* (1798), the tone of which is set by the epigraph:

> From Virtue's blissful paths away
> The double-tongued are sure to stray;
> Good is a forth-right journey still,
> And many paths but lead to ill.

(*Wieland* [New York, 1973], p. 5)

23

> History is inseparable from the earth, struggle is underground, and, if we want to grasp an event, we must not show it, we must not pass along the event, but plunge into it, go through all the geological layers that are its internal history . . .

(Deleuze, *Cinema 2: The Time-Image*, trans. Hugh Tomlinson and Robert Galeta [Minneapolis, 1989], p. 119)

24 Thomas Hardy, 'While Drawing in a Churchyard', in *Collected Poems* (London, 1968), p. 504.

25 Cf. Claire Colebrook, 'Inhuman Irony', in *Deleuze and Literature*, eds Buchanan and Marks, p. 126:

> Both Foucault and Deleuze were insistent that power or desire could not be reduced to the human. And both insisted that certain literary styles could take us back to the inhuman buzzing of discourse, to a white noise that plunges us from the heights of meaning to the depths of materiality.

26 See Helen J. Nicholson, *The Knights Hospitalier* (London, 2001); Piers Paul Read, *The Templars* (Cambridge, MA, 1999); Roger Peyrefitte, *Knights of Malta*, trans. Edward Hyams (London, 1960).

27 The echo is of Walcott, *Another Life* (1973), in *Collected Poems*, pp. 143–294:

> There
> was your heaven! The clear
> glaze of another life,
> a landscape locked in amber, the rare
> gleam. The dream
> of reason had produced its monster . . .

(p. 145)

28 The authority here remains John Bowlby: see the three volumes of his *Attachment and Loss*: *Attachment* (1969), *Separation: Anxiety and Anger* (1973), and *Loss: Sadness and Depression* (1980). See also Jeremy Holmes, *John Bowlby and Attachment Theory* (London, 1993).

29 See Blake, especially *Vala, or, The Four Zoas*, Nights the First and Seventh, in *Complete Writings*, pp. 264–80 and 320–32.

30 See Jacob Kinnard, *Imaging Wisdom: Saying and Knowing in the Art of Indian Buddhism* (Richmond, 1999); Richard S. Cohen, *Beyond Enlightenment: Buddhism, Religion, Modernity* (London, 2006); and, more obliquely, Jan Nattier, *Once Upon a Future Time: Studies in a Buddhist Prophecy of Decline* (Berkeley, CA, 1991).

31 A classic account of the resurrection of the pet and the child is King, *Pet Sematary* (New York, 1983).

## **9** Some Tales of Erythron

1 See Heidegger, *The Basic Problems of Phenomenology*, trans. Albert Hofstadter (Bloomington, IN, 1982), pp. 289–90; Sartre, *Being and Nothingness: An Essay on Phenomenological Ontology*, trans. Hazel E. Barnes (London, 1958), pp. 43–5; Derrida's essay, 'The Pit and the Pyramid: Introduction to Hegel's Semiology' (1971), in *Margins of Philosophy*, trans. Alan Bass (Brighton, 1982), pp. 60–108.

2 See Deleuze and Guattari, *Anti-Oedipus: Capitalism and Schizophrenia*, trans. Robert Hurley *et al.* (Minneapolis, 1983); also Eugene Holland, *Deleuze and Guattari's 'Anti-Oedipus': Introduction to Schizoanalysis* (Oxford, 1999).

3 Particularly in the form of object-loss; see Freud, 'Inhibitions, Symptoms and Anxiety' (1926), in *Standard Edition*, XX.129–31, 136–9, 167–72.

4 See Freud, *Civilisation and its Discontents*, in *Standard Edition*, XXI.69–71: 'in mental life nothing which has once been formed can perish' (p. 69).

5 The immediate reference, of course, is to Martin Luther and the 95 Theses. Luther, as it happens, was a sufferer from Ménière's disease, which is manifested in vertigo and tinnitus (buzzing in the ears) as well, in later life, as angina. Ménière's disease also, naturally, affects the ability to hear.

6 There is from Great Eternity a mild and pleasant rest
Nam'd Beulah, a soft Moony Universe, feminine, lovely . . .

(Blake, *Vala, or, The Four Zoas*, Night the First, ll. 94–5, in *Complete Writings*, p. 266). See also Petronius, *Satyricon*, trans. P.G. Walsh (Oxford, 1997); Richard Seaford, *Dionysos* (Oxford, 2006); Rosemarie Taylor-Perry, *The God who Comes: Dionysian Mysteries Revisited* (New York, 2003).

7 Big clumsy people all around, they don't mean to break things but they do. Inside her head the precious fragile toys. . . . She packs her head full of good things so that there won't be room for the other things, the things she hates.

(Rushdie, *Shame* [London, 1983], pp. 213–14)

8 See Blake, *Milton* (1804–8), 18.5–25, in *Complete Writings*, p. 499.

9 See, e.g., Donald Preziosi, *Brain of the Earth's Body: Art, Museums and the Phantasms of Modernity* (Minneapolis, 2003); Steve Pile, *Real Cities: Modernity, Space and the Phantasmagorias of City Life* (London, 2005); *Tracing Modernity: Manifestations of the Modern in Architecture and the City*, eds Mari Hvattum and Christian Hermansen (London, 2004).

10 But they smile, they find a music centred in a doleful song
Steaming up, a lamentation and an ancient tale of wrong,
Like a tale of little meaning tho' the words are strong . . .

(Alfred Lord Tennyson, 'The Lotos-Eaters' [1832], in *Selected Poems*, ed. Aidan Day [London, 1991], p. 62)

11 'By virtue of their prior chronic drug use, the pleasure/reward circuits of their brains have been forever changed' (Gardner and David, 'The Neurobiology of Chemical Addiction', in *Getting Hooked*, eds Elster and Skog, p. 120).

12 Nor is there voice: 'If the heart is totally absorbed, all the other members are totally obliterated in it and there is no need of the tongue' (Arberry, *Discourses of Rūmī*, p. 55).

13 See, e.g., Fred Botting, 'Candygothic', and Jerrold E. Hogle, 'The Gothic at our Turn of the Century: Our Culture of Simulation and the Return of the Body', in *The Gothic*, ed. Botting (Cambridge, 2001), pp. 133–51, 153–79.

14 Cf., e.g., Nina Auerbach, *Our Vampires, Ourselves* (new edn, Chicago, 1997); Allin Cottrell, 'Sniffing the Camembert: On the Conceivability of Zombies', *Journal of Consciousness Studies*, 6 (1999), 4–12; Robert Kirk, *Zombies and Consciousness* (Oxford, 2005).

15 See J. M. Barrie, *Peter Pan, or The Boy who Wouldn't Grow Up* (1904); J. Randy Taraborrelli, *Michael Jackson: The Magic and the Madness* (new edn, London, 2004).

16 With Ronell, we can perhaps reconnect this with the world of soul or spirit: 'The spirit is flaming, and only perhaps in this sense is it something flickering in the air', she says of Trakl (although possibly also of Heidegger) (*The Telephone Book*, p. 176).

17 Slowly the poison the whole blood stream fills.
It is not the effort nor the failure tires.
The waste remains, the waste remains and kills.

(William Empson, 'Missing Dates', in *Collected Poems* [London, 1962], p. 60)

18 See Haraway, *Primate Visions: Gender, Race and Nature in the World of Modern Science* (New York, 1989), e.g., pp. 129–32.

19 Siegfried Morenz has an especially illuminating passage on the Egyptian dimension in his *Egyptian Religion*, trans. Ann E. Keep (Ithaca, NY, 1973), pp. 183–213.

20
> No such sweet sights doth Limbo den immure,
> Wall'd round, and made a spirit-jail secure,
> By the mere horror of blank Naught-at-all,
> Whose circumambience doth these ghosts enthral.
> A lurid thought is growthless, dull Privation,
> Yet that is but a Purgatory curse;
> Hell knows a fear far worse,
> A fear – a future state; – 'tis positive Negation!

(Coleridge, 'Limbo' [1817], in *Poetical Works*, pp. 430–1)

21
> About a fortnight before he was assassinated, Abraham Lincoln recounted a dream in which he heard the sound of sobbing. 'I went from room to room; no living person was in sight, but the same mournful sounds of distress met me as I passed along'. He eventually discovers a catafalque; the corpse resting on it is his own.

(*Theatre of Sleep: An Anthology of Literary Dreams*, eds Guido Almansi and Claude Béguin [London, 1986], p. 161)

22 Or, indeed, on a *mise-en-abŷme*, one classic locus for which would be Calvino's *If on a Winter's Night a Traveller* (1979), whose opening already 'opens up' the possibility of infinite regress.

23 Two examples of the 'reversed gaze' would be Gulfishan Khan, *Indian Muslim Perceptions of the West during the Eighteenth Century* (Karachi, 1998) and Tapan Raychaudhuri, *Europe Reconsidered: Perceptions of the West in Nineteenth-Century Bengal* (2nd edn, New Delhi, 2002).

24 Even in the merest detail which connects addiction and the dark:
> . . . I see very clearly [*sic*] in my head the tube of luminal and the bottle of whisky. In case . . .
>
> Just as I have got to my door there is a click and everything is in darkness. Impossible to get the key in. I must cross the pitch-black landing . . .

(Rhys, *Good Morning, Midnight* [London, 1939], p. 148)

25 At the end,
> It seemed to me that the house would collapse before I could escape, that the heavens would fall upon my head. But nothing happened. The heavens do not fall for such a trifle.

(Conrad, *Heart of Darkness*, p. 121)

26
> Therein lies literature's secret, the infinite power to keep undecidable and thus forever sealed the secret of what it says . . . It is the secret place in which it establishes itself as the verypossibility of the secret . . .

(Derrida, *Geneses, Genealogies, Genres and Genius*, p. 18)

27 As with, for example, the Cumaean Sybil whom Eliot invokes at the beginning of *The Waste Land*, whose only reply to taunts and questionings is, 'I want to die' (see *Collected Poems*, p. 61).

28 One of Kierkegaard's superbly suggestive section headings comes to mind:

> Despair is a Sickness in the Spirit, in the Self, and So It May Assume A Triple Form: in Despair at Not Being Conscious of Having a Self (Despair Improperly So Called); in Despair at Not Willing to Be Oneself; in Despair at Willing to Be Oneself.

(Kierkegaard, *The Sickness unto Death* [1849], in *'Fear and Trembling' and 'The Sickness unto Death'*, trans. Walter Lowrie [Princeton, NJ, 1954], p. 6)

29 See Lewis-Williams, *The Mind in the Cave*, pp. 124–9, 273–7.

30 See Hillman, *The Dream and the Underworld*, pp. 27–32.

31 The 'difference' of the Chinese supernatural, its constant overlap with the everyday, and the ever-presence, for better or worse, of the ancestors are laid out well in Karl S.Y. Kao's Introduction (pp. 1–51) to his *Classical Chinese Tales of the Supernatural and the Fantastic: Selections from the Third to the Tenth Century* (Hong Kong, 1985).

32 See *Dhammapada*, trans. dGe-'dun Chos-'phel and Dharma Publishing Staff (Berkeley, CA, 1985), pp. 189–205.

## 10 Constructing a White Space

1 See, e.g., Michael Schmidt, *A Reader's Guide to Fifty Modern British Poets* (London, 1979), pp. 297–304.

2 The reference is to Barthes, *Writing Degree Zero* (1953), trans. Annette Lavers and Colin Smith (London, 1968). The phrasing:

> This erect discourse is full of terror, that is to say, it relates man not to other men, but to the most inhuman images in Nature: heaven, hell, loneliness, childhood, madness, pure mother, etc. (p. 56)

while in many ways entirely baffling nonetheless seems the most apposite to Graham and, perhaps, to rapture in general.

3 Thomas Blackburn, *The Price of an Eye* (London, 1961), p. 131.

4 See Robert Coover, 'The Hat Act', in *Pricksongs and Descants* (London, 1971), pp. 194, 206. But for the 'drink-induced delirium' which is an essential accompaniment to Graham's poetry, see, e.g., David Cameron, 'The Printed Snow: On W.S. Graham', *The Dark Horse*, 19 (2006), 58–64.

5 'The Narrator', in Graham, *The Seven Journeys*; see Graham, *New Collected Poems*, p. 3.

6 'There was when Morning Fell', in Graham, *Cage without Grievance*; see Graham, *New Collected Poems*, p. 22. Perhaps this bears comparison and contrast with Prynne's 'cavernous heart' and 'tacit gleam'.

7 'I, No More Real than Evil in My Roof', in *Cage without Grievance*; see *New Collected Poems*, p. 29.

8 'I, No More Real than Evil in My Roof', in *Cage without Grievance*; see *New Collected Poems*, p. 29. The key, the differentiating term here is without doubt 'trundle'.

9 'His Companions Buried Him', in *2ND Poems*; see *New Collected Poems*, pp. 37–8. The intervening stanzas refer to the mythical three ships 'cast to perish'.
10 Calvin Bedient, *Eight Contemporary Poets* (London, 1974), p. 162.
11 'The White Threshold', in *The White Threshold*; see *New Collected Poems*, p. 92.
12 We need, perhaps, here – although absorbed into the deathly, all-encompassing rapture of the sea, into the wake and the drowning, the drowning and the wake – to remind ourselves of Freud on the 'oceanic'; particularly relevant, it seems to me, are his remarks in *Civilisation and its Discontents*. See Freud, *Standard Edition*, XXI.64–5, 72–3, where he also touches upon rapture.
13 'The Children of Lanarkshire', in *The White Threshold*; see Graham, *New Collected Poems*, pp. 70–1.
14 Or the beached, abandoned boat which is such an uncanny focus of feeling in Kazuo Ishiguro's haunted and haunting novel about cloning and loss, *Never Let Me Go* (London, 2005).
15 'The Search by a Town', in *The White Threshold*; see Graham, *New Collected Poems*, p. 65. The call, the beckoning, of 'her wandering voice' (p. 66) seals this strange affinity with Blake as Lyca and her siblings are led into the wild; or we, as readers, are led there by them.
16 'Three Poems of Drowning', 3, in *The White Threshold*; see Graham, *New Collected Poems*, p. 86. The terror of being drowned (not once but thrice) and of working despite the imminence of death are both, of course, for addicts matters of the utmost delicacy, inviting a filigree, a latticework.
17 'Two Love Poems', 1, in *The White Threshold*; see Graham, *New Collected Poems*, p. 79.
18 'The Nightfishing', 6, in *The Nightfishing*; see Graham, *New Collected Poems*, p. 118.
19 Bedient, *Eight Contemporary Poets*, p. 168.
20 'The Nightfishing', I, in *The Nightfishing*; see Graham, *New Collected Poems*, p. 106, and while seeing, I suppose, also observe: observe in particular the complexities of the 'turning', the turning away or the turning aside, the turn which maintains dignity or which destroys it.
21 'The Nightfishing', 1, in *The Nightfishing*; see Graham, *New Collected Poems*, pp. 106–7; and think twice before you turn the page.
22 'The Nightfishing', 2, in *The Nightfishing*; see Graham, *New Collected Poems*, p. 107.
23 For an interestingly relevant account, see John Jones, *John Keats's Dream of Truth* (London, 1969), e.g., pp. 225–6.
24 'The Nightfishing', 3, in *The Nightfishing*; see Graham, *New Collected Poems*, p. 113. The first eight lines of that quotation are a mere example of the verse form followed, with tremendous aplomb against the despair of drowning, throughout this section of the poem.
25 'The Nightfishing', 5, in *The Nightfishing*; see Graham, *New Collected Poems*, pp. 117–18.
26 'The Nightfishing', 7, in *The Nightfishing*; see Graham, *New Collected Poems*, p.

119. The crucial word would presumably be 'becomes'; are we talking about admiration or about an otherwise inevitable future?

27 'The Nightfishing', 7, in *The Nightfishing*; see Graham, *New Collected Poems*, p. 120.

28 'The Nightfishing', 7, in *The Nightfishing*; see Graham, *New Collected Poems*, p. 120.

29 'Letter II', in *The Nightfishing*; see Graham, *New Collected Poems*, pp. 122, 124. Cf. Ronell on Heidegger:

> 'But language *is* monologue. This now says two things: it is language *alone* which speaks authentically; and, language speaks *lonesomely*'.

(Ronell, *The Telephone Book*, p. 161, quoting Heidegger, *On the Way to Language*, p. 134). As Ronell goes on to say, 'Language will *not* leave me alone'.

30 'Letter V', in *The Nightfishing*; see Graham, *New Collected Poems*, p. 132.

31 'Two Ballads: Baldy Bane', in *The Nightfishing*; see Graham, *New Collected Poems*, p. 148. The relevant comparison for this mode of mythologisation would be with the bizarrely politicised Glaswegian pornography of a book like Alexander Trocchi, *Thongs* (London, 1971).

32 'Malcolm Mooney's Land', in *Malcolm Mooney's Land*; see Graham, *New Collected Poems*, pp. 153, 157.

33 'Malcolm Mooney's Land', in *Malcolm Mooney's Land*; see Graham, *New Collected Poems*, pp. 154, 156–7, 153.

34 'Malcolm Mooney's Land', in *Malcolm Mooney's Land*; see Graham, *New Collected Poems*, p. 154. Cf., obviously, Ronell, *passim.*; an echo of ringtones.

35 'Malcolm Mooney's Land', in *Malcolm Mooney's Land*; see Graham, *New Collected Poems*, p. 155.

36 'The Beast in the Space', in *Malcolm Mooney's Land*; see Graham, *New Collected Poems*, p. 157.

37 'The Beast in the Space', in *Malcolm Mooney's Land*; see Graham, *New Collected Poems*, pp. 157–8. The space of allusion is perhaps not so unlikely as it sounds: one of the messages the 'Great Beast' Crowley tries to convey in *Diary of a Drug Fiend* and elsewhere is that magic has to do with the mastery and manipulation of linguistic and quasi-linguistic codes. See also Arthur Conan Doyle, 'The Terror of Blue John Gap', in *The Conan Doyle Stories* (London, 1929), pp. 506–25.

38 'The Lying Dear', in *Malcolm Mooney's Land*; see Graham, *New Collected Poems*, p. 159.

> A thinking dialogue with poetry runs the risk of interfering with the saying of the utterance, instead of allowing it to sing from within its own inner peace. The response to the call of the poem, however thinkingly grasped, still resonates the alarm that started the thinking which has roused the thought from its reserve.

(Ronell, *The Telephone Book*, p. 173)

39 'Dear Who I Mean', in *Malcolm Mooney's Land*; see Graham, *New Collected Poems*, p. 161.

40 'Dear Who I Mean', in *Malcolm Mooney's Land*; see Graham, *New Collected Poems*, p. 161.

41 'The Constructed Space', in *Malcolm Mooney's Land*; see Graham, *New Collected Poems*, p. 162.
42 'Malcolm Mooney's Land', in *Malcolm Mooney's Land*; see Graham, *New Collected Poems*, p. 155.
43 'The Dark Dialogues', in *Malcolm Mooney's Land*; see Graham, *New Collected Poems*, p. 167.
44 'Approaches to How They Behave', in *Malcolm Mooney's Land*; see Graham, *New Collected Poems*, p. 179.
45 'Clusters Travelling Out', in *Malcolm Mooney's Land*; see Graham, *New Collected Poems*, p. 192.
46 The specific reference is to Fredric Jameson, *The Prison-House of Language* (Princeton, NJ, 1974); Jameson's brilliant account of the problems of structuralism is deeply relevant to the nature of Graham's enterprise.
47 Douglas Dunn, 'For the Love of Lumb: New Poetry', *Encounter*, L.1 (1978), 82.
48 'What is the Language Using Us for?', in *Implements in Their Places*; see Graham, *New Collected Poems*, pp. 203–4.
49 'Imagine a Forest', in *Implements in Their Places*; see Graham, *New Collected Poems*, p. 204; and we, of course, have been lost in this forest (where it turns out there is 'elephant bark') before.
50 'A Note to the Difficult One', in *Implements in Their Places*; see Graham, *New Collected Poems*, p. 207. Cf. Rumī:

> Your name is upon my tongue,
> Your image is in my sight,
> Your memory is in my heart:
> Whither then shall I write?

(Arberry, *Discourses of Rūmī*, p. 178)
51 'Language Ah Now You Have Me', in *Implements in Their Places*; see Graham, *New Collected Poems*, p. 207.
52 'Ten Shots of Mister Simpson', 1, in *Implements in Their Places*; see Graham, *New Collected Poems*, p. 210.
53 'Ten Shots of Mister Simpson', 2, in *Implements in Their Places*; see Graham, *New Collected Poems*, p. 211.
54 'Enter a Cloud', 5, in *Implements in Their Places*; see Graham, *New Collected Poems*, pp. 218–19.
55 See *Contemporary Poets of the English Language*, ed. Rosalie Murphy (Chicago, 1970), p. 436.
56 'Johann Joachim Quantz's Five Lessons', in *Implements in Their Places*; see Graham, *New Collected Poems*, p. 229. The films which spring most immediately to mind are Fassbinder, *Fear Eats the Soul* (1973) and Herzog, *The Enigma of Caspar Hauser* (1974).
57 'Implements in Their Places', in *Implements in Their Places*; see Graham, *New Collected Poems*, p. 240.
58 'Implements in Their Places', in *Implements in Their Places*; see Graham, *New Collected Poems*, pp. 249–50.
59 'Implements in Their Places', in *Implements in Their Places*; see Graham, *New*

*Collected Poems*, p. 254; although, as we have seen, according to a certain logic of the secret the wood will always be 'the wrong wood'.

## 11 Towards a Homeopathic Erotics

1 See Deleuze, e.g., *Essays Critical and Clinical*, pp. 2–5; *Expressionism in Philosophy*, trans. Martin Joughin (New York, 1990), pp. 254–7; *Spinoza: Practical Philosophy*, trans. Robert Hurley (San Francisco, 1988), pp. 41–3.

2 The essential text is Hermione de Almeida, *Romantic Medicine and John Keats* (New York, 1991); see also Donald C. Goellnicht, *The Poet-Physician: Keats and Medical Science* (Pittsburgh, PA, 1984).

3 See, of course, Al Alvarez, *The Savage God: A Study of Suicide* (London, 1971); but also, for background to these further reflections on the crypt, Abraham and Torok, *The Wolf Man's Magic Word*, *passim*.

4 As, perhaps, the tense of the addict always is. There is a curious moment in Burroughs where a narrative of the past changes abruptly into an impossible present: 'He dies many years ago' (*Nova Express*, p. 90).

5 See Derrida, Foreword to Abraham and Torok, *The Wolf Man's Magic Word*, pp. xxv ff.; and Louis Althusser, *'L'avenir dure longtemps', suivi de 'Les faits'*, eds Olivier Corpet and Yann Moulier Boutang (Paris, 1992).

6 See Sylvia Plath, 'Lady Lazarus', in *Ariel* (London, 1965), p. 17.

7 'O Come, All Ye Faithful'; see *Hymns Ancient and Modern* (new edn, London, 1924), p. 47.

8 Some of the references here are to Eliot, 'The Dry Salvages' (1941), in *Four Quartets* (see *Collected Poems*, pp. 205–12) and Ballard, *The Atrocity Exhibition*.

9 See, e.g., von Franz, *Shadow and Evil in Fairytales* (Zurich, 1974).

10 The reference is to Coleridge, 'Frost at Midnight' (1798), in *Poetical Works*, pp. 240–2; in this poem, it is all too obvious that Coleridge is rapt.

11 Plath, 'Nick and the Candlestick', in *Ariel*, p. 40.

12 In the all too appropriate words of 'Dark as a Dungeon', an American industrial folk song; see Alan Lomax, *The Folk Songs of North America* (London, 1960), p. 295.

13 See Hughes, e.g., 'A Childish Prank', in *Crow: From the Life and Songs of the Crow* (London, 1974), p. 19.

14 The reference here is again to Hillman, *The Dream and the Underworld*, esp. pp. 23–45:

> Because the underworld differs so radically from the underground, that which has its home there, dreams, must refer to a psychic or pneumatic world of ghosts, spirits, ancestors, souls, daimones. . . . This world is fluid, or dusty, fiery, muddy, or aetherial, so there is nothing firm to hold on to – unless we develop intuitive instruments for seizing impalpables that slip through our fingers or burn at the touch (p. 40).

15 See Freud, 'Mourning and Melancholia' (1917), in *Standard Edition*, XIV.243–58.

16 The reference is to Eugène Ionesco, *Tueur sans Gages*, in, e.g., *Théatre complet*, ed. Emmanuel Jacquart (Paris, 1991), pp. 467–535.

17
> A long-standing clinical observation of addicting drug action is that a more intense 'high' is produced when self-administered than when exogenously administered.

(Gardner and David, 'The Neurobiology of Chemical Addiction', in *Getting Hooked*, eds Elster and Skog, p. 103)

18 Or, perhaps we might say, the 'huge and birdless silence' being towed by the 'black-/Sailed unfamiliar' in Larkin's 'Next, Please' (1951); see Larkin, *Collected Poems*, p. 52.

19 The relation between mother and baby forms, of course, an obvious model for rapture and for its withdrawal/absence; see, e.g., Kathryn Harrison, *Seeking Rapture: Scenes from a Mother's Life* (New York, 2003).

20 The reference is to Andrew Marvell, 'The Gallery', in, e.g., *The Complete Poems*, ed. E. S. Donno (Harmondsworth, 1985), pp. 40–1. See also Punter, *Writing the Passions*, pp. 63–73.

21 I am thinking of Heathcliff's curious disappearance and his return, changed in wealth and culture, in Emily Brontë, *Wuthering Heights* (1847).

22 See Larkin, 'The Explosion', in *Collected Poems*, p. 175.

23 See Hillman, *Anima: An Anatomy of a Personified Notion*.

> Anima is the function that gives psyche to multiplicity by being the psychological correlate to polytheism and to individual symbol formations (p. 167).

24 On this point see Lacan, *The Language of the Self: The Function of Language in Psychoanalysis*, trans. Anthony Wilden (New York, 1968), pp. 66–7.

25 Originally, in the thinking of William Hogarth and others, a mark of painterly and architectural perfection; since, as most typically in Alan Hollinghurst, *The Line of Beauty* (new edn, London, 2005), adapted as part of the discourse of cocaine use.

26 There is a copious literature on trickster figures across a wide range of cultures and mythologies: for useful links see <members.aol.com/pmichaels/glorantha/foolsparadise>.

27 See, e.g., Joshua C. Gregory, *A Short History of Atomism* (London, 1981); Robert Hugh Kargon, *Atomism in England from Hariot to Newton* (Oxford, 1966); Geoffrey Lloyd, *Early Greek Science: Thales to Aristotle* (London, 1970).

## **12** Rapt

1 Clark, *The Poetics of Singularity*, p. 83.

2 See Beckett, *The Unnamable* (London, 1975); also Lovecraft, 'The Nameless City' (among many others) in *The Doom that came to Sarnath*, ed. Lin Carter (New York, 1971), pp. 106–21.

3 The echoes are of Beckett, *Endgame* (1957) and *Not I* (1972). In *Not I*, we are made more than aware that we are in the presence of a pre-linguistic 'buzzing'

of language; rumour has it that women (for the mouth which is the only protagonist of the play is a woman's mouth) who take on the part go mad, lose their wits.

4 Clark, *The Poetics of Singularity*, p. 70, quoting Gadamer, 'Thinking and Poeticising in Heidegger and in Hölderlin's *Andenken*', trans. R.E. Palmer, in *Heidegger Towards the Turn: Essays on the Work of the 1930s* (Albany, NY, 1990), p. 154.

5 Here is an interesting if bizarre sidelight:

> Machinic desire can seem a little [*sic*] inhuman, as it rips up political cultures, deletes traditions, dissolves subjectivities, and hacks through security apparatuses, tracking a soulless tropism to zero control. This is because what appears to humanity as the history of capitalism is an invasion from the future by an artificial intelligent space that must assemble itself entirely from the enemy's resources.

(Ned Land, 'Machinic Desire', *Textual Practice*, 7 [1993], 479)

6 De Quincey, *Confessions of an English Opium-Eater* (1821), illus. Willy Pogany (London, 1856), pp. 98–9.

7 Which could return us to the animal world, in, for example (again), Kafka – the musical dogs, the singing apes and mice, the ineradicable cry of the jackal . . .

8 See Virilio, e.g., *War and Cinema* (London, 1989); *The Art of the Motor* (Minneapolis, 1995); *The End of Modernity* (Cambridge, 1998).

9 The song is by Robert Earl Keen, and can be found on *West Textures* (1989).

10 De Quincey, *Confessions of an English Opium-Eater*, p. 99. Cf. Richard Walker, 'A Change in Physical Economy: Identity and the Rejection of Modernity in Thomas De Quincey's *Confessions*', in *Inhuman Reflections*, ed. Brewster *et al.*, pp. 150–68.

11 Larkin, 'Dockery and Son' (1963), in *Collected Poems*, p. 153.

12 Nietzsche, *Thus Spoke Zarathustra: A Book for Everyone and No One* (1886), trans. R. J. Hollingdale (Harmondsworth, 1961), p. 151.

13 Nietzsche, *Thus Spoke Zarathustra*, p. 101. It is also worth bearing in mind Heidegger's remark that 'for Nietzsche rapture means the most glorious victory of form' (Heidegger, *Nietzsche: The Will to Power as Art*, trans. D. F. Krell [New York, 1973], p. 119).

14 Cf. Rūmī:

> The Master said: It is good if you are helpless all the time and at every moment, and see yourself helpless in the state of capacity just as in the state of incapacity. For above your capacity there is a greater Capacity . . .

(Arberry, *Discourses of Rūmī*, p. 25)

15 On Fitzgerald as well as Faulkner, Blake, Genet and many others, see Mottram, *The Algebra of Need*, e.g., pp. 44, 64, 165, 177, 182.

16 Scott Fitzgerald, *The Beautiful and Damned* (Harmondsworth, 1966), pp. 120–1.

17 Fitzgerald, *The Beautiful and Damned*, p. 153.

18 For an interesting sidelight on the 'state of rapture', see Cleanth Brooks, *William Faulkner: Toward Yoknapatawpha and Beyond* (Baton Rouge, LA, 1990), pp. 42 ff.
19 Bernard De Voto, 'Witchcraft in Mississippi', in *William Faulkner: The Critical Heritage*, ed. John E. Bassett (London, 1997), p. 200.
20 Joel Williamson, *William Faulkner and Southern History* (Oxford, 1993), p. 238.
21 This is hinted at in, e.g., Rebecca Rio-Jelliffe, *Obscurity's Myriad Components: The Theory and Practice of William Faulkner* (Lewisburg, PA, 2001), p. 99.
22 Faulkner, *The Sound and the Fury*, introd. Richard Hughes (London, 1989), p. 257.
23 See Conrad, *The Secret Agent*, ed. Martin Seymour-Smith (London, 1984), e.g., p. 216 where, after Stevie's catastrophic death, Mrs Verloc sits 'in the place where poor Stevie usually established himself of an evening with paper and pencil for the pastime of drawing those coruscations of innumerable circles suggesting chaos and eternity'.
24 The references are to Sartre, *Saint Genet: comédien et martyr* (Paris, 1952) and to Genet, *Notre Dame des Fleurs* (Lyon, 1948). See also Derrida, *Glas* (1974), trans. John P. Leavy, Jr, and Richard Rand (Lincoln, NE, 1986), pp. 204–5.
25 Genet, *Miracle of the Rose*, trans. Bernard Frechtman (Harmondsworth, 1971), p. 176.
26 Genet, *Miracle of the Rose*, p. 138.
27 Genet, *The Thief's Journal*, trans. Frechtman (London, 1973), p. 180.
28 Genet, *The Thief's Journal*, p. 217.
29 Or a perversion beyond perversion; see, e.g., Poppy Z. Brite, *Lost Souls* (New York, 1992), on a regime within which perversion itself is (theoretically) sublated.
30 Rechy, *City of Night* (2nd edn, New York, 1984), p. 92.
31 Rechy, *City of Night*, p. 338.
32 Gao Xingjian, *Soul Mountain*, trans. Mabel Lee (London, 2001), pp. 503–4. Gao's thoughts on the possibility of a language of transcendence are remarkable: see pp. 351–2.
33 Gao, *Soul Mountain*, p. 506.

# Index